Bella Merlin

Bella Merlin trained as an actor in both England and Russia. Her theatre credits include Wedekind's Lulu and Henry James's Governess, alongside writing and performing on London's fringe circuit. She has worked in television, film and radio as well as tutoring in Drama and Theatre Arts at the University of Birmingham.

Her experiences as a postgraduate on the actor-training course at Moscow's State Institute of Cinematography led her to practical research, resulting in a doctorate from Birmingham University in 'The Russian School of Acting'. Since then she has led master classes in Poland, France, London and various drama schools, and co-hosted a series of Russian Summer schools and an International Michael Chekhov Symposium in Birmingham. She also serves as Book Reviews Editor for *New Theatre Quarterly*.

She has directed a number of productions exclusively using Stanislavsky's Active Analysis.

Although she has published several articles, *Beyond Stanislavsky* is her first book to date.

Beyond Stanislavsky

The most exciting thinking about acting has always come from Russia: this remains true today, despite the successive political and economic crises of the recent past. Woefully little of what has been and is being discovered there now reaches the West. Seventy years ago, Norris Houghton went to Soviet Russia to find out about the thrilling artistic upheavals of that period and wrote two seminal books about it. Bella Merlin has written a seminal book for today. She has been there to find out about it in the best possible way (better even than that of the passionate amateur, Houghton): by undergoing the training. Her personal odyssey has enabled her to write an outstandingly lucid account of current Russian practice, analysing its sources and vividly conveying the excitement of what it has to offer a Western theatre which in its constant struggle for survival is in no position to explore the further possibilities of acting. In *Beyond Stanislavsky*, Bella Merlin opens up a debate about acting which is desperately necessary if the art is to move forward, go deeper: for audiences and practitioners alike, it is essential reading.

SIMON CALLOW

Beyond Stanislavsky

The Psycho-Physical Approach to Actor Training

BELLA MERLIN

Routledge
Taylor & Francis Group
New York   London

Beyond Stanislavsky
first published in Great Britain in 2001
as a paperback original by
Nick Hern Books Limited, London

Published in the U.S.A and Canada in 2001
by Theatre Arts Books/Routledge
270 Madison Avenue, New York NY 10016
www.routledge-ny.com
by arrangement with Nick Hern Books

This edition published 2011 by Routledge:

Routledge	Routledge
Taylor & Francis Group	Taylor & Francis Group
711 Third Avenue	2 Park Square, Milton Park
New York, NY 10017	Abingdon, Oxon OX14 4RN

British Library Cataloguing data for this book
is available from the British Library
ISBN 978 1 85459 613 0 (UK)

Cataloging-in-Publication data is available
from the Library of Congress
ISBN 978 0 87830 142 3 (USA)
ISBN 978 0 87830 143 0 (USA hardback)

For S. B. Isumel

Acknowledgements

Completion of this book owes much to many, professionally, psychologically and practically. First and foremost huge thanks must go to Nick Hern, whose commitment to the project has been unflinching, along with the support of Max Stafford-Clark, whose belief in my Russian experiences was inspiring. Thereafter, the encouragement and hard work of Caroline Downing provided the final spur to completion. Of course, there would have been no book at all had it not been for Vladimir Ananyev, Katya Kamotskaya and Albert Filozov: their insight as practitioners and patience as teachers continues to be extraordinary. Jimmy Donoher, Mark D'Aughton, Sohail Khan, Jane Millar, Mark Babych and Jenny Stephens proved to be colleagues and friends of talent and invention, as well as generously allowing me into their working methods and enabling me to pursue my theatrical 'experiments' effortlessly. I am also indebted to Olga Polyakova, Lorena Aggrey, Jeremy Criddle and Tatiana Storchak for their translation skills, and to Jonathan Dockar Drysdale for his contribution to the front-cover photograph. The support and wisdom of colleagues in the Drama and Theatre Arts Department of Birmingham University has been immense, not least the stimulation and provocation of Dr Robert Leach. And the on-going encouragement from Simon Callow of all things Russian has worked miracles on many occasions. Simon Trussler and Clive Barker of *New Theatre Quarterly* must be thanked for their inclusion of infant-versions of certain ideas expanded within this book in Volumes XV, Part 3 (NTQ 59), August 1999 ('Albert Filozov and the Method of Physical Actions') and Volume XVI, Part 3 (NTQ 63), August 2000 ('Mamet's Heresy and Common Sense: What's True and False in *True and False*'). I would also like to thank hugely Natasha of Natasha Stevenson Management, for patiently tolerating my unavailability when deadlines were pressing. Finally, to end with the very beginning, special acknowledgements are owed to Rebecca Lenkiewicz, who first suggested the Moscow trip one rainy July afternoon in Fulham, London. Thereafter, the faith and generosity of my remarkable parents provided me at five weeks' notice with the means to embark on the Russian training. Without the continual reassurance of the 'Reverend Doctor', this book would have been extremely difficult. Without Alexander Delamere (unofficial editor, invincible comrade and cover-design inspirer), it would have been impossible – thank you.

Contents

Foreword

The two strongest theatre cultures in the world are unquestionably those of Russia and of England. It is a matter for constant reproach that the two have so little understanding of each other's methods and that practitioners make so little effort to find out. Economic and political circumstances in the respective countries have led to very different theatre systems. Here in England, we long for the permanent ensembles or 'theatre families' that gave such depth to Soviet theatre, where a director would create an ensemble that then worked together for twenty years or more. In turn, Russian actors envy the freedom of movement and diversity that characterizes the working lives of their English colleagues. Many English practitioners think their system preferable while Russian actors know theirs to be superior. Bella Merlin is one of the very few English actresses to have made a working journey to the heart of the Russian system. It is a journey which proves to be invaluable, not just for Bella herself, but also for the enquiring reader.

Stanislavsky is much quoted but little understood in this country either by students or by actors. Bella Merlin studied in Moscow under three 'masters' who were all connected with Stanislavsky's work in some way, and one of whom was in fact taught by Stanislavsky's assistant, Mikhail Kedrov. The first lesson to be negotiated by Bella is how to discard the result-orientated rehearsal methods essential in England because of the shortness of rehearsal time. Indeed, I was once working with a group of directing students in St Petersburg who politely enquired how many weeks of rehearsal were customary in London. I replied that four weeks was the norm but that occasionally five weeks was possible. The translator dutifully gave my reply but clearly the students were baffled . . . even upset. After several vigorous exchanges, the translator apologised saying that she must have misunderstood my answer... Did I mean four months or four years? The idea that a play could possibly be rehearsed in four weeks was ludicrous to a serious theatre student in Russia.

In the first half of this compelling book, Bella struggles to understand and to implement the techniques of Michael Chekhov and of Stanislavsky himself. She is working in a foreign language with a disparate group of British and Irish actors who are in Moscow for very different reasons. Her effort to understand first her mentors and then to apply these lessons makes fascinating reading and gives us a working understanding of the value of this methodology. In the second half, Bella Merlin returns to England and tries to implement her new-learned technique in English Rep. The results are always instructive and sometimes hilarious.

This is a book which is vital both to practitioners and to all serious students of theatre.

MAX STAFFORD-CLARK

Beyond Stanislavsky

Prologue

*This is the story of an English actor in Russia
at the end of the twentieth century.*

It is an account of a ten-month actor-training programme at
Moscow's State Institute of Cinematography (otherwise known
as VGIK), a training which I undertook as one of ten English-
speaking actors in September 1993. Up until this point, I'd been
working in Britain for a variety of theatres and in a variety of
companies, and on the whole the work had been rewarding and
interesting. Yet all the time I felt as if I had an unmined seam of
creativity that was never accessed in the short rehearsal periods
of most theatres or in the instant action of television. My
training in Britain had certainly been very challenging. After
three inspiring years as an undergraduate in the Drama and
Theatre Arts Department of Birmingham University, I'd spent a
rather less inspired time on a one-year postgraduate course at a
drama school. At the end of one term, I remember sitting
opposite my acting tutor who said, 'You're going to find it hard
to get work when you leave here. You're so dumpy, dowdy, plain
and common.' That was when I grew the first epidermis of the
thick skin needed in this marvellous profession. I was a little
disappointed that my Rosalind, or my Mrs Pinchwife, or my
Nora hadn't been commented on. Yet – despite my tutor's warn-
ings – within a month of graduation, I'd secured my first job.

Most actors experience some degree of humiliation, often on
a more public scale and usually followed closely by a complete
incomprehension of what the whole thing's about anyway. And
when we're in those circumstances, we have to remind ourselves:
There is art in acting. There must be, or it's a dead profession.

And it's the actor's responsibility to him or her self to remember that art, and to work upon and value it. And that requires training. Or to coin a certain phrase: Life-long Learning. And this book is about such training. Psycho-physical training. While the term might sound esoteric, the reality isn't. Psychophysical training is one in which body and psyche, outer expression and inner sensation, are integrated and inter-dependent. The *brain* inspires the *emotions*, which then prompt the *body* into action and expression. Or the *body* arouses the *imagination*, which then activates the *emotions*. Or the *emotions* stir the *brain* to propel the *body* to work. All the components – body, mind, and emotions – are part of the psycho-physical mechanism which makes up the actor: psychology and physicality are part of one continuum. 'Psycho-technique' was a term coined by Stanislavsky and developed by Michael Chekhov; it was the complete integration of psychology and physicality which formed the basis of the Russian actor-training as I experienced it in Moscow. And this is where my account can fill in a small blank on a large canvas...

During the final stages of his life, Stanislavsky devoted himself to unlocking the psycho-physical nature of acting and finding a truly integrated psycho-technique. This period of Stanislavsky's work has not gone unrecorded. In fact a significant part of *Stanislavsky in Focus*,[1] a thorough study by American writer, Sharon Carnicke, examines these final stages. She pays particular attention to the Method of Physical Actions (a term being used more and more frequently in contemporary Western practice), and beyond that to what became known as 'Active Analysis'. In many ways, the Method of Physical Actions and Active Analysis are very similar in their rehearsal techniques: rather than using sedentary textual analysis or imaginative visualisations, the actor now accesses a character through *experience*. In other words, by *getting up and doing it* through a process of improvisation. However, there is a crucial difference between the two approaches. The Method of Physical Actions is concerned with finding a logical line or 'score' of individual actions through a scene, while

Active Analysis is an holistic system integrating body and mind, and most importantly *spirit* (as I'll discuss in further detail in Chapter 1). 'What exactly is *spirit?*' you may well ask; but turning to the works of Stanislavsky won't help very much, as Soviet censorship made sure that he kept to a minimum all seemingly esoteric references. In stark contrast, the idea of *action* was seized by the Soviets as being in line with their Marxist dialectic: it was physical, visual, provable, scientific. Hence the Method of Physical Actions was keenly welcomed and promoted by politicians and practitioners alike. And it's certainly a rehearsal approach adopted in America and not unheard of in Britain; it even appears on A-level Drama syllabuses.

'Active Analysis', though, is a comparatively unknown phrase. Stanislavsky died before the first students of his Active Analysis had graduated, and he was too sick in his last years to maintain his own accounts of the work. What this incompletion means is that the 'system' – as Carnicke explains – has had to pass from *fact* to *lore*. (Though Stanislavsky would undoubtedly balk at the idea that it was ever considered 'fact' in the first place.) Certainly the 'lore' of Stanislavsky's system continued immediately after his death, with his assistants, protégés and students furthering his work according to their own biases and understandings. And it's being constantly explored and perpetuated in Moscow today, whether it be in drama schools or rehearsal rooms or laboratory studios. The nature of 'lore' is that it is based in practice rather than theory and, as Carnicke suggests, it differs from the available published sources in that it accommodates much of Stanislavsky's '*integrative* thinking'.[2] But as Carnicke points out, the trouble with this lore is that 'English descriptions remain incomplete and fragmentary, when set against the tradition of Russia's lore.'

My experience in Moscow was a 'hands-on' training in the integrative approach to acting proposed by Stanislavsky. The practitioners under whom I studied combined their disciplines in a synthesised, holistic way whereby the actors' emotions, imagination, body and spirit – or 'superconscious' as Stanislavsky sometimes called it – were stimulated without their even realising. It was a truly active analysis, engaging script, character and actor all at the same time. I can seize the opportunity now to feed that experience back into the English language and keep the lore developing. In Moscow, I was a comparatively open book, I was hungry for new approaches. While of course I questioned and challenged the work that I was undertaking, I also had sufficient experience in the British acting profession to compare and contrast. At the time of my Moscow training, I knew nothing of Stanislavsky's later work, and I'd never even heard of the Method of Physical Actions. I simply found that the Russian tutors used little cerebral analysis of text in rehearsals; everything was discovered through improvisation. It was only on my return to England that I found out through research that what I'd experienced in Russia was 'Active Analysis'. My ignorance while I was involved in the training meant that I wasn't trying to fit my experiences into a particular system or structure: I had no personal agenda, or superior knowledge. There was no need to bend my results to fit the proposed methodology; I simply did what was suggested, wrote copious journals and, at a later date, analysed, notated and labelled.

As I've said, there's no definitive explanation of Stanislavsky's system: even Stanislavsky didn't have one, his theories were still in a state of on-going development when he died. Understanding the 'system' is now dependent on contemporary practitioners' lore. Since society is in a state of continuous development, so too is theatre, and so must any 'system' be for getting inside representations of human behaviour. In other words, the changing nature of lore is legitimate, as it prevents method becoming museum. The acting process described in this book is based on the work of three particular actor-tutors with whom I studied: Vladimir Ananyev (Scenic Movement), Katya Kamotskaya (Actor-Training) and Albert Filozov (Acting 'Master'). Their disciplines correspond to Working on Your Self, Working in the Ensemble and Working on the Role, each of which constitutes an important aspect of the actor's on-going development. All of the tutors had trained as actors in Moscow, and – as will be revealed – their work is heavily influenced by Stanislavsky. But in many ways Stanislavsky is only a starting point: Michael Chekhov and Jerzy Grotowski also form an intrinsic part of much of the work, along with a multitude of other influences. The combination of these three practitioners – Ananyev, Kamotskaya and Filozov – was timely and serendipitous. Their unique methods and personalities homogenised into an actor-training which embraced action, emotion and experience. Although this account is a personal journey through a very particular method, I ardently believe that many of the elements can be applied by most actors, whether they be engaged in toothpaste commercials or *Hamlet*.

To begin with, I'll address the heart of Physical Actions and Active Analysis to try and understand how Stanislavsky got there in the first place. Then the meat of this book is devoted to a hands-on assessment of a contemporary actor-training. I conclude with a brief look at the application of the training during a season at a British repertory theatre immediately following my return. If I highlight the difficulties as much as the successes, it's not to undermine the work in any way, but rather to infer that this account is by no means intended as gospel.

Using various aspects of the Russian approach in the time since I returned, I've put the work to the test in a diversity of environments with varying degrees of success. I've acted, I've directed, and I've led workshops for professional actors and actor-students (both undergraduate and A-level) in Britain and abroad. In other words, I haven't taken anything at face value; I've challenged, questioned, and sometimes blatantly failed. To cover the range of circumstances in which this approach can be used, I've included exercises and ideas that may be applied to text, improvisation, audition or workshop. At the core of the whole training is Stanislavsky's Active Analysis *as I have interpreted it*. And it's important to remember that: this is only my interpretation of others' interpretations of their own tutors. Albert Filozov trained under Mikhail Kedrov, who was Stanislavsky's Assistant Director at the time of his death: so, if you like and for what it's worth, this account is three degrees of separation from Stanislavsky!

The fact that 'system' has now become lore doesn't imply a watering-down of the principles. Given the fashionable 'postmodern perspective' – i.e. that there is no grand narrative, there is no objective truth – then experience can be the only true teacher. And that experience is what I strive to access for the reader in this book. I could have provided a simple handbook of exercises. However, as Michael Chekhov points out in his Foreword for *To The Actor*, it requires considerable collaboration on the part of the reader to practise the exercises and thereby understand their potency. By adopting a highly subjective stance in this account, I hope to take you part-way on that collaborative voyage. While such an intimate 'voice' might not appeal to everyone, I simply didn't want to offer a handbook. I specifically wanted to invite that 'shared experience', so that through my illuminating the difficulties and highlighting the benefits of psycho-physical training, you might take away something more from *Beyond Stanislavsky* than just a provocative read. And so the journey through this book is a personal struggle with a strange and intangible craft. The lofty – or humble? – intention is to reveal to the actor the holistic nature of our art.

ACT 1
Myths, Methods, Systems and Superstitions

Why bother with Stanislavsky?

When it comes to acting, there are many myths about methods and suspicions about systems. What did Stanislavsky say? When? Why? Who adopted it? Who adapted it? Who decreed it? Who decried it? And what's the relevance of it all today? Before answering any of these questions, it's important to remember that Stanislavsky was first and foremost a practitioner, an *amateur* of theatre in the true meaning of the word. He wasn't a professed theoretician: his reluctance to publish his ideas (a reluctance eventually vitiated by financial need) indicates that he didn't want his words to be taken as gospel. That aside, there are certain elements of his theories which are as pertinent today as they ever were and ever will be, as he was simply untangling, and as far as possible systematising, natural human responses. We should also remember that he was an experimenter: he didn't confine his acting and directing to naturalistic Russian plays. He tried his hand at operetta, symbolism, Shakespeare, Molière. Despite popular belief, his search for 'truth' – whatever that might mean – was as much a search for *stylistic* and *theatrical* truth as it was for psychological truth. For him, theatre was a laboratory, and if somebody didn't mix the chemicals, there would never be a reaction.

The reason why we should still bother with Stanislavsky today is that maybe it's only now, at the dawn of a new millennium, that his ideas are starting to make sense. For the last century, practitioners from Brecht to Brook to Barba and beyond have been arguing that theatre is dying. Ask Joe Public why he doesn't go to the theatre, and the answer will probably be 'Because it's boring!' And why is it boring? Because the art of theatre acting is just as stagnant now as it was in the 1960s, when Brook despaired of 'deadly' theatre. If we don't invest theatre with real humanity, the resonances of live performance quickly diminish. And this was what Stanislavsky was seeking – real human emotions on stage, an end to which he thought all actors should address themselves if they really want to keep theatrical art alive. He knew that every gifted performer possesses the appropriate raw materials for the task: it was just a question of finding 'the right bait' to lure him or her.[3] The trouble was that he was only too aware that we can't consciously manipulate our emotions, yet herein lies the inherent contradiction of the acting process. We need humanity on stage, based on true connection with our heart and soul, but how can we turn that humanity on at 8pm each evening for a six-month contract or at five seconds' notice when the director shouts 'Action!'? This contradiction provided the stimulus for Stanislavsky's endless investigations into acting techniques, as he grappled to find the very bait with which to ensnare those capricious emotions.

What's wrong with affective memory?

Given Stanislavsky's interest in emotion, you could be forgiven for thinking that his main contribution to acting practice was his introduction of the term 'affective memory'. Affective memory has received a lot of bad press over the past few decades. It was Stanislavsky who certainly brought it into acting terminology, though doubtless the great actors were using it long before he gave it a name. Since then Lee Strasberg has been tarred with a brush of vitriol by many practitioners for arguably basing the American 'Method' on emotion recall. But if the heart of vibrant acting is true human content, why does 'affective memory' cause so much concern and consideration? To some extent, it's fair to say that if you find you have an analogous situation which presents you (without any effort or inner contortion) with a trigger into a character, then it's a gift and you're crazy to ignore it. However, you only have to take a brief look at some of the scientific ideas promulgated since the late 19th century – from around the same time that Stanislavsky began his own serious explorations – to see that the use of affective memory quickly becomes questionable.

Affective memory implies that the imaginative remembrance of things past can cause present-tense changes in an individual's psychology. And in fact in everyday life, we're constantly using it to make all manner of major and minor decisions. The psychologist Magda B. Arnold describes affective memory as playing a very important part in the appraisal and interpretation of everything around us, calling it 'the matrix of all experience and action'.[4] She goes on to say that, of course, it's intensely personal, as affective memory is the living record of the emotional life-history of each individual person: it reflects his or her unique experiences and biases. This is one of the dangers of affective memory. Because of the intense subjectivity, Arnold actually advises against relying on affective memories, as they continually distort the individual's judgement.[5] This also applies to the acting process, where aligning a character with the actor's personal memories can lead to a distortion both of the writer's original intention and of the actor's creative emotions. Who's to say that an actor will even be able to locate at will an appropriate affective memory, when often we unconsciously suppress an emotion at source through our own involuntary self-censorship? Stanislavsky himself wrote that the more an actor violates an emotion, the more that emotion resists and 'throws out invisible buffers before it and these . . . do not allow emotion to approach that part of the role which is too difficult for it.'[6] Recent experience of a television shoot in which I had to play a beaten-up young mum reminded me of that danger only too well: the more my brain nagged me that the script said, 'The tears begin to fall', the more those invisible buffers pushed the emotion away from me. And the situation can perpetuate itself: the more the buffers are developed, continues Stanislavsky, the harder it is for the emotion to appear when it's needed and the more an actor then has to appeal to 'old stencils and stagey craftsmanship'. And we all know how dreadful those 'stencils' or dry imitations of feeling can look looming large on a TV close-up . . .

Another limitation of affective memory is that every time an event is recalled, the individual's perception of it shifts slightly, so that the affectiveness of the memory constantly changes. This is, after all, the positive use of affective memory in some psychotherapy: a patient is invited to relive over and over again in detail a disturbing experience. Eventually, the point is reached at which the memory has been transferred from the left-hand brain, where it exerts subconscious control over the patient's life, to the right-hand brain, where it can be rationalised and 'diffused'. To add to the suspicions surrounding affective memory, Théodule Ribot, the scientist from whom Stanislavsky adopted the term, even went so far as to doubt its very existence, stating that 'the emotional memory is nil in the majority of people.'[7] If the very man who coined the phrase says that, then what are we mere actors supposed to think?

Throughout his life, Stanislavsky maintained that his system was nothing more than an application of natural laws of biology and behaviour to the conventions of the stage.[8] Along with this, we have to remember that he was reacting strongly against formal theatrical traditions. He didn't want his actors declaiming their roles, as was the customary practice on the international stage. He wanted them to invest their characters with real emotions, or rather with human truth: obviously he thought that affective memory could be a springboard into that truth. Whether or not affective memory exists, is reliable, is accessible, or creatively helpful, there's another far more significant consideration when it comes to analysing emotion. What prompts it – is it the mind or is it, in fact, the *body*?

What is an emotion?

Even with the early (and by current standards, fairly primitive) investigations into emotion, the emphasis was clearly on body, not mind. In 1884, William James wrote his famous essay, *What is an Emotion?* – an essay with which Stanislavsky was probably familiar. James described how the entire circulatory system acts as a 'sounding board' within the human body, 'which every change of our consciousness, however slight, may make reverberate'.[9] He went on to say that regardless of whether any outward change appears, tension within our inner musculature adapts to each varying mood. So, if every emotion makes a biological impression, each individual could be described as possessing a physiological compendium of emotions imprinted on his or her musculature. The conclusion that James drew from his findings was that the various permutations and combinations of these organic activities make it possible that every shade of emotion, however slight, has a unique bodily reverberation. So muscle and mind are completely interdependent. This was certainly something that influenced Stanislavsky as his enquiries into acting practice developed away from memory to body. *He* suggested that the power of a muscular memory was dependent on the strength of the original emotional experience, which makes the most ordinary sensations the hardest ones to locate. In other words, when we experience moments of great emotional tension, the muscles preserve the memory of the sensation more lastingly than they do with daily experiences.[10] Yet it's often daily experiences we need to portray on the stage. How many times has the simple task of pouring a cup of tea turned a perfectly decent actor into a lump of physical clumsiness? Indeed, in one of his most famous examples in *An Actor Prepares*, Stanislavsky's semi-fictional director, Tortsov, invites his students to look for a brooch in a curtain, using the exercise as an illustration of the unnecessary complexities we add to the most simple of actions on stage.

While this chapter in no way offers any deep scientific analysis of emotion (there are plenty of excellent books which do that),

I want to look at some of the ideas which Stanislavsky would have known about.[11] They might give us clues as to why he moved from affective memory to physical actions in the development of his system. In *What is an Emotion*, William James famously challenged the belief (commonly held at the end of the 19th century) that external stimulus – real or imaginary – arouses emotional response, which in itself leads to a corresponding action or expression. Or to put it more directly, (1) we meet the bear; (2) we feel afraid; (3) we run. By way of a challenge, James postulated that (2) and (3) were reversed: we meet the bear; we run instantly *before* we've had time logically or emotionally to assimilate the situation, and only then do we register our feeling of fear. In other words, he suggested that the instinctive physical reaction (running) to the stimulus (the bear) caused the emotion (fear). It's our sensation of biological activities, taking place within us *after* the action but *before* we've had a chance consciously to recognise what's going on, which *is* the emotion. So to some extent the sequence really has a fourth stage – (1) the *stimulus* leading to (2) the *physical action*, swiftly prompting (3) the *physiological activity*, rapidly perceived as (4) an *emotional state*.

If in fact the natural sequence of biological activity in emotion is stimulus / physiological reaction / emotion, then the use of affective memory on stage does seem to be an extremely bizarre practice. Distilled to its most simplistic, the basic premise underlying affective memory goes like this: (1) I meet a theatrical bear; (2) I recall the moment in my life when I saw a real bear and remember the details of all the sensory stimuli which surrounded that moment; and finally (3), if my memory is sufficiently potent, I'll begin to experience the fear towards the theatrical bear which I originally experienced towards the real bear, and in that state of genuine re-experienced fear, I run. Phew! The process surrounding affective memory is both *reflective* (as my attention is turned to the past) and *reflexive* (as I focus in on my own sensations). The actual on-stage reality of being here, now, with this partner and that audience, is superseded by the actor's independent recollection of a personal event, an event which might not necessarily have anything to do with the action of the play. There's certainly a belief that affective memory can assist an actor in penetrating a complex character during the *rehearsal* process, but relying on this tool in *performance* can be limiting, unhelpful and often very difficult.

Looked at it in terms of the whole of Stanislavsky's life, affective memory was really only a tiny part of his investigations. After years of trial and error, he came to realise that true life on the stage would never arise from the demonstrational acting which adorned the 19th-century theatre. Or from the director superimposing activities on the actor (as he himself had done in his early years). Or from dredging up emotions through a process of affective memory. Or from intellectual analysis of text through round-the-table discussions. He had to discover an alternative technique, and, indeed, by the end of his life, he believed he'd found a possible solution to the doing/feeling dichotomy. Instead of considering true emotion as the *end*-product of an acting technique, he sought to crystallise a process in which experience of an emotion might be an inevitable *by*-product.

From emotion to action

Stanislavsky acknowledged that emotion (or feeling) forms only a part of a human being's intricate mechanism, which also comprises body (or will) and mind (or thought and imagination). These three centres – emotion, will and thought – Stanislavsky named the 'inner motive forces'. If emotion *was* so elusive, perhaps it could be more effectively stimulated, not through directly assaulting the emotion-centre itself, but *indirectly*, by provoking the will-centre (the body) and coercing the thought-centre (the imagination). In other words, if the performer actively *did* something and imaginatively *committed* to what he or she was doing, appropriate emotions would arise accordingly. After all, emotion isn't static. As Daniel Goleman proposes in his assessment of *Emotional Intelligence*, 'All emotions are, in essence, impulses to act, the instant plans for handling life that evolution has instilled in us.'[12] He goes on to point out that the very root of the word *emotion* is *motere*, the Latin verb 'to move', plus the prefix 'e' to indicate 'move away'. This suggests that there is a tendency to act implicit in every emotion. And attention to action was the underlying principle of Stanislavsky's final experiments: if emotion was to be aroused on the stage, stillness (be it inner or outer) had to be replaced from the very first moments of rehearsal by some kind of action (be it inner or outer). As he declared to his opera students in 1935: 'Now we shall proceed differently. We shall create *the line of physical action*,' [13] believing that this line of physical action would engage the actor's body, which, in turn, could ignite the life of his or her humanity and spirit.

This transference of attention from inner emotion to on-stage action was described by his actor-protégé, Vasily Toporkov, as 'one of Stanislavsky's greatest discoveries'[14], though it wasn't really so much a 'discovery' as a culmination of a journey which can be traced throughout his life. It led to an approach which is most commonly known as the Method of Physical Actions or, in its later development, Active Analysis. In both cases, the actor was drawn *towards* physical actions and *away* from worrying about emoting in performance, so that the process actually freed up the actor's subconscious, inducing it to work spontaneously and creatively.[15] Through this *forward-moving* impulse, all the physiological, psychological and emotional components of the actor's apparatus were aligned almost effortlessly, making it a truly psycho-physical technique, where body and psychology (brain, emotions, and imagination) were mutually dependent. Sounds wonderful, but how do you do it?

Finding the physical actions

It's quite possible that without his previous exploration of round-the-table textual analysis (focusing on the thought-centre) and his notorious affective memory (focusing on the emotion-centre), Stanislavsky might never have reached the conclusion that it was in fact the *body* (via the will-centre) which was most accessible to the performer. With both analysis and affective memory, the actors were really starting at one remove from the stage experience. They were sitting round a table or conjuring up imaginative memory: they weren't actually experiencing the encounter. The potential of the Method of Physical Actions, however, lay in its *immediacy*.[16] The actor didn't ask, 'What would I do *if* I were in this situation?', but simply said 'Here I *am* in the concrete reality of this stage environment, so what do I do *now*?' Paradoxically, it was by acknowledging the actuality of being in a theatrical situation that the actor's imagination was liberated, rather than being constrained within pretend circumstances. This was the magic of physical actions.

But what exactly were they, these physical actions?

Basically, physical actions were an organic blend of several of the existing elements of Stanislavsky's system, including inner actions, objectives and activities. They were expressed through small, achievable tasks of an outer nature (which could be as simple as 'I turn on/off a light switch') and an inner nature (such as 'I charm you', 'I intimidate you', 'I reject you', etc.). What was important about physical actions is that they were usually directed towards the on-stage partner or they created an effect on a partner. So, I turn on the light switch to make the room more comfortable for you and then it is easier for me to charm you. Or, I turn off the light switch so that you can't see me and then it's easier for me to intimidate you. On the one hand, these achievable tasks could encapsulate great psychological complexities. On the other hand, their simplicity and directness was such that they could be accomplished effortlessly by the actor. This meant that carrying out physical actions wasn't an end in itself, but rather it set in motion the actor's transition from everyday life into complex psychological and emotional experiences pertinent to the play in hand.[17]

The rehearsal technique for finding the line of physical actions was in fact very simple. It was no longer a question of engaging in extensive textual knowledge and prolonged discussion of a play; instead the actors were asked to come to a rehearsal, read a scene through – after which there would be some brief discussion of the structure and content of the scene – and then they would get up and improvise it.[18] After each improvisation, the actors considered what they had done, both in terms of the line of physical actions and the sensations which had arisen out of those actions. They then assessed how appropriate those actions and sensations were to the characters and the scene. And at each subsequent rehearsal, they made the necessary adaptations to the physical actions to enable them to draw closer to the experience of the characters and the intentions of the playwright. They didn't worry about directly changing the *sensations*. They didn't think, 'Oh, I must play it happier here, angrier there.' They just changed the physical actions to try and find the ones which would arouse happiness, arouse anger or whatever the appropriate sensation might be. *Doing it* was the key to *understanding* it.

There was nothing particularly new in this approach. Extensive improvisation had actually been instigated by Meyerhold in the 1905 Theatrical Studio, much to the exasperation of the Moscow Art Theatre's co-founder, Nemirovich-Danchenko. At the time, he was astonished that Stanislavsky could endorse a process, which demanded nothing more of the actors than to rehearse 'as the spirit moves' them.[19] Meyerhold had overthrown analysis, psychology and reason, and instead had drawn the material for the production from whatever the actors intuitively presented without any knowledge of the characters or the overall tone of the play. Although Nemirovich-Danchenko was outraged, it's clear to see how Meyerhold's anarchic method in the 1905 Theatrical Studio pre-empted the techniques promoted by Stanislavsky some thirty years later. Once more, in 1935, analysis was subordinated and the improvisation of words and actions became the main rehearsal principle.

It's important to realise that, with the Method of Physical Actions, these improvisations were far from generalised or haphazard: for Stanislavsky, identifying truthful physical actions required just as much attention to detail as with round-the-table analysis. After all, however simple the actions might be, the actors still needed to break the scenes into bits and objectives, to give a logic and consistency to their actions and feelings. What this meant was that each time the scene was improvised and the appropriate actions identified, the sequence of physical actions (known as the 'score') was noted, adjusted and ultimately fixed to form a skeleton for the scene. Once a precise score had been identified and fixed, it could then be repeated and invested each time with the actors' own colours, to the point where habit became easy and ease became beautiful. It's quite possible that the final 'score' bore a strong resemblance to the kind of prompt copy that Stanislavsky forced upon his actors during his early days at the Moscow Art Theatre, or even to the results of endless hours of collaborative round-the-table analysis. However, the process of discovering the score of physical actions was significantly different. The performers didn't act out the director's predetermined choreography, neither did they sit at a table with their heads in the scripts and a pencil in their hands: 'No, we remained on the stage and we acted, we searched in our action, *in our own natural life*, for whatever we needed to promote our objective.'[20]

Finding the playwright's text

Note that Stanislavsky says that the search for physical actions began by looking 'in our own natural life'. What this meant was that with the immediacy and spontaneity of the early improvisations, *character* wasn't a primary concern. Instead, Stanislavsky insisted that the actors started with *themselves* and their own justification of any chosen action. He believed that if they drew on their personal perspective of life, habits, artistic senses, intuition, or whatever was needed to help them execute their actions, they would find that their own nature would guide them towards the first stages of characterisation. A dynamic, immediate connection with the physical actions would provide them with a rock-solid, human foundation for the creative process, from which a fully-rounded interpretation could develop and grow, rather than superficially putting the character on like an overcoat.

Starting with 'themselves' certainly had a significant effect on how text was used in rehearsals, particularly with Active Analysis. The script was, of course, *the starting point* for locating the line of actions in terms of the initial read-through and discussion of a scene, but then (for a while) the playwright's words ceased to be 'holy'. During the early rehearsals, the author's exact text wasn't required, but rather the actors used their own understanding of the ideas and actions embodied in the play.[21] Little by little, through improvisation and continuous re-readings of the script, the words the actors used to express ideas and actions drew closer and closer to the playwright's text, to the point at which they were dead-letter-perfect. What was important for Stanislavsky was that the actors found their own journey towards those words, rather than learning them by rote. He believed that 'between our own words and those of another, the distance is of most immeasurable size. Our own words are the direct expression of our feelings, whereas the words of another are alien until we have made them our own, are nothing more than signs of future emotions which have not yet come to life inside us. Our own words are needed in the first phase of physical embodiment of a part because they are best able to extract from within us live feelings, which have not yet found their outward expression.'[22] In fact, Stanislavsky actively *forbade* the memorizing of the playwright's text. He even went so far as to consider that those actors, who depended on the words of the script, betrayed their reluctance to embody fully the characters' life and express it through physical actions. He was confident that if the actors simply discovered what physical actions they needed, they would reduce their dependence on learning the spoken word and bring the play truly to life.[23]

That doesn't mean that Stanislavsky left the actors floundering in their improvisations. There would come a time in rehearsals when he felt that the actual text was now necessary to the actors. At this point he gradually fed them from the sidelines – like a football coach – with the writer's words. The actors grabbed these words hungrily because, by this stage, they knew that the author's text expressed a thought or carried out a piece of action far better than their own words could.[24] The result of this process was a seemingly effortless passage from (1) the actors' improvised speech, through (2) the director's side-line promptings from the author's text, to (3) an ultimate state of knowing the lines because those were the words that the actors needed. They didn't have to learn them in a formalised manner. By working this way, Stanislavsky believed that the actual speaking of a text could become the 'creation of the living word'[25] with its roots running deep into the actor's soul and emerging as an expression of his or her true inner action.

Summing it all up, Stanislavsky described the Method of Physical Actions, and Active Analysis, as being carried out simultaneously by all the intellectual, emotional, spiritual, and physical forces of our nature. This isn't theoretical, 'but *practical research* for the sake of a *genuine objective*, which we attain through *physical actions.*'[26] In other words, it was a kind of textual analysis which was carried out by the actor's entire being, and not solely the brain. This led to a synthesis of the actor and the play, rather than the dissection of the text. This synthesis connected *natural* physical phenomena to a creative technique, and that creative technique could then be used to tackle theatrical *artifice*.

Where does emotion fit into all this?

William James proposed that in life the *external stimulus* – let's call it 'the bear' – is the catalyst in the emotion process. It's exactly the same on stage: the first link in the chain of reaction is the external stimulus, be it atmosphere, music, set, props, partner and audience. The *root* of these stimuli is of course the play-text, but in the actual moment of on-stage encounter, it is the flesh-and-blood negotiation of the environment (music, audience, partner, etc.) which breathes life into the action. If an actor's contact with the partner is not *unlimited*, it's quite possible that there will be absolutely no truthful engagement with his or her own body, emotions, imagination or humanity. In that case, the audience may be presented with a very aesthetic construct – wonderful *mise-en-scène*, lovely delivery of text, beautiful line of movement – but the actor is really giving nothing more than form without content. And in fact it's possible to see it all the time, even in the West End or on Broadway: actors playing in a bubble, without *really* listening to each other or their surroundings. They may be picking up their cues and therefore *seeming* to listen to each other, but the space between them isn't reverberating, isn't alive, isn't in a state of constant adaptation. I repeat, it's contact with the environment which stimulates emotion. As James puts it, 'The most important part of my environment is my fellow man. The consciousness of his attitude towards me is the perception that normally unlocks most of my shames and indignations and fears.'[27] And loves, and joys, and pleasures – both social pleasures and artistic pleasures.

In dramatic terms, the attitude of one's fellow man – i.e. what do people think of me? – becomes part of the pursuit of *objectives* and *actions*. An objective usually stems from the desire to change the on-stage partner's attitude towards you, and distilled down to its essence it's often to do with one of two primary instincts: *attraction towards* ('I want you to love me') or *repulsion from* ('I want you to fear me'). Suppose the actor's objective is 'I want to get my partner to leave the room'. The actions employed by the actor to achieve this objective may be, for example, 'to offend him', 'to provoke him', 'to threaten him' or 'to repel him'. Each of these actions is a tactic employed in an attempt to provoke the partner to alter his attitude towards the provocateur, so that ultimately he *wants* to leave the room. At that point, the provocateur's objective will have been achieved. Just as affective memory informs our moment-by-moment decisions, the pursuit of objectives also underlies all human behaviour. All our actions in life stem from desires or needs, the most fundamental objective, or super-objective, being 'I want to survive.' To obtain that super-objective, we have to execute a whole series of smaller objectives: 'I want to solve the murder investigation because I need to impress the boss. I want to impress the boss because I need to keep my job. I want to keep my job because I need to earn money. I want to earn money because I need to buy food. I want to buy food because I need to eat. I need to eat because I want to survive.'

The extent to which we try to achieve an objective depends upon our appraisal of each and every situation in which we find ourselves with any other person. We assess, sometimes almost instantaneously, the importance with which we endow the meeting and how deep our need to change that person's attitude towards us. I walk into the audition room and I so badly want this film job that I make sure I do everything I possibly can to change the director's attitude towards me. I don't want him thinking, 'Is she right for the part?'; I want him to believe, 'Wow, she's the one to play in this movie and guarantee us Oscar nominations'. Our appraisal of a situation stems from the spontaneous assimilation of our past experience (affective memory) and our projected future (imagination). Or as Magda B. Arnold suggests, 'Anything that is appraised as good here and now will result in an impulse towards it. And what *is* so appraised depends as much on memory and imagination as it does on the here-and-now experience'.[28] So the past, present and future are working together all the time to determine our actions and decisions: 'I don't want to be a temp any more' (affective memory) – 'I want to live in Hollywood' (imagination); 'Oh, and by the way, I really like this director!' (present-tense appraisal). The value we give to a situation produces within us a particular emotion, and that emotion then prompts us to take specific actions. All the time, we're subconsciously and instantaneously organising our emotion according to our evaluation of the situation that produced it. In other words, the emotion produced by the way in which we appraise a situation leads us to take a specific, or 'organised' pattern of action. Or as Stanislavsky put it: 'a line of physical action'.

If it happens in life, it can happen on the stage

As human beings, we are constantly and spontaneously determining objectives and setting in motion *organised patterns of behaviour* – or *lines of physical action* – to achieve those objectives. So once again, there's a natural, biological and psychological backdrop to the processes proposed by Stanislavsky for getting inside a role through Active Analysis. Pursuit of objectives is discussed very clearly by psychologist Karl Pribam, who calls objectives 'Plans'. If something stops us in an important situation from achieving our Plan (or objective), then anger, frustration, maybe even fear can arise. This emotion can either open us to make further attempts to achieve our Plan, or close us completely. If the blocking of our Plan continues, Pribam describes how we either enter a state of considerable regression or we alter our Plan to a version we feel fairly confident we can successfully achieve.[29] In each scenario – whether we're blocked or whether we're successful in attaining our objective – emotion arises. Although Pribam is discussing human behaviour in life, it corresponds precisely to the pursuit of dramatic objectives on the stage. Does the character within the play retreat from a blocked objective or alter the tactic and begin another assault? Either way, the psychologists' analysis shows that emotion is an unbidden by-product of persevering with a Plan or objective through a line of physical actions. In other words, play your action, pursue your objective and you can't help but feel the emotion. Active Analysis places you at the heart of that pursuit, putting you in a position where you're constantly developing a dual consciousness. Dual consciousness enables you to commit physically and imaginatively to the actions in hand, while simultaneously assessing how relevant those sensations are for the character and the scene. So part of you is doing the action: part of you is watching the action. Through this dual consciousness, the actor can gradually align his or her real sensations with the given circumstances of the playwright's text.

Pursuit of action can be wholly absorbing. This leads to another paradox: if a person (or actor) is completely absorbed in an action, then not only is his or her attention *deflected* from the emotion, but also the emotion actually *increases* for the very reason that the person (or actor) isn't concentrating on it.[30] So we'll find that we're being emotional on stage, because we're being *active*: we no longer need to fake the emotion or squeeze it out like a tube of toothpaste. The psychologists' perspective goes to reinforce the fact that Stanislavsky's shift from emotion to action (in the Method of Physical Actions and Active Analysis) was a true alignment of biology with art, and nature with nurture. This endorses the protest against those who pigeon-hole Stanislavsky's theories as cerebral, obsolete, and theoretical. Far from it: they're artistic, vibrant and practical. Above all, they're transferable from one genre to another, as it's simply a question of human interaction. And I would argue that any genre of theatre is essentially about human communication at some level or another. Psycho-physical acting isn't concerned purely with the genre of psychological realism. It's an approach to acting encompassing all styles and '-isms', because it's concerned with body and psychology feeding each other on the inner/outer continuum discussed by practitioners as diverse as Meyerhold, Grotowski, Brook and Chaikin. Physical Action is an organic method of interaction both *within* the actor (in terms of will, thought and feeling) and *between* actors (in terms of dramatic dialogue). In the realms of science lies the drama of objectives and obstacles, the pursuit of needs and desires: it's a natural instinct, not a theoretician's conceit. The question is how to put it all into practice in a manageable, logical and inspiring actor-training, and so get to the heart of Active Analysis. It was at this point that my journey to Moscow revealed all. So without further ado, let's go there . . .

ACT 2
Working on Your Self

What do you mean – 'psycho-physical'?

The ten-month Russian training was geared towards developing an actor's psycho-physicality. Well, what on earth does that mean? In a nutshell, the basis of psycho-physical acting is that *inner feeling* and *outer expression* happen at the same time. In other words, whatever emotion you may be experiencing, your physical response to that emotion is instantaneous. And *vice versa*: whatever physical action you execute, the inner sensation aroused by that action is spontaneous. That doesn't necessarily mean that if you feel upset, you show that sorrow, as we all know that in everyday life we often hide or disguise or deny our real emotions. What it does mean is that there has to be a genuine and dynamic connection within each actor between seen action and unseen sensation. Let's be clear that at this stage we're dealing with actor-training and not with what goes on inside an actor during performance. I'll come on to that shortly. But we have to wake the actor up before we can arouse the character.

Many practitioners divide acting into 'inner/outer' techniques (for example 'Method' acting) and 'outer/inner' techniques (for example 'character' acting). But in reality these distinctions aren't so clear. In effect there's no *divide* between body and psychology, but rather a *continuum*; as we go about our daily lives, different experiences stimulate us at different points along that continuum, not simply at one end or the other. What we're doing in psycho-physical actor-training is simply harnessing all those natural responses and channelling them into the artificial

circumstances of the stage, so that, when we're playing a character, the inner/outer dialogue takes place truthfully and simultaneously. Then, and only then, will an audience really understand
what's going on before their eyes. As Michael Chekhov describes
it, we are 'transforming the outer thing into the inner life, and
changing the inner life into the outer event.'[31] And the continuum between inner and outer – body and emotion – is the crux
of psycho-physical co-ordination.

Are you listening?

The whole process should be very easy: after all, we do it all the
time in normal life without even thinking about it. On stage,
however, the connection between outer experience and inner
sensation is incredibly elusive, because the degree of sensitivity
required by the actor demands that he or she lives entirely *in the
moment*. Or as Stanislavsky puts it, the actor has to lay 'the *total*
bestowal of all his powers on the transient 'now', without a
thought of how he will act and sustain himself until the fifth or
sixth act'.[32] As most actors know – especially if a role is particularly demanding – it's not always easy to sweep the troublesome
parts of the play from your thoughts and simply get on with the
scene in hand. Even if your mind doesn't wander to the dodgy
scene in the second act, it's extremely difficult to listen *truly*
to the words of your partner in the actual moment that they're
spoken. Too often we unconsciously wait for cue lines, or
go through the motions of rehearsed reactions. *Real* listening
doesn't rely on the ear, but rather on the whole of the actor's
body and psychology, and to engage in this all-consuming activity of real listening, the actor needs to be in a state of *constant
inner improvisation*. What that means is that, as you listen to the
words spoken on-stage, you allow those words really to touch
your heart; this in turn prompts the right response, which
(ultimately) is the playwright's text. Putting it another way, the
words on the page become exactly the words you need in order to
express yourself truthfully, rather than simply being a series of

learned and rehearsed responses. Nothing preconceived or repeated is brought into the stage-space: every impulse is born in *that* moment, in that 'transient now'. It goes without saying that this kind of constant improvisation has to remain entirely within the realms of both the playwright's text and the director's overview: it's the actor's *inner* adaptation, not an invitation to complete anarchy.

Inner adaptation needs supreme attention to the other actors on-stage: the slightest change in your partner's tone or the subtlest turn of the head will create a different response within you every night if you're really listening to your partner. But the listening doesn't stop there. In fact, it doesn't even *start* there. If it's essential for you to listen to your on-stage partner, it's even more important to develop the ability to listen to *yourself.* And this requires the absolute complicity within each actor of the 'inner motive forces'. As I discussed in Chapter 1, the inner motive forces comprise the 'emotion-centre', the 'thought-centre' and the 'action-centre', and the dialogue that goes on between these centres is a very subtle one. If you want to tap into this dialogue as an actor, you have to understand how your body affects your psychology, and how your psychology affects your body in everyday life.

Since 'psychology' is a fairly amorphous, ungraspable concept, the easiest way into this process is through the body, which isn't amorphous and is utterly graspable. Fine-tuning the body will help us to fine-tune the other parts of our psycho-physical mechanism (imagination, emotion and will). If the key to what Stanislavsky calls the 'life of the human spirit' on stage really is the interplay between what you do and how you feel, then we *need* our creative tools to be this finely tuned. Tuned to the extent that the subtlest gesture can inspire an emotional response, or the gentlest shift of emotional sensation can arouse the body. While most actors would undoubtedly like this fine-tuning to be an inherent part of their natural talent, in reality it often isn't and a thorough physical-training programme seems not only to be inevitable, but essential. To this end, Stanislavsky suggested daily exercises for the actor, such as those practised by the dancer, the athlete or the musician. The intention was that, like our fellow artists, the constant repetition of certain exercises would ensure that the muscles could be conditioned; through this physical conditioning, Stanislavsky believed that the 'creative state' – the realm of inspiration – could be developed. If an actor regularly practised these physical exercises, the 'creative state' could become the *natural* state for the performer, for ultimately (as Stanislavsky insists) all such training 'must become habitual'.[33] After all, any technique is only useful once it becomes second nature.

Finding a suitable psycho-physical work-out

Most actors are lazy when it comes to physical preparation. We're more than happy to participate in sport or dance or work-outs at the gym, or even a quick stretch before a performance. But the kind of psycho-physical preparation required of acting, which after all employs the complex and simultaneous combination of body, mind and emotions, is rarely practised. The training offered in Russia addressed this very task: *to condition the muscles of the body* in readiness for *expressing the spirit of the character*: this training constituted much of the work led by Scenic Movement teacher, Vladimir Ananyev. Ananyev had a pithy little epigram stating that 'in the beginning was the word, but the word was false', and so he turned to the *simplest human movement* as the most immediate means of expression. As Stanislavsky advised, 'An actor, like an infant, must learn everything from the beginning, to look, to walk, to talk, and so on',[34] and from the start of his training programme, Ananyev set about teaching the actor to do this very thing: to 'walk again'. This he did through a series of simple physical exercises, believing that through the thorough breakdown of technical movement, then slowly but surely the actor can rediscover just how intelligent and versatile the body is. And more than that: he or she can penetrate the sophisticated interplay between body and emotions. Once you're armed with this new insight, you no longer have to depend upon the brain to do all the detective work on a script; instead, you can turn to the *body's* connection with the text, as a channel for discovering a character. At the end of the day, Ananyev believed that simple physical tuning can enhance complex psychological sensitivity.

The roots of Ananyev's work were fairly eclectic, ranging from martial arts, tumbling, gymnastics and Meyerhold's Biomechanics to classical dance, eastern philosophy, Michael Chekhov's principles and yoga. So the exercises in this chapter are definitely Ananyev's idiosyncracy rather than any closely defined interpretation of Stanislavsky or Chekhov. Added to which, this account is definitely *my* interpretation of Ananyev's exercises, which in itself further perpetuates the 'lore' of actor-training as I discussed in the introduction. Ananyev himself had trained as an actor at Moscow's State Institute of Theatre Arts (GITIS), before working in the experimental, almost underground, Theatre of Plastic Drama from 1974 to 1988. As his understanding of psycho-physicality increased, he began to coach dance, plastic movement, stage-fighting and pantomime in various dramatic, musical and puppet theatres throughout Moscow, and eventually throughout Europe.

By the time I met him as the Scenic Movement pedagogue at the State Institute of Cinematography (VGIK), Ananyev was also Associate Director of Moscow's Theatre of Clowns. This was no small coincidence, clowning being an important discipline for combining bright fantasy with broad physicality. As Michael Chekhov points out, 'Clowning will teach you *to believe in whatever you wish*'[35], and you need this kind of imaginative liberation when you're dealing with the complexities and inhibitions so often tied up with physical expression. And Ananyev certainly invested much of his teaching at VGIK with his knowledge of physical theatre. He encouraged the actor, like the clown, to explore the psychology of a character through bold physicality. Incorporating *movement* into *psychology* in this way proved to be extremely important. One of the fundamental

problems for us as actors is that the primary tool for creativity –
our selves – is also used each day for a range of activities, most of
which are not particularly creative. How do we turn an
instrument of everyday mundanity into one of potential genius?
This can be very difficult for many actors, particularly in our
rather cerebrally-orientated British culture: body and psychology quickly become separated, rather than integrated. This
might explain why some actors shy away from physical warm-
ups: there's a kind of fear that muscular stiffness is a reflection
that other acting tools – emotions and mind – are atrophied too.
But as Michael Chekhov suggests, when the body *does* become
integrated into our psychology, 'this same body which we use the
whole day through for going here and there . . . is a different one
when we are on the stage.'[36] And the subtle adaptation of our
own everyday body into that of a created character is integral to
psycho-physical acting.

   Physical adaptation was at the heart of Ananyev's work. He
wanted to help us find ways of 'transcending' our everyday
physicality and personality, and to find a path into each new
character that might take us by surprise and excite us as performers. His training programme assailed this 'transcendence' in
three particular ways. First, by developing each actor's physical
vocabulary through exercises and improvisations. Secondly, by
finding a way of accessing personal energies and resources rarely
used in daily life. (This corresponded to Michael Chekhov's
'higher consciousness' and focused on energies that might,
through their metaphysical properties, raise the actor's work to a
truly artistic plane. Although this may sound frighteningly esoteric, it could in fact be hugely liberating, and I'll discuss it in
further detail later in this chapter.) Thirdly, Ananyev seemed to
propose that, by harnessing this 'higher consciousness', an actor
could break away from his or her own particular mannerisms and
clichés to develop a character's 'creative individuality'. Although
I'll also go on to explore this at greater length, let me sum it up
by saying that in fact Stanislavsky and Chekhov believed not
in *three* inner motive forces, but in *four*: the will-centre, the

thought-centre, the emotion-centre, and the *spirit*. I'm aware from experience that the concept of 'spirit' and 'spirituality' can ring alarm bells in some practitioners, but all Stanislavsky and Chekhov were suggesting was that our daily, conscious life is the tip of the iceberg: the realms of the subconscious are vast. By creating an environment in which we allow ourselves to delve deeper into that creative subconscious – or rather, by freeing ourselves from the dominance of our analytical brains (which aren't always that intelligent anyway) – we can begin to access a kind of 'creative spontaneity'. A state in which we can experience flashes of inspiration, when we do things on stage that we didn't know we were going to do, or that we didn't even know we were capable of doing. In this state of creative spontaneity, the tempo-rhythm of the character (or the 'creative individuality') starts to take on a life of its own. It's nothing spooky or schizophrenic, it's simply unexpected and inspiring. And – most importantly – it all lies within the confines of the text and the artifice of the stage; in no way does it send you to the therapist's couch. But I will return to all this in due course . . .

Possessing your personal space

All these concepts of 'higher consciousness' and 'creative individuality' may seem fairly remote and of little relevance to an actor doing three lines in an episode of a TV soap. On the contrary. Just as a pianist can apply arpeggios to Mozart or Mantovani, and the *port de bras* will help a West End chorus or a Pina Bausch ensemble, so the 'psycho-physical work-out' developed at VGIK proved to be as applicable to pantomime as to Shakespeare. As with any technique, the first step is always the hardest, and the starting point in Ananyev's psycho-physical programme was the painstaking return to simple movement. This occupied the first two months of the ten-month programme. Two or three sessions were held per week, each of which lasted from 1½ to 2 hours, and the regularity of these sessions in the early stages was essential if every actor's body was to engage fully in the tough re-learning process. (Ideally, they should be held daily.)

Each class began with a physical warm-up conducted by Ananyev, the first stage of which involved us all assuming a 'primary' or 'vertical' position. For Ananyev, this was a very specific pose not unlike the statue of Yuri Gagarin in Moscow, and at first it wasn't particularly comfortable. With the feet together in parallel, the weight of the body was shifted slightly forwards onto the balls of the feet, as if the ten toes were lightly gripping the floor. Keeping a feeling of extension up the back of the calves, the knees were gently pushed backwards and turned outwards, with the hips also turned out from the pelvis, like an open book. The sensation in the upper legs was as if the feet were actually in 1st position, not parallel. This created a sense of dynamic tension up the legs: although the feet were pointing forwards, the thighs were opened out from the hip joints at 45 degrees. As for the rest of the body, the pelvis was slightly curled forward as if the 'tail' was tucked underneath, and the stomach was gently drawn in. The extension of the chest went in three directions – forwards, upwards and open to the sides – with an expansive, but not inflated, feeling. The extension of the shoulders went in two directions: slightly back, and downwards. The elbows were bent away from the body a little, with the flats of the palms placed lightly on the outsides of the mid-thighs to allow the air to circulate between the body and the inner arms. (Your arms should feel as light as wings in repose.) The eye-line was focused just above the horizon as if there was a rose opening in front of the throat beneath the chin. The image of a cord extending from the top of the head to the heavens allowed the actor's spine to elongate and the energy centre in the solar plexus to feel active and open. Added to all this was – a smile!

Although it could feel rather phoney at first, the smile served two specific purposes in terms of psycho-physical awareness. In the first place, Ananyev incorporated into exercises elements of eastern philosophy (also an essential aspect of Michael Chekhov's practices and much of Stanislavsky's early work with

Leopold Sulerzhitsky in the Moscow Art Theatre's First Studio). If the actor smiled, he or she could begin to open the seventh chakra – the Hindu energy centre in the crown of the head. This could provide a conduit through which higher consciousness (or inspiration) might enter the human body, igniting like fireworks all the energy centres down the spine. Secondly, and rather more tangibly, the smile created an atmosphere of fun, which was the key to assimilating knowledge. This echoed Michael Chekhov's 'Feeling of Ease', which is 'related to humour, a crucial aspect of art. The more hearty gaiety the actor brings into all his exercises the better.'[37] There's no doubt we all found that a great deal of physical and mental effort was required to re-educate our physicality, and as Stanislavsky maintained, 'When an actor is making too much effort, it is sometimes a good idea for him to introduce a lighter, more frivolous approach to his work.'[38] And so, Ananyev insisted on a smile!

Although the various cross-tensions of the 'vertical' position felt strange at first, it was surprisingly empowering. In fact, it resembled a relaxed prone position, the kind of position you naturally fall into lying in bed: it's just that we were doing it standing up.

The position was very important for Ananyev in terms of creating character. Our natural standing posture usually lies outside the vertical line of the spine: either falling forwards or leaning back. Unless we identify our natural perversions of the vertical position, we'll never be able to create characters which can 'transcend' our everyday physicality. We'll always be dragging them back to and caging them within our own individual unconscious physical contortions. Because the vertical position aligns the spine with all its energy centres, it can be incredibly invigorating. At the same time, it gives the actor a physical 'blank canvas'. Once we'd adopted this position, a very simple but remarkably revealing exercise ensued. Each actor leant as far forward in this position and as far backwards as possible without falling over or losing the line of the spine. The psychology of the physical exercise is to explore how I feel inside, when I possess my personal space (leaning forward), when I find my neutral space (standing in the vertical position) and when I retreat from my personal space (leaning backwards). On stage, the actor must always possess his or her own personal space, even if the *character* is either retreating or pro-active. It's by possessing our personal space that we put ourselves in the maximum position of activity: I can advance, or I can retreat at a moment's notice. Even if the character is a couch potato (therefore clearly existing in the relaxed space), the actor must be in possession of his or her space *within* the character's retreating posture.

Re-negotiating the body through joints and straight lines

Having explored the sensations of the entire body existing within its own space, a process of re-negotiating the details of the body began. The first step was to understand the most basic movement: the movement within *the joints of the skeleton*. Although it may sound obvious, we wouldn't be able to move very far without our joints, and yet so often we allow them to stiffen or atrophy (particularly our spines), in our tendency to concentrate on developing muscles and physical strength. Now was the time to tackle this head on. In the main sessions of the first few weeks, Ananyev focused intensively on isolating the action of a single joint – such as a wrist or ankle or hip. To clarify the exercise even further, the movement was restricted to only one joint at a time and the trajectory could only be *in straight lines*. It was a matter of breaking physical action down to its absolute simplest. What was important though was that, even in these early stages, exercises weren't locked in the realm of dry technicality: the imagination always had an active part in the physical work. So, in this instance, we were to imagine that our bodies were like the small wooden figurines used by artists in preparing drawings, so that a vivid imaginative picture could help with the physical task of isolating individual joints.

Theoretically the exercise was extremely simple. Each actor was to describe a series of straight lines through the air, each straight line being led by a particular joint with the rest of the limb following like a kite-tail. Every movement had to be very specific: so, if we were focusing on the wrist joint, for example, it wasn't a question of observing how the hand flexes forwards and backwards *from* the wrist, but how the wrist joint itself can describe straight lines in the air. Inevitably this movement does involve the hand flexing to and fro as it follows behind the wrist like a watch-chain, but the wrist joint is the focus, not the hand. The important thing to remember in all this is that the point of the exercise wasn't simply to *execute* the movement, but to allow a *sensation* of the movement to permeate the whole body. After all, this is the basic premise of psycho-physical training: the body, imagination and emotions are all working, all the time, whether the exercise is apparently technical, emotional or imagination-led. If the actor allowed the *sensation* of movement to be as significant as the *execution* of movement, it soon became clear that each joint could arouse a profoundly different feeling. For example, if the knee was leading, the quality of the movement might have a certain gravitas; if the middle joint of the forefinger was leading, the movement might be nimble and intricate. So a feeling of solemnity on the one hand (knee) or mischief on the other (finger) could swamp the whole body, just from the starting point of a single joint.

Concentrating on limited movement (simply *one joint at a time in a straight line*) was crucial for developing psycho-physical awareness, and yet horrifyingly difficult. I found that having lived in my body for some twenty-odd years and worked as an actor for five of those years, it was strangely humiliating suddenly to discover just how little I actually knew about that body. Ironically, I found that returning to a movement as simple as isolating one joint seemed to *freeze* the body at first, not free it. But as Michael Chekhov says, 'Realise that the joints are not given you to make you stiff, but on the contrary to enable you to use your limbs with utmost freedom and flexibility.'[39] The joint is the simplest cog in the machine of the body, and yet understanding its movement proved to be extremely hard. The task was actually made easier by repeating the exercise in pairs. With one actor as the figurine (usually with their eyes closed so that they could intensify their personal circle of attention), the other actor took the role of artist or sculptor, and moulded the figurine by manipulating just one joint at a time. The 'figurine' had surrendered the decision-making part of the brain, as the choices about which joint to move next were now being made by the sculptor. This allowed the possibilities of the body to be more freely explored. All the 'figurine' had to do was to submit to the *sensation* of particular movements, and to notice how outer movement affected inner emotion or feeling. It was funny how much easier it was to awaken a sense of psycho-physicality when you didn't have to take responsibility for your own body's movements.

Focusing on straight lines quickly revealed just how little our bodies actually move along a flat plane. Bending the lower arm to the upper arm (so that the hand meets the shoulder) was a movement on a *curved* plane, therefore outside the realm of this exercise, and so other possibilities of moving the elbow joint had to be explored. This basically meant discovering that the only way for the elbow to describe a straight line was to move the entire arm through space. Similarly, the knee wasn't allowed to bend, the head couldn't turn, and it was certainly a big no-no for the jaw to yawn wide open. In fact the natural predominance of body movements proved to be on a *curved* plane. Taking the time to rediscover the body in this way felt both wildly frustrating and strangely privileged. While the question sometimes nagged, 'Why do I *need* to know that the body hardly uses straight lines?', I was aware that without this physical knowledge – and further-more, without the opportunity to *discover* this knowledge – I was blurring the edges of my own understanding of the basics of psycho-physicality. In other words, by painstakingly developing *physical* co-ordination, we were preparing ourselves for the tougher task of developing *psycho*-physical co-ordination: that is, the effortless connection between inner sensation and outer expression.

Waves and physical plasticity

Having spent several sessions exploring in detail isolated movements on a *straight* line, it was time to introduce the *curved plane*. At this point, the artist's figurine (with moving joints only) was exchanged for the image of a plasticine model, like Morph or Wallace. This meant that we were no longer limited to just our skeletons: we could now picture muscles, sinews, and tendons, and in fact the softness of the plasticine image enhanced the sensuality of the curved movements. We were still restricted to one isolated limb at a time, but now the elbow could bend, the knee could genuflect and the torso could bow. And with this increased *physical* vocabulary came an increased range of *sensation*. To thrust your head forward in *a straight line*, like a turtle from a shell, could arouse a sensation of strange curiosity, of peering at the world: the movement was essentially outward-flowing. In contrast to that, bowing your head forward *on a curved plane* could arouse a sensation of humility, contemplation, and reverence: the movement was essentially inward-flowing. It was important that the approach to this intense training was slow and precise to allow the actor time to experience this kind of *sensation* of movements, as well as how those movements provoke different emotional qualities. This was enhanced when we worked once again in partners: like the 'figurine', the 'plasticine' actor was able to relinquish the decision-making part of the brain to the sculptor. This left him or her free to experience both the sensation of the pose and – importantly – *the movement through space* to achieve that pose. It's only when technical movement and inner sensation go hand in hand that psycho-physical awareness can develop.

These early sessions focused on the significance of joints and their isolated movement on both straight and curved planes. The next step was then to put a series of joint movements together to form a *physical wave*. Why bother doing that, then? Well, the wave is the basic impulse of all natural and human existence. We're constantly involved in the continuing sequence of (1) action,

(2) reaction, (3) decision, whether it's in private experiences or social encounters. Someone greets us in the street (action), we like that person (reaction), and we choose to greet them back (decision). The psycho-physical wave sequence is at the root of our ordinary, spontaneous lives. The trouble is that, as with many of the things that we do spontaneously in real life, when we try to apply it to the artificiality of the stage, it ain't so easy. Psycho-physical waves are complex; they involve us *completely*, in terms of our emotions, our imaginations, our decisions, as we take information from the world, chew that information around and spew out our response to it. So in actor-training, rather than tackle psycho-physical waves head on, we can approach them first by assessing their tangible, *physical* properties. And in that way we can begin to unlock the more complicated elements of their *psychological* properties. If we start like this – with something physical and manageable – eventually we ought to be able to understand what's going on in our spontaneous responses. We can then apply that understanding to the artificial conditions surrounding our on-stage interactions.

As with all the other exercises in Ananyev's training programme, the first step was to break the wave down to its simplest execution. So, to begin with, exercises were often confined to one part of the body, such as the arm. The way to explore the wave motion in a single limb was for each actor to hold both arms out at right angles in front of his or her body like a Native American chief with one arm placed on top of the other. A wave motion was then directed along the top arm by isolating and activating single joints in consecutive order. It began with the elbow, then the wrist, then the knuckles, then the joints of the fingers, and finally the finger tips. By laying one arm on the other, it was easier for the actor to keep the wave on a horizontal plane, making sure that the task was executed as precisely as possible. This is in fact an extremely difficult exercise, especially as most actors find that they simply can't isolate the finger tips. What frustration arises when we discover how little control we have over our own bodies! And this single exercise quickly highlights just how difficult the actor's task is. If we can't even isolate and control simple joints, how on earth can we begin to understand the complex nature of the inner 'psychological waves' of action, reaction, decision? If the smallest *physical* task challenges us, how can we begin to control the intangible elements of our craft?

Articulating a wave motion through the entire body is even harder. To make it a bit easier, Ananyev suggested that the actor stands facing a wall. First the head is gently thrust forward on the horizontal plane so that the nose touches the wall; as the head is brought back into line with the spine, the shoulders are thrust forward to touch the wall. As the shoulders are returned to neutral, the chest is thrust forward and so on through the stomach, the groin and the knees. If using the wall isn't very helpful, the actor can lie on the floor while an obliging partner passes a stick underneath the various parts of the body – first under the head, then under the shoulders, the chest, and so on. Each part of the wave is executed by raising the appropriate section of the body off the floor *in sequence*. And this is why the wave movement is so crucial: it's about executing a series of individual actions *in sequence* to make a natural and logical flow of movement. This is at the heart of both the Method of Physical Actions and Active Analysis. Every action must come from what preceded it and lead to the next logical moment. That doesn't mean that the actions are predictable or unimaginative; but the spectators have to *believe* what's happening. They have to understand the cumulative sequence of action / reaction / decision. If, as actors, we skip a stage in the sequence of physical actions, our on-stage activity (inner and outer) will seem contrived and artificial. That's why a mastery of basic physical waves can have profound knock-on effects in terms of psycho-physical control.

Ananyev complicated the wave exercise even further by asking the actors to stand in the middle of the room (without the guidance of floor or wall) and to execute the sequence free-standing. We did this exercise many times during the year, often badly, usually frustratingly so. If it's regularly practised – and perfected! – the wave movement should eventually feel quite natural. And a sense of ease with the wave movement is really a prerequisite of this kind of training, since waves are central to psycho-physical (i.e. inner/outer and outer/inner) co-ordination. It demands great patience, control and attention to execute waves precisely and sequentially. Once again, it also requires an awareness of the *space through which the limb moves*, as well as the movement of the limb itself. For Ananyev, *space* was an important partner, with which an actor can work as closely on stage as with any *human* partner. It's through space that we connect with our fellow actors and with the audience; it's by filling space that we create atmosphere and energy, and so space becomes another essential component in psycho-physical awareness. (This will become clearer in Chapter 3.)

And in this way, isolations and their co-ordination into wave motions formed the basis of early psycho-physical training. What emerged after the first two weeks with Ananyev was that this kind of training is a long, slow process. Although much of what we were doing was in principle very simple, it all felt terribly strange. But the goal is that everything which at first feels alien to the body will eventually become habit, and habit makes everything feel easy. Basic psycho-physical training is working towards a sense of ease, since that sense of ease will ultimately become artistically beautiful and aesthetically pleasing for both performer and spectator alike.

The psychology of re-learning

The journey from the alien feeling to the 'beautiful ease' is often frustrating and – to be perfectly honest – plain boring. The first stages of developing a psycho-physical technique can present problems, particularly to those actors who have already had a fair amount of film and stage experience, as they quickly crave *results*. The problem at VGIK was that some of the actors in our English-speaking group were used to taking the necessary short-cuts demanded by brief rehearsal periods or, as in the case of television, by no rehearsal at all. The consequence of which was that they found Ananyev's process pretty slow, and they assumed that the exercises were all too easy, with little to show for their efforts in the early stages. Understandably, they grew impatient, but inevitably their impatience impeded their development. One fact remains inescapable: these exercises have to be *as simple as possible*, otherwise we start to cheat ourselves. Or as Michael Chekhov puts it, 'If we start with complicated exercises, our bodies will change them so that they become comfortable. We must defeat our body through simple basic means.'[40]

In many respects, Ananyev didn't see his Scenic Movement discipline as 'training', but rather as a process of physical 'liberation': liberation from our individual clichés, habits, muscular atrophy and physical inexpressiveness. This liberation can only be achieved through re-educating the body, and re-education can only be achieved through the simplification of movement. Actors who were frustrated by the slowness of the training programme were – subconsciously – trying to circumvent their own limitations. Re-education of any sort, particularly of the body, is neither easy nor particularly enjoyable. It's especially painful if we're experienced performers, as we don't even like to *hear* about our physical limitations, let alone try and confront or change them. But for Ananyev, that was exactly what the struggle of learning was all about: 'You take information, you analyse its use, you test its use for you personally, and you use it until it becomes second nature. But look how long it takes for a child to learn to walk, eat, talk – and that's starting from zero. How much harder to *un*learn before you can start to *re*learn.'

What emerged from the experience of those actors who became frustrated with the Russian training was that the very process of physical re-education is in itself a *psychological* challenge, in that it requires the actor to make a particular *mental* adjustment towards the *physical* exercises. Michael Chekhov anticipates this problem: as he points out, the psychology of someone who exercises for artistic purposes is quite different from the someone who exercises without knowing that '*repetition is actually the growing power*'. He stresses that it's important not to think that 'I'm doing something which is becoming stale and dull for me'. Instead, each time we do the simple lifting and lowering of the arm, we must 'do it with a fresh approach and a desire to do it again and again, as if for the first time'.[41] This is the key idea: that repetition is the growing power. After all, that's what rehearsal is all about, and interestingly the Russian word for 'rehearsal', not unlike the French, is *repetitsia*. In fact, the psychology required for exercise is exactly the same as that required for performance: that is, the participant needs to live in the moment, in the 'transient now', and to fill the activity with as much *imagination* as *physical precision*. Again, Michael Chekhov addresses this combination of technique and imagination, by suggesting that we approach a physical exercise with the psychology of a creative person, rather than as an athlete or technician. In this way, the exercise 'will not be somewhere else, and we, as creative persons, be here. The exercise must be where our creative spirit is'. Every simple task we undertake has to be done with a fresh approach, 'so that each small thing is an accomplished piece of art'.[42] If we *do* consider each small exercise to be 'an accomplished piece of art', then the training programme itself actually *becomes* the psycho-physical process, and not just a means of *developing* psycho-physical versatility. In other words, the result is here and now in the exercise, rather than somewhere in the future when we hope to reap the benefits of the hard work. Endorsing this theory, Ananyev believed that when there is a 'very exact process', that process could be presented to an audience at any moment and there would be something interesting to watch, so that, the process itself becomes the result. To maintain this 'very exact process', he advocated that 'it is better to go slowly and feel as though you've achieved nothing, than to push on and achieve wrong results.'

From the very beginning of psycho-physical training, the imagination (the thought-centre) and the body (the active will-centre) are necessary ingredients in exploring basic isolations and wave movements. I suggested in Chapter 1 that when imagination and body work in unison, the third motive force – emotion, or feeling – is inevitably aroused. In terms of Ananyev's work, the simplest exercise can begin to energise and integrate the entire psycho-physical apparatus comprising body, mind and feeling. It became clear among the group in Moscow that, in the cases where particular actors *didn't* fill the exercises with imagination, boredom ensued. In fact, these classes weren't at all popular with some of the English-speaking actors who found it difficult not to perceive *result* in terms of final product, rather than process. It was a bit like a piano student who gets impatient with scales and arpeggios and gives up before he's had the chance to develop the skills he needs for tackling the concerto. The pronounced reaction provoked among mature, experienced per-formers confirmed the fact that, if an actor is going to engage successfully in intensive physical re-education, he or she may well need to adapt their psychology and outlook before physical training can really take effect. Or to put it slightly differently, before we can begin to transform ourselves physically towards our characters, we have to transform ourselves psychologically towards our craft. Easy to understand, but much harder to do.

Dynamic meditation

In fact, Ananyev had various strategies to assist an actor with his or her psychological transformation, strategies which (in the words of Michael Chekhov) may 'occupy and electrify' the body and, therefore, activate the emotions.[43] The first task was to nurture an environment, in which the participant's attention could be diverted away from the difficulty of learning new techniques, towards finding a kind of pleasure in the work. Ananyev believed that when an actor is conscious of the limi-tations and 'inadequacies' of his or her own body, it's very difficult to develop any degree of physical versatility. There's a voice inside your head, saying '*That* looks stupid . . . You're doing that exercise wrong . . . Everyone else can do it . . . You're no good . . . ' Most of us are haunted at some time or another by a critical inner voice. And it's totally unhelpful, because it's impossible to *play* (act) and *judge* at the same time: they are quite simply contradictory actions. To play is outward-flowing, interacting with the partner and the environment; to judge is inward-flowing, analytical and self-reflective. So we have to find ways of silencing our critical inner judge.

One way to do this is by creating a state of 'dynamic meditation', a state in which the creative aspect of our psyche isn't disturbed by our boring old reason and judgement. Developing this kind of creative relaxation once again requires us to invest technical exercises with an emotional and imaginative quality. To help with this, Ananyev used *music* during most of his movement classes, for, as Stanislavsky believed, 'our feelings are directly worked upon by *tempo-rhythm*.'[44] Because of its emotive potential (via the speed – *tempo* – at which we do something and the intensity – *rhythm* – with which we do it), tempo-rhythm was a vital part of Ananyev's work. And so he selected music with a wide range of different tempo-rhythms and, consequently, a wide range of varying emotional appeals. This music was sometimes very rhythmical, sometimes very humorous and usually fairly emotive, to some degree even manipulative. It was used to form a backdrop to the technical exercises, encouraging us to experience the way in which the body responds to varying melodies and tempo-rhythms, and how those physical responses arouse numerous inner sensations. Often Ananyev drew upon film-underscoring by composers such as John Williams and Vangelis since, in its original context, this kind of music had been used evocatively and provocatively to stir a spectator's emotions. And here it was used to inspire the actors as they executed technical exercises.

In many respects, we were encouraged to use the music as another on-stage partner, just as we were with the *space*. In other words, we were to strike up a kind of dialogue with the music, so that our physicality was liberated and unselfconscious, not unlike the ways in which dancers react instinctively to music in a nightclub. Our mental concentration wasn't locked blinkeredly into the technicalities of joints or waves; instead, our bodies were the driving forces, responding freely, but intelligently, to the dynamics of the music. Of course, the focus of the exercise was still on isolations or waves or whatever the particular exercise might be, but the emphasis had changed. It was no longer a question of intellectually breaking down a specific movement and trying to execute it physically; now, the *music* inspired the body. So we could shut up our brains for a while. In this way, a state of dynamic meditation could be developed, in which the body was free to expand its vocabulary; there was minimum interference from the mind and maximum enjoyment of the movement. In this state of dynamic meditation, even the simplest exercise (such as the 'figurine' or 'plasticine' partner exercise) could arouse a remarkably profound sense of serenity and exhilaration. The smallest physical movement was endowed with a powerful emotional life. Michael Chekhov describes this kind of sensation as a 'Feeling of Beauty', created when the actor begins 'with simple movements and "listens" attentively within himself to the pleasure, the satisfaction, limbs experience while moving'.[45]

Opening and closing: the gateway to the universe

Step by step in the course of this training, movements were combined and complicated in a slow progression towards psycho-physical versatility. At this stage in Ananyev's programme, the emphasis was primarily on how physical movement arouses emotion, i.e. how the changes in our body affect our inner feelings. But as we know, the premise of psycho–physical activity is that the impulse might go either way – from inner mechanism to outer expression, or vice versa at any point along the continuum. We also know that this inner/outer dialogue is a complex one. And as practitioners in the art of human behaviour, we somehow need to develop our ability to understand the complexity.

Wave motion symbolises our interaction with the big wide world. It illustrates our assimilation of the information we receive and our unique response to that information, through the process of action / reaction / decision. This instantly illuminates

another principle of psycho-physical activity – the movement
from centre to periphery, and from periphery to centre. If the
wave motion originates *from my centre*, it's an indication of the
information I'm *giving to the world*. I walk forward: the wave
motion in my legs goes from hip to knee to ankle to heel, and the
world clearly sees that I'm taking a decision, making an action,
and moving in a particular direction. If a wave motion originates
at the periphery, it's an indication of the information I'm *receiving*
from the world. I walk backwards: I'm less confident, I don't
know where I'm going, I'm receiving information from my
surroundings. The wave movement in my legs is from periphery
to centre, as I check out where I'm going through my toes, my
ankles, my knees, my hips.

   Closely allied to the wave movements of giving information
(centre to periphery) and receiving information (periphery to
centre) is the extent to which I *open* myself up to the world, or I
close myself away from the world. In effect, there are only two
actions in life – to open and to close, and in between lies the
universe. In every moment of our lives, we are drawn towards
something (having a cup of tea, buying a blue coat, making love)
or we retreat from something (going out in the rain, discovering
a spider in the bath, opening a bank statement). Our instantaneous attraction to or repulsion from someone can affect a whole
myriad of responses. Waves movements, central and peripheral
activity, opening and closing are intricately interwoven. To combine these complex psychological activities, Ananyev introduced
a very simple but evocative exercise. It was based on the
principles of a *torch beam*, although a different image could be
used, such as the expansion and contraction of daisy petals. The
joy of the exercise was that it combined physical action, imagination, and communication with a partner, in an extremely direct
way. Each actor was to imagine that the bright gold centre of a
torch beam was located about three centimetres below the navel
from which six 'shutters' extended. The arms and legs constituted four of the shutters, the head was the fifth and the coccyx
was the sixth.

Accompanied by various styles of music, the actor began to explore both the physical and the inner sensation of opening and closing the six shutters. The options were various, but finite. The right side could open or close; the left side could open or close. The upper shutters could open or close; the lower shutters could open or close. All six shutters could expand. All six shutters could contract. Added to this, the expansions and contractions could be complete or partial, giving an infinite repertoire of combinations. If the actor engaged imaginatively as well as physically with the exercise, contrasts very quickly became apparent between harmonised movements (where all the shutters moved in the same direction) and conflicting movements (where some shutters closed and some shutters opened). The lower shutters, for example, might be fully closed (with the knees bent together in a knock-kneed way and the pelvis tucked under the body as if the tail shutter was furled beneath) whilst the upper shutters were partially opened (so that the arms were semi-extended and the head slightly raised). The physical contrast between upper and lower shutters within this movement could provoke a feeling of inner conflict, as the actor's psychology was torn between opening and sending out light to the environment, and contracting and withdrawing light from the environment. By exploring combinations like this, a whole spectrum of sensations and psychological nuances could be experienced and accessed.

In theory, the exercise seems simple, but it's imperative that the shutter movements are articulated very precisely if the actor is going to experience the true inner sensations aroused by extreme openness (brightness), extreme closedness (darkness) and the myriad of degrees in between. Ananyev was quick to correct positions if an actor's arms were flung too far back when fully open, or if the head was thrust backwards beyond the vertical of the spine when the 'head shutter' was fully extended. Sometimes an actor unwittingly shifted the centre of the torch from the belly up towards the chest or down towards the groin: again, this would undercut the technical precision needed for the exercise. Here we go back to the issue of physical re-education: although the torch-beam movement seemed easy, individual bodies were quick to adjust the positions to make them more comfortable. So we had to be alert to our bodies' surreptitious cheating.

After exploring the torch-beam movement on our own, a dialogue with a partner was introduced: one actor would 'communicate' with an opening or closing of his or her 'shutters', and a fellow actor would reply with his or her own expansion or contraction. Again, seemingly easy, but again a whole new set of conditions arose. The consequence of working with a partner was that another person's objective and status had now been introduced. This was no bad thing as it diverted the actor's immediate attention from him or her self, and directed it towards the partner with the result that each individual's inner/outer activity became more spontaneous. What happened now was that the external stimulus of the partner's contraction or expansion provided the first component in the action / reaction / decision sequence. My partner contracts (action), I feel protective (reaction), I contract too to show that I'm not threatening (decision). Or my partner contracts (action), I feel powerful (reaction), I expand to my full extension to intimidate (decision). A wave was being transmitted between the two participants, based on opening and closing.

(My experience of using this exercise with novice student-actors is that they suddenly find that they're mirroring their partner's movements, so in fact for a while they become less spontaneous and more self-aware as they try to be more original. This isn't a problem: the mirroring simply illustrates that the *particular* dialogue that they are engaged in is a co-operative, friendly one rather than an antagonistic exchange, which they might perhaps experience with a different partner on a different occasion. Fear of imitating is a passing phase. The more you relax into the torch-beam dialogue, the more you surrender up your brain and let your body do the talking.)

Introducing the idea of dialogue to the exercise contributed further nuances to the opening and closing. Opening all the shutters to a partner could arouse either a sense of pride and power, or the opposite – a feeling of nakedness and vulnerability. In turn, when all the shutters were closed, the sensation could be one of fear and defence or, by contrast, a feeling of comfort and security. It all depended on the impulse received from the partner. And of course that impulse will change according to whom you're working with. Whatever the multitude of emotions and nuances might be, isolations and wave movements remained the basic physical vocabulary at the root of the dialogue. With very little effort a technical exercise had been transformed into dramatic action. In one simple task, all aspects of the actor's psycho-physical motor were activated: body, imagination, emotions, and the radiation of energy between partners.

Cherez pauza – through the pauses

In all the exercises explored so far – joints, curves, waves, torch beam – there has been one essential ingredient, which in many ways gives each exercise its meaning. And that ingredient is the *pause*. On stage, an actor is always in dialogue: with the audience, with the other characters, the music, the space, the atmosphere, or with his or her own self. We've already said that this kind of inner/outer dialogue is a complex one. It becomes even more complex if we don't know how to listen to it, and it becomes almost impossible if we don't *take the time* to listen to it. And it's the pause that provides us with that valuable listening time. For Ananyev, any dialogue, whether it be spoken text or movement, could only acquire any meaning at all *cherez pauza* – 'through the pause'. It's the basis of the actor's art, our tool for really experiencing the subtleties of physical and emotional sensations, and assimilating that information into our psycho-physical apparatus. Only through the pause can we truly understand what's going on both within ourselves, and between partners and ourselves. It's not cerebral understanding, it's inner understanding. In some respects, it goes even deeper than that into what we might call 'spiritual' understanding. Echoing the vocabulary of Stanislavsky, Michael Chekhov and Grotowski, Ananyev maintained that the pause was 'the only door into the *spiritual* world: only when the actor *stops*, might he or she sense the inner movement.'

A pause is a very specific moment: I'm sure we've all watched performances in which we yearn for the actors to get on with it and stop indulging in a quagmire of 'inner life'. At the other extreme, I've worked with directors who have screamed in rehearsals, 'Pick up your cues! I could drive a bus through that pause!' But here we touch upon the difference between speed and pace, and sometimes the one gets mistaken for the other. As often as I've yearned for actors to 'get on with it', I've also wished on other occasions that they would slow down and allow the reality of the situation to touch them in some small way, instead of heading for the curtain line as if it's the last call at the bar. It's not a question of pauses having to be 'earned', as if speeding through the first scene means that you've deserved the right to relish the second scene. It's more a question of understanding that a pause is an inherent part of the tempo-rhythm of a play. The true life of a dramatic text depends as much on the silences as it does on the words, just as our heart depends as much on the pauses between the beats as it does on the beats themselves. It's an uncomfortable feeling when our heart starts pounding if we're nervous or excited or we've exerted ourselves physically: the beating needs to slow itself down and the pauses need to be longer. It's really no different with life on the stage.

But if the pause is such a specific movement, why is it so and what exactly is it? As far as Ananyev was concerned, a pause had the potential to be as articulate as an action: it was neither an empty space nor a diffusion of energy. And perhaps this is where the idea of truly 'earning' a pause comes in: an 'earned' pause is literally a 'pregnant' pause, one that's full of life. As Michael Chekhov stresses, a pause cannot *exist* as a pause: it has always to be the result of what's just happened, or the preparation for what's about to happen. And ultimately, 'the most beautiful pauses are those which are the continuation of something, and then the turning point or preparation for . . . a new action.'[46] In

Ananyev's Scenic Movement, action and pause were inextricably linked: just as moments of silence turn sound into music, the pause turns random movement into action. It's an essential part of psycho-physical development, as a pause in the action is crucial for *interpreting all the information that we receive from the outside world.*

Information comes to us in the form of various sensory perceptions that we have of the world at large, and also in the form of *exchanges of energy* with other people. Ananyev explained that 'we have to develop the ability to understand where that information-energy comes from and how it affects emotions, actions, thoughts. Each movement may stop in space, but the energy continues like a ray, a beam, through space and onwards.' This receipt and communication of information, this transference of energy from outside world to inner being and from inner being to outside world, is yet another application of natural behaviour to the circumstances of the stage. If pauses are an intrinsic part of our *heart beat*, so inner/outer activity is an integral part of our *breathing*: in other words, a movement which passes from outside to inside to outside (peripheral-central-peripheral) corresponds to our instinctive breathing pattern. We breathe in oxygen. We take it into our lungs. We breathe out carbon dioxide.

This relates directly to the action / reaction / decision wave-sequence in which we're all involved in every moment of our lives. First of all, I 'inhale' my partner's action; Michael Chekhov called this 'an absorption of experiences'[47]: a movement from periphery to centre. In a pause – which might be split second or momentarily sustained – I assimilate the information. This assimilation (or inner reaction) will provoke one of my inner motive forces. It might be an impulsive reaction (action-centre), or it might set me thinking (thought-centre) or I might be instantly amused or distressed (emotion-centre). Based on which centre was most proactive in my reaction, I 'exhale' my resultant decision; Michael Chekhov called this 'an expression of self': the movement from centre to periphery. Of course, all this assimilation and exhalation needn't be a great moment of pontification and suspense: it can, and usually does, happen instantaneously.

Taken to its grand conclusion, the metaphor of inhaling information and exhaling expression encapsulates the entire process of acting. The actor inhales all the details of the character, studying it through the text and allowing it to percolate through his or her body, mind and emotions. Then there's an extended pause of three or four weeks, during which a lot of assimilation goes on. After this time, the actor exhales the character as a fully realised, expressive performance.

Psycho-physical technique and the inner motive forces

The bit in the middle – between breathing in and breathing out – is the pause. And Ananyev's work convinced me that pauses are necessary for actors if we're really going to 'hear' the complex dialogue within ourselves. In fact, this complex inner dialogue soon became the next point of focus in Ananyev's training. He approached the development of psycho-physical sensitivity through two distinct branches of *co-ordination*: physical co-ordination (which as we've seen was addressed through isolations and waves) and inner co-ordination (which involved the *inner motive forces*, or *centres*). These, as we know, are the thought-centre, the emotion-centre and the will- (or action-) centre. Stanislavsky himself advocated that the key to uniting inner action and outer expression is understanding the interaction between these three centres, as 'they support and incite one another with the result that they always act at the same time and in close relationship. When we call our minds into action, by the same token we stir our will and feelings. It is only when these forces are co-operating harmoniously that we can create freely.'[48] To ensure that the centres do 'co-operate harmoniously', Stanislavsky challenged practitioners 'to evolve an appropriate psycho-technique', which would take advantage of the interdependence of the inner motive forces. The purpose of this psycho-technique wouldn't be just to arouse the centres as an end in itself, but to harness them in order to 'stir other creative elements'. (These 'other creative elements' could well include 'spirit' or inspiration, which we'll look at in due course.)

Ananyev rose to Stanislavsky's challenge. In an attempt to evolve 'an effective psycho-technique', he turned once again to the wave movement as the essence of 'inner dialogue'. He suggested that when we're dealing with psycho-physical behaviour, we need to locate the point at which a wave begins, not simply in terms of external physical movements ('Is it my hip? Is it my shoulder? Is it my elbow?'), but also in terms of the *inner* wave. What he meant by that was the sequence in which the centres (action, emotion and thought) connect. Again, it seems fairly obvious, but how can you do it when it all sounds so ungraspable? How can we catch an emotion? How can we label an impulse to move? How do I know whether it was my head or my heart which provoked me to do something? Ananyev addressed himself to these very questions. To try and translate the potentially esoteric concepts of intellect, will and emotion into something tangible and accessible, he divided the whole body into three sections, each of which corresponded to an inner motive force. The first section, the *head*, represented the thought-centre; the second section, the *chest and torso*, represented the emotion-centre; and the third section, *pelvis, arms and legs*, represented the action-centre. This is nothing new, as Michael Chekhov had already proposed these divisions. However, Ananyev went further.

Within each of the general sections, he suggested that qualities of the other centres could be found in more localised areas. The *thought-centre* (the head) featured *feeling* in the *eyes* (consider the nuances of emotion we betray through our eyes); *thought* in the *nose and ears* (consider the curious cat poking its nose into every crevice, and the eavesdropping neighbour with the glass to the wall); and *action* in the *chin and mouth* (consider Desperate Dan and his spade-like chin, having 'more brawn than brains'). The *emotion-centre* (or *feeling*) (the chest and torso) is more complex as it involves energy centres (referred to in Eastern practices as chakras, a term with which Stanislavsky was probably familiar through the teaching of Leopold Sulerzhitsky). Therefore, it's easier to consider the emotion-centre in its totality, rather than breaking it down into areas. The *will-centre* (or *action*) (the groin, arms and legs) featured *feeling* in the *knees* (consider how our knees shake involuntarily when we're nervous) and *shoulders* (consider how we carry our tension in our hunched shoulders); *thought* in the *feet* (consider tapping of toes and kicking of heels) and *hands* (consider how we gesticulate when we communicate our thoughts); and *action* in the *hips* (consider the root of sexual expression) and *elbows* (consider elbowing people out of the way).

Armed with this matrix of body parts and energy centres, we embarked on a series of improvisations. To begin with these were very simple. For example, we might walk around the room with the head leading the movement as an exploration of the thought-centre. The back might lead the movement as we explored the qualities of the emotion-centre. The left hip might lead the movement in an exploration of the action-centre. Once we'd tried this, a more localised part might be singled out, so that the chin might lead the head in an exploration of 'action in the thought-centre'. The hand might lead the torso in an exploration of 'active thought in the emotion-centre'. The knee might lead the lower body in an exploration of 'feeling in the action-centre'. At first, this sort of exercise encouraged fairly generalised movement, although it was still very enjoyable: as we walked around the room with the movement stemming from the hips (the action-centre), we all started to swagger confidently like cowboys. As we walked around the room with the nose leading the movement (thought in the thought-centre), we all poked about like nosy neighbours.

Quickly, though, the exercises became more complicated, focusing on curves and waves. We might, for example, explore a wave movement through the arm, as it journeys from thought in the hands, through action in the elbows to emotion in the shoulders. Or a wave movement involving the middle section of the body, as it progresses through emotion in the chest, action in the pelvis, and emotion in the knee. Other times, improvisations were completely free, so that we could move entirely where and how we wished. All the time, however, a kind of dual consciousness was in operation, whereby part of the brain constantly observed the movements, trying to catch which centre emitted an impulse to move. Was it an emotional impulse, an action-based impulse, or a thought-provoked impulse? While the brain was doing this bit of analysis, the body carried on executing the movements as freely as possible, usually responding to the accompanying music. Identifying which centre initiated the movement wasn't always straight-forward: as Ananyev reminded us, 'the part of the body which *expresses* the movement may not be the centre which *gave birth* to the movement. The actor must be in touch with the connection between the *birth* of the impulse and the *expression* of the impulse.' Gee whizz, human beings are complex . . .

Although this compendium of body parts and centres wasn't intended to be exhaustive, it provided a means of alerting the actor to the way in which particular parts of the body can express thought, feeling and action. It was a direct means through which intangible concepts (like emotion) were made manifest (through the chest, knees and eyes). Once again, it was a question of decoding ways in which we behave in everyday life and applying them to the stage. In deep thought, for example, we might trace patterns on the floor with a toe (the feet being an ally of the thought-centre). If we want someone to know how determined or intransigent we're going to be about something, we jut out our elbows (the elbows being action-centre allies), by thrusting our hands on our hips or in our pockets. In deep sorrow, we might sit hugging our knees (which are emotion-centre allies). The joy is that this information can have an instant practical use: taking the television close-up, for example, you can subtly convey to your screen audience whether you're being thoughtful, emotional or pro-active, just by radiating your energy from your nose, your eyes or your mouth. It's a very 'hands-on' means of unlocking and applying intangible issues to acting practice. But, however useful it may be, dissecting the body like this was only a preliminary exercise. It didn't take long in Ananyev's classes to realise that the centres communicate with each other almost simultaneously. This was revealed through a series of improvisations.

Summary of the Psycho-Physical Warm-up

The Psycho-Physical Warm-up develops the actor's inner/outer co-ordination; i.e. the co-ordination between inner experience and outer expression. This is connected to the transference of information between the environment (the periphery) and the individual (the centre). If the actor can begin to 'hear' this dialogue, he or she can develop his or her awareness of personal psycho-physicality and the continuous, inner wave motions of action/reaction/decision. Through this awareness, the actor's future on-stage interaction may become more vital and spontaneous. The key component in all this is *the pause*.

• **The Vertical Position**
Feet in parallel
Toes lightly gripping the floor
Extension up the *calves*
Knees in two directions – slightly backwards and rotated gently out
   to the sides
Hips open like a book
Tail tucked under the body
Stomach drawn in (though not tensely)
Chest in three directions – forwards, upwards and out to the sides
   like an open book
Shoulders in two directions – slightly back and downwards
Elbows out to the side
Palms lightly resting on the outside of the mid-thighs
Arms bent, with the sense of air circulating between inner arms
   and body
Eyeline at the individual's own horizon (not too high, not too low)
The sense of a cord gently pulling the crown of the *head* to extend
   the spine
Smile

- **Isolations**

One joint at a time in a straight line (like an artist's figurine)
(Individually and in partners, with sculptor and sculpted)
A series of joints in a curved trajectory (like a plasticine model)
(Individually and in partners, with sculptor and sculpted)

- **Wave motions**

Through one limb
Through the whole body

- **Opening and Closing**

The Torch Beam exercise, with six 'shutters' (two arms, two legs,
head and coccyx)
(Individually and in dialogue with a partner)

- **Inner Motive Forces, or Centres**

THOUGHT	FEELING	ACTION
(or Mental-centre)	(or Emotion-centre)	(or Will-centre)
HEAD	**TORSO**	**PELVIS/ARMS/LEGS**

THOUGHT:	Nose	(It is simpler to	Fingers & Toes
FEELING:	Eyes	consider this centre	Shoulders & Knees
ACTION:	Mouth & Chin	as the entire torso)	Elbows & Hips

Using this matrix:
One body-part leads the movement in an exploration of a single centre
Combinations of body-parts lead the movement in an exploration of
the 'dialogue' between centres

The Object Exercise

Exploratory improvisations became a central part of the Scenic
Movement programme, as technical exercises became more
complicated. They were invariably accompanied by music and
could last for anything from five minutes to an hour. In most
improvisations, Ananyev gave us neither text nor visual imagery
for stimulation. The challenge for the actor was to take
inspiration from the movement of the body itself, and from the
sensations created by that movement as the centres spontaneously interconnected. Occasionally, we *were* given a specific ob-

jective, which would then focus the activity of the inner motive forces on a particular task. One such improvisation proved to be quite revelatory in understanding the connection between psycho-physical technique and the inner motive forces. I've used it on several occasions with actors and students alike, and each time, the outcome has surprised and delighted all. I've called it The Object Exercise.

First of all, we were asked to find our own space in the room and to place an item of clothing on the floor in front of us. We then had to endow this item, whatever it might be, with great value or importance, though, at this stage, we didn't have to know *why* it was so important to us. For the next fifteen minutes, we were to allow the music, the space, and the object to affect us in whichever ways aroused us. But, despite how important this object was to us, our underlying objective throughout the whole exercise was *to prevent ourselves from touching the object*. Under no circumstances could we come into contact with it at all. This objective instantly established an inner contradiction: if you have to prevent yourself from doing something, it suggests that part of you wants to do it, and part of you certainly doesn't. There's a dynamic set up between attraction and repulsion, between desire and denial, between opening up to and closing away from the object. During this exercise, the contradiction would stimulate the inner motive forces in a multitude of ways, as long as we engaged imaginatively with the objective and the object. It's the sort of exercise you can't talk about too cerebrally or think about beforehand: you just have to get stuck in.

This exercise revealed a very important truth: when you're in a state of dynamic meditation, your imagination develops a vivid life of its own. Throughout all our exercises, Ananyev reiterated that we mustn't impose any kind of conscious narrative on our movements. However, if we found that a narrative developed almost unwittingly, we were to be brave enough to follow those imaginative ideas, seeing what emotional and physical discoveries we made. During my first exposure to this particular 'object' improvisation I found that, by listening to the music and to my own body, my imagination suddenly and bizarrely 'transformed' my inanimate sweater into the head of John the Baptist. This certainly wasn't an image that I'd consciously chosen, but it appealed to me and so I accepted it. In doing so, I began to experience a spontaneous 'conversation' with the object. Without imposing anything, I discovered that at every moment in this crazy dialogue, there was a justification for why I valued but couldn't pick up the 'disembodied head'. Sometimes I wanted to touch it, then I wanted to reject it, then to ignore it, to embrace it, to kick it, to lick it, to stroke it, to spit upon it, to fondle it. Sometimes I hated it, sometimes I worshipped it, sometimes it fascinated me, other times it bored me. It was all very strange because it wasn't as though I imagined black hair, dead eyes, a bloodied mouth: I simply saw the folds of my sweater. Strangely, they meant as much to me as if I were Salome and they were the locks of John the Baptist's hair. Following Ananyev's incentive to be brave in one's imaginings, I'd awoken unexpected, unpremeditated reactions, some of which were *emotional*, some of which were *rational* and some of which were impulses to *action*. It was a startling moment of *Eureka!* for me. It felt as though for the first time in my acting life, I'd truly experienced the uninhibited dialogue of the inner motive forces. I'd dared myself to allow my *body* to lead the improvisation instead of my conscious mind.

'Ouch! My brain hurts.'

Although moments like this were truly inspiring and creatively invigorating, they were relatively rare, and the development of a psycho-physical technique was by no means easy. Much of the problem has to do with 'our heads getting in the way'. Until we reach the point as actors where we've learnt to trust the decisions made by our psycho-physical apparatus (body, imagination and emotions), we usually rely on our brains (or thought-centre) to do the hard work. We think the brain is our most intelligent facet (it isn't, our bodies are far cleverer, otherwise we'd die in our sleep). More significantly, we think the brain is the centre that we can most consciously control. This is exacerbated in a learning environment (like a rehearsal room or drama class) where nothing has quite become second nature yet. So it's unavoidable that the head has to do a lot of the assimilation work. The exercises that Ananyev proposed often required us to identify which centre (thought, emotion or will) inspired an impulse to action. In other words, we were being asked to *analyse* an exercise and *engage* with it at the same time. It was impossible. All the inner activity went straight to the *thought-centre*, as it tried to do the analytical work, and that in itself short-circuited the exercise. I was besieged with questions: 'If we've got to identify the motivating centre, and if we need our rational minds to make that identification, how is it possible for any *spontaneous* inter-action to take place between the centres? Surely the mind will always and inevitably be the governing force?'

To some degree, that's true, but what became apparent in psycho-physical training was that this initial appeal to the thought-centre was simply part of the learning process. It's a bit like a musician who has to dissect a musical score intellectually at first in order to learn the notes and the dynamics. Once he's done this preparatory work and he has an analytical grasp of the score, he can begin to release this technical knowledge from his conscious mind. From thereon in, he can allow his creative brain to be more organically employed in expressing and interpreting the music. It's an unavoidable paradox of learning: acquiring technique seems to be intellectual, while creative performance has to be integrated. Michael Chekhov clarifies this paradox, saying that 'If this division of thought, feeling, and will *seems* to be intellectual and dry, it only seems to be because when you feel that you can really manage these three levels concretely, you can plunge into the realm of ideas, or you become absolutely filled with the realm of feelings. You can live in the realm of the heart, as well as the realm of the will.'[49] We have to go through this process of dissection followed by reintegration if we really want our psycho-physical awareness to evolve. As Michael Chekhov promises us, 'this temporary anatomizing will lead us later on to such a composition of things in us, such a harmonious composition, that we shall be able to discover in ourselves many things which want to be awakened, but we don't [usually] allow them.' Setting up an environment of dynamic meditation and free improvisation helped to accelerate the move from 'temporary anatomizing' to 'harmonious composition'.

Free improvisation and the Psychological Gesture

At this point, I should clarify the exact nature of free improvisation. The premise behind Ananyev's psycho-physical training was that once the actor had begun to liberate the body, he or she would find that the body stimulates the imagination, which in turn provokes stories, which in turn stimulate emotions. These stories aren't superimposed by the actor; they just arise from the mental and emotional impulses which are activated once the physical body starts to move. This requires a very delicate handling of body and imagination: we mustn't allow our minds to manipulate the story, and neither must we curb the natural flow of our fantasies. It's a matter of nurturing an imaginative narrative without forcing it, and, if a narrative arises spontaneously, it's about having the courage to follow and develop it: this had been my experience when my sweater turned into 'the head of John the Baptist'. Sometimes these spontaneous stories may have specific imaginative settings, such as catching butterflies, crawling through muddy tunnels, bidding a sweetheart farewell or awaking on a new planet. Other times, they may simply be emotional or physical impulses that follow one after another, with no specific setting but a sequential logic of their own. In either case, what's important is that the actor doesn't consciously predetermine the choices made, but simply fans the creative flame to follow the unfolding story. As David Mamet puts it, 'Invent nothing, deny nothing.'[50]

I discovered that the success of free improvisation was dependent on the thorough practice of technical exercises such as isolations and wave movements. Through these technical exercises, the body acquired its own versatility or 'intelligence'. The free improvisations then provided a kind of laboratory in which the actor could test out this newly acquired physical intelligence. It enabled him or her to percolate all the sensory information received from various sources (be it music, actors or the space itself) through the whole psycho-physical instrument and then channel it into uninhibited expression. In terms of Scenic Movement, the nature of free improvisations corresponded to Michael Chekhov's approach to 'Psychological Gesture'.[51]

Chekhov saw each individual psychological state as 'a combination of thoughts (or Images), Feelings and Will-Impulses'. He believed that the actor could filter all that information about a character into a simple repeatable movement. So the Psychological Gesture is a self-contained combination of *one physical posture* – followed by *a transition* – followed by *a second physical posture*. Chekhov usually used Psychological Gesture for unlocking a character: you find a small repeatable sequence of pose/transition/pose, which sums up the superobjective of the character to give you an encapsulated, bite-sized way of expressing the character's personality. To be most effective, a Psychological Gesture should combine *form* and *movement* using varying tempi, amplitudes, directions and speeds as you move from the first static form to the second. For Michael Chekhov, the combination of the three stages – form, transition, new form – harmonised the interaction of the inner motive forces. Form (thought) prompts movement (action) with the consequent arousal of sensation (emotion). By studying and practising the Psychological Gesture, Chekhov maintained that you could experience its 'threefold influence upon your psyche'.[52] Through the simple choreography of moving from one pose to another, you could activate all your inner motive forces – provided the positions were carefully chosen. In fact, some actors use a Psychological Gesture just before an audition or performance as a quick and immediate means of reminding themselves of what the character is all about.

Michael Chekhov then took it a step further: Psychological Gesture needn't be a single isolated moment, but rather as 'an incessant movement'. He suggested that the actor construct a series of Psychological Gestures which, once familiar, could be repeated and expanded. So you start with your first Psychological Gesture, move to your second, then add your third, fourth, fifth and so on. Soon 'you will feel yourself so free that you will not need to start again from the first Psychological Gesture, but can go on indefinitely, adding one Psychological Gesture to the other, creating them and their organic connections, spontaneously and entirely intuitively.'[53] And this was the premise from which Ananyev's concept of free improvisation grew. Of course, Ananyev constantly reminded us to *pause* during these sequences, in order that we could listen to how our inner impulse was directing us, and allow *our bodies* to determine what the next gesture would be.

Chekhov wasn't the only significant influence in Ananyev's free improvisations: he also harnessed many elements of Rudolf Laban's dance-movement work. Central and peripheral movements, bound and free flow, a constant variation in direction, tempo and amplitude, were all incorporated into the vocabulary of repertoire. What was important was that the emphasis wasn't simply on acquiring physical vocabulary, but rather developing psycho-physical *experience*. As each actor's body became more versatile, and the psycho-physical mechanism became more liberated, a greater number of spontaneous narratives arose. The narratives ensured that there was always a task or an objective behind the free improvisations, so that the movement (whether it be expressionistic or plastic or completely realistic) never became purposeless. When all the elements of technical exercises, free improvisation and the inner motive forces were combined in this way, it became clear that Ananyev's discipline wasn't really a *movement* class, but actually an *acting* class led by the body.

From abstract to everyday

We worked like this for a number of weeks – reminding ourselves
of the intricacies of our own instruments, tuning them up and
testing them out. Then, after a while, the work subtly shifted from
actor-training to the first tentative steps of building a character.

One day, Ananyev asked us to remember a monologue. I chose
the speech from Act III, Scene I of *Henry VI, Part 2*, when
Queen Margaret addresses Henry with the words:

> Can you not see? Or will you not observe
> The strangeness of his altered countenance?
> With what a majesty he bears himself,
> How insolent of late he is become,
> How proud, how peremptory, and unlike himself?
> We know the time since he was mild and affable,
> And if we did but glance a far-off look,
> Immediately he was upon his knee,
> That all the court admired him for submission;
> But meet him now, and be it in the morn,
> When everyone will give the time of day,
> He knits his brow and shows an angry eye,
> And passeth by with stiff unbowèd knee,
> Disdaining duty that to us belongs.
> Small curs are not regarded when they grin,
> But great men tremble when the lion roars;
> And Humphrey is no little man in England.
> First note that he is near you in descent
> And should you fall, he is the next will mount.
> Me seemeth then it is no policy,
> Respecting what a rancorous mind he bears
> And his advantage following your decease,
> That he should come about your royal person
> Or be admitted to your highness' Council.
> By flattery hath he won the commons' hearts,
> And when he please to make commotion,

'Tis to be feared they all will follow him.
Now 'tis the spring, and weeds are shallow-rooted;
Suffer them now and they'll o'ergrow the garden,
And choke the herbs for want of husbandry.
The reverent care I bear unto my lord
Made me collect these dangers in the Duke.
If it be fond, call it a woman's fear;
Which fear if better reasons can supplant,
I will subscribe and say I wronged the Duke.
My lord of Suffolk, Buckingham, and York,
Reprove my allegation if you can;
Or else conclude my words effectual.

Ananyev then applied a series of exercises to the monologues, the text of which remained entirely in our heads (i.e. unspoken!) during the course of the improvisation. As ever, a musical background was provided at first to create a state of 'dynamic meditation'.

First of all, we had to decide which was the predominant centre in the text. In other words, was it a thoughtful or emotive or action-based speech? We then chose a corresponding part of the body from the matrix of centres and body-parts, with which we were now familiar. It could be the wrist, knee, shoulder, ear or whichever part befitted the text's overall tenor in terms of its predominant inner motive force. We then moved around the space, all the time going through our monologues in our heads, with that *one part of the body* leading the movement and the rest of the body following like a kite-tail, responding to the changing dynamics and directions. The character of Margaret was very manipulative in my chosen speech, her manipulation having both an analytical and an active aspect. So I used my hand as the instigator of movement, the hand being the expression of 'thought in the action-centre'. What was clearly important in this exercise was that, however abstract the movement may be, it must always be specific. You have to be aware of your physicality on-stage and set up a kind of dialogue with your body in order that the movement doesn't become generalised and, consequently, not understood by the audience.

This first exercise was reasonably simple and led to a shift from mind to body as a way into a text. The second exercise built on the first, only this time, as the impulse of the speech changed from moment to moment (i.e. from action to feeling to thought), a series of *different parts of the body* initiated the movement, selected according to their centre-quality. So if the character was being impulsive at one point, one of the *action*-centres in the body might lead – chin, elbow, hip, butt. If the timbre changed to a more contemplative tone, a thought-centre might lead the movement – nose, fingers, toes or the whole head. I discovered in this exercise how surprisingly flexible my chosen speech could be. The subtext of many of Margaret's words is *emotive*, and yet her 'manipulation' bears the qualities both of *intellectual* cunning and of inciting her partner to *action*. This combination of action, imagination and emotion meant that I was able to explore the whole range of centres and body-parts through this speech, with varying degrees of success.

In the third exercise, we progressed from what had been fairly abstract movement towards a much more naturalistic activity. We 'spoke' our monologues *internally* whilst applying three very specific *external* actions: *walking, sitting and turning*. At this point the idea of 'character' was overtly introduced in that, although each actor was obviously using his or her own body and movements, the choice as to whether to walk, sit or turn stemmed from the decisions and motivations of the *character*. This exercise proved to be extremely fruitful in exploring Margaret's character: while the more abstract exercises had unlocked her 'subtext', the simple naturalistic activities relocated that subtext in Margaret's compressed and rather introspective style. The progression from abstract, plastic movement to naturalistic activity was seamless and remarkably enlightening. The naturalistic movements in no way felt pedestrian, as they might've been had we begun with them. Instead, they'd acquired a kind of creative composure, informed by the preceding, more expressionistic exercises.

In the fourth exercise, the three activities of walking, sitting or turning were repeated, but this time, the motivation to move stemmed directly from the *inner motive forces*. In other words, there was a matrix of *actions* (sitting, turning, walking) and *qualities* (wilfully, thoughtfully and emotionally). The permutations of these changed from moment to moment according to whatever motivation lay behind the text. What this exercise highlighted was how the centres throughout the body can often be *in conflict*: your thought-centre might propel you to sit, while the impulse of your emotion-centre might be to turn. Alternatively, your action-centre might have the energy to pace, while part of you wants to sit and contemplate. Although this exercise was interesting, it wasn't wholly successful for me, partly owing to the problem we've touched upon before. Technical exercises inevitably call upon the brain to do a lot of the analytical work, and even if you're trying to engage in an exercise to *integrate* the centres, it's nigh on impossible to by-pass the brain. In fact if you're being called upon to make conscious decisions and observations in an exercise, how can you possibly avoid the thought-centre dominating and ensure that your psycho-physical co-ordination is spontaneous? The answer is: you can't – it's part of the learning process. You have to go back to Chekhov's belief that 'temporary anatomizing' will ultimately lead to 'harmonious composition'.

Exercise Five explored the speech for the final time, *combining all the preceding exercises* and varying them as and when it felt appropriate. The freedom of this exercise proved to be very helpful, as it encouraged exciting shifts from abstract to naturalistic movement, from the prosaic to the poetic, from technique to imagination, as the content of the text changed from moment to moment. An exercise like this can unlock problematic points in a play, since you're free to explore both text and character in a range of ways – from broad expressionistic gesture to detailed naturalistic activity. This liberation enables you to sniff out the tools or physical processes which may be effective in activating your own personal psycho-physical expressiveness. The exercise demands that you constantly shift between precise technical execution, liberated abstract movement and a direct, concrete transference onto the text of various everyday activities. This constant shift allows body and brain to work together more and more harmoniously. Once again, Ananyev's work in this field closely resembled Michael Chekhov's application of Psychological Gestures: Chekhov invites the actor gradually and carefully to make Psychological Gestures resemble realistic, naturalistic acting. 'By doing this slowly, step by step, you will have a long chain of gestures whose first link will be a purely abstract, purely musical, rhythmical one, in close connection to your subconscious creative impulses, and whose last link will become the gesture of everyday life, concrete, and naturalistically true. The long series of gestures in between will be a slow transition from the 'abstract' to the 'concrete' gestures and words.'[54] This transition from abstract to everyday can liberate the actor's mind and activate the imagination.

Dialogue with an object

By the end of the first semester, it was clear to see how Ananyev had taken us through the slow breakdown of technical movements in isolations, co-ordinations and physical waves, to the more complex interaction of the inner motive forces. This had involved our exploration of abstract plastic movement and naturalistic everyday movement, and we'd begun to focus on the relationship between the physical actor and the imaginary character in reference to a text. To a greater or lesser extent, we were becoming psycho-physically awake. During the second semester, the work progressed in three particular directions: (i) mime (or *pantomim*) and the role of real and imaginary objects; (ii) exploring the intangible communication of energy between two actors (Stanislavsky called it 'irradiation'[55]); and (iii) the development of 'creative individuality'. I'll go on to explore each of these in turn.

For Ananyev, the discipline of Pantomime in actor-training was of paramount importance. The Russian word *pantomim* refers to classical Mime, and has nothing to do with the British Christmas Pantomime tradition of Principal Boys and Widow Twankeys. And the work of Jean-Louis Barrault and Marcel Marceau had certainly been great influences on Ananyev. He believed that Pantomime had the capacity to strengthen your imagination, and a strong imagination could give clarity to your action on stage. Most actors know how difficult any level of Pantomime is, and yet if the simple task of drinking from an imaginary cup exposes our creative skills, how much more so can working with imaginary murders, ghosts, and daggers in mid-air. Through physically describing invisible objects, Pantomime can provide the actor with the freedom to strike up a relationship with anything: with music, with the space, with the floor or with imaginary people. As Ananyev claimed, 'All the actor is restricted by is his or her body and his or her imagination, and the aim of my work is to expand both of those.'

It was to this end that much of the second semester was devoted. Many classes incorporated isolations and co-ordinations into traditional pantomimic études, such as pushing and pulling imaginary ropes, marking out invisible walls, or opening non-existent doors. I'd done this sort of work before at drama school and university, and I'd always found that I was hopeless at it, and quite frankly it bored me silly. But there was a difference here. In the past, the focus had been on the monochrome repetition of difficult and rather empty, technical tasks, as we'd all stood obediently in a line flexing and relaxing our hands against an invisible wall. But Ananyev's approach was technicolour, as there was always an imaginative backdrop. In other words, it wasn't just the analytical brain doing the work; once again, all the inner motive forces were drafted into the exercise. The result was that we were diverted from the rather pleasureless execution of dry technique, and immersed in creative objectives. So, marking out an imaginary wall became an adventure through a labyrinth, with sudden chasms over which rope-bridges hung, and where our hands might plunge into warm water one moment and into a termites' nest the next. Sometimes, an Aladdin's cave was discovered, with rocky surfaces into which doors to secret passages would suddenly open and treasure chests could be unlocked. Physical development was effortlessly combined with imagination, spontaneous narratives, and a rare old serving of fun.

But it wasn't only invisible objects that were taken into consideration: Ananyev believed that *every* stage object, whether it was real or mimed, could be endowed with certain imaginary qualities. To some extent, I knew this from the exercise where my sweater turned into the head of John the Baptist. With this kind of imaginary freedom as an actor, you can respond to any object with the same attention that you'd respond to a human partner. And focusing all your attention on an object can often alleviate potentially difficult given circumstances. Stanislavsky touches upon this when he refers to the powerful emotions that have to be called upon if you're playing the part of a murderer. Rather than fretting about the fact that 'you've never murdered anyone so how can you possibly play Macbeth?', he suggests that you divert all your attention to the murder weapon. His words of wisdom are worth quoting here in full: 'The only thought . . . with which you should enter the circle [of attention] is your knife. Concentrate on the physical action: examining the knife. Look at it closely, test its edge with your finger, find out whether its handle is firm or not. Transfer it mentally into the heart or chest of your rival. If you play the villain try to estimate the force of the blow that would be needed to thrust the knife into your rival's back. Try to think whether you would be able to deal the blow, whether the blade should have been a little stronger, or whether it would stand the blow without bending? All your thoughts are concentrated on one object only: the knife, the weapon.'[56] With this kind of concentration, the dialogue with an object can provide you with a powerful imaginative inroad into a character's psychology without ever having to conjure up or squeeze out any kind of affective memory.

Continuing the work we'd done with the internal monologues, we went on to integrate inherently physical exercises into scenes that we were working on in text-based Acting classes. During one session when I was playing Sonya in *Uncle Vanya*, Ananyev noted a strange contradiction between my inner intention and my outer action. At the moment in Act II when Sonya steers Yelena's conversation onto talking about Doctor Astrov, I'd been absentmindedly stabbing an apple with a knife. Seeing it from a spectator's perspective, Ananyev declared that at that point he'd simply stopped believing me, as the contradiction between Sonya's internal feeling (love) and my external action (stabbing the apple) was too acute. That's not to say that contradictions like that are not only permissible, but also *fundamental* to interesting drama; it was just that the particular moment he'd isolated revealed that my inner life as an actress was not fully awake. The prop should be a partner, and as such it can texture and colour the performance. Ananyev made a similar observation a little later in the scene, when I drank a slug of vodka from a small glass on the table. He drew my attention to the fact that this was the glass from which, only minutes before, my beloved Doctor Astrov had drunk, so the object itself could feed my inner life as Sonya. My sip might be like a secret kiss, touching the glass that I knew his lips had just touched. You can even work like this with the entire atmosphere of a room: the person Sonya dearly loves has just been sitting in this room with her, so everything has an aura, a specialness. In order to texture my performance as Sonya, I could let this specialness subtly permeate my actions, not overstating or telegraphing the connection, but simply alerting myself to the relation between objects, atmosphere and inner sensation. These are the kind of details which will subconsciously resonate for an audience.

Levels of consciousness

Ananyev sought various means by which we could texture our work, and develop a deep connection between ourselves, the other actors and the objects inhabiting the on-stage world. To this end, he concentrated much of the second semester on evolving a sense of non-verbal communication. This was based on the notion of 'radiating' *Prana* energies and building a sense of what Stanislavsky calls 'communion' or 'irradiation'. *Prana* is a Hindu word, which, in a nutshell, describes the energy that radiates from your emotion centre, and is focused in your solar plexus. Tapping into this energy may sound terribly weird and esoteric, but in fact we're responding constantly to the energy that others are unconsciously radiating all the time. All that Stanislavsky, Chekhov and Ananyev were trying to do was to awaken the actor to how potent this energy is, and how energizing on-stage activity can be if we even glimpse the tip of the iceberg of this kind of communication.

To alert us to these energy fields, Ananyev introduced some very simple exercises, which were not entirely unfamiliar to me, but I'd never experienced quite the same results before. One such exercise involved an actor standing, with eyes closed, and holding the palms of his or her hands out, as if they were pressed up against a wall. One by one, the rest of us placed our own palms on the subject's hands and said our names. The hands remained in contact until the point at which the subject had sensed the other person's energy, and then he or she broke the contact. This was the easy part of the exercise. The next part was a little harder. Each member of the group anonymously placed his or her hands on the palms of the subject, who – with eyes still closed – attempted to identify the energy of the unknown communicator. Of course, there were other factors besides energy that helped with identifying the hands, such as size, heat and texture, as well as the sound of the footsteps approaching or the smell of a particular perfume. Despite all these factors, the communication of *energy* was to some extent discernible. This was certainly the case when Ananyev placed his own hands on the subjects: the transmission of energy through his palms seemed to cause subjects' hands almost to vibrate. The exercise went one stage further: instead of actually touching palms with the subject, a gap of several centimetres was left between the hands. The subject then had to identify the energy being directed from the other person through the space towards his or her palms.

There was no doubt that Ananyev had developed his own energy communication to a significant degree, and this was demonstrated for me one day in another exercise. The group was divided into male (A) and female (B) partnerships. Whilst Partner B's eyes were closed, Partner A tried to move B around the room by placing his hands no less than fifteen centimetres from B's body. In other words, there was no direct contact: simply by radiating energy through the palms of his hands, A was to lead the 'blind' partner B around the space. Unbeknownst to the blind B, Ananyev occasionally 'interfered' with the communication between partners by exerting his own energy through his palms, in an attempt to break the connection between A and B. After some time, the exercise was then repeated the other way around, with the sighted females guiding the blind males round the room with no other contact that the energy radiated through their palms.

Personally, I was almost incapable of budging my partner a millimetre with my radiated energy alone, but I experienced the most extraordinary sensation when *I* was 'blind'. I found it a very difficult exercise as, from start to finish, I struggled to silence my conscious mind. There was a voice in my head which insisted on discrediting the notion of 'irradiation', believing it to be a load of old nonsense. I tried as hard as I could to 'hear' the energy commands of my partner A, and move when I *thought* I felt an impulse, but I was never really sure and I suspected that I was probably making the whole thing up. Besides which, it's not the kind of exercise where 'trying hard' really helps. Then, in the midst of all my blind stumbling around, oblivious to my partner's guidance, I suddenly felt this huge surge of energy. I was overwhelmed by a tremendously physical sense of confusion or turmoil, as if I was being pulled from one place to another in some kind of energy whirlwind. It was such a disquieting sensation that I had to open my eyes just to re-orientate myself and stop myself falling over. As I looked around, I discovered that Ananyev and my partner were on either side of me – neither of them closer to me than a ruler's length – and a battle of energies had indeed been in progress. Each of them was trying to divert my energy in contradictory directions through the space. There was a non-physical, non-verbal tug-of-war going on, which I'd experienced through the radiated currents pushing and pulling me around the room. I don't think I'd ever experienced such non-verbal communication so powerfully before. In fact, this kind of communication, which is quite alien to a materialistic culture, opened up avenues of consciousness with which we just weren't familiar. Although the sensation was pretty unsettling at first, it was absolutely exhilarating. It was a bit like being on a roller-coaster but without the rubber harness. Tapping into this level of creative energy (or 'higher consciousness') requires a very particular approach, one that isn't necessarily reverent, but on the contrary – fun. For Ananyev, the creative process must be a *game*. Contact with the emotion-centre must always be accompanied by what Michael Chekhov calls a 'Feeling of Ease'[57], so that even darker emotions may be explored with a sense of lightness, a sense of pleasure, a sense of enjoyment and safety.

Working with higher (or deeper?) levels of consciousness requires both personal openness and a trust of the process, so that the actor can transport him or her self into the character's pains, without that pain being worked into his or her own psyche. Whatever happens, we mustn't play Ophelia and end up mad. We can't play Othello and finish up on a murder charge. To this end, Ananyev introduced into his training programme certain aspects of psychology to which we could relate in a very tangible, physical way. Essentially, he was building up a vocabulary of psycho-physical images with which we could develop our own consciousness; through that developed consciousness, we could then broaden our ability to create character. In order to build up this vocabulary of psycho-physical images, Ananyev drew illustrations from Dr Eric Berne's structural analysis of human psychology, referred to in his book *The Games People Play*. In his analysis, Berne talks about three ego-states, which co-exist within each human being, and they are the states of the *Adult*, the

Parent and the *Child*.[58] I'm sure we all know Peter Pan-type figures, whose youthful energy remains eternal (Child). Or little children whose responsible attitude outweighs that of their elders (Parent). Or certain individuals whose wisdom and extraordinary insight exceeds their experience or years (Adult). While we may all exhibit a dominant tendency in one particular direction, these three ego-states combine to make up our unique personal psychology. Applying them to the theatre, Ananyev explored the ego-states through a series of improvisations, which directly connected with the inner motive forces of emotion, thought and action. In these improvisations, Ananyev compared each ego-state with an *image* and an *energy-quality* which the actor could then explore physically. (All the time we were to remember the other components of tempo-rhythm, amplitude, dynamic and direction, and constantly punctuate the movement with the pause, of course.) Again, Ananyev's interpretation of Berne's ideas was idiosyncratic, presenting the actors with a correlation of imaginative picture, philosophical interpretation and physical manifestation.

The first of these 'ego-states' was the *Adult*, which was visualised as *a beam of Light*. The Adult was closest to a serenity which Ananyev allied with higher consciousness or 'God', whatever that might mean to an individual. We physically explored the idea of Light by imagining we were standing on a high mountain, overseeing a landscape of problems, with long rays extending from our finger tips and other extremities. While we were engaged in the physical and imaginative process, we were also to observe what kind of inner sensation was aroused, as well as which qualities were accessed in each of the centres. How did that quality of Light affect the emotion-centre? The thought-centre? How did it affect action? I discovered that a feeling of incredible calm and powerfulness quickly arose through the combination of imagining the picture and then physically embodying it. It was really rather pleasurable.

The second ego-state was the *Parent*, which was visualised as a *Point*, like a piece of chalking moving from one specific point on a blackboard to another. The inner Parent within each of us plans, manipulates and constructs stratagems, and through its cunning, it aims to achieve certain results without being at all capricious. Once again, we explored the image physically, by making decisive movements of the body from one precise point in space to another. We could move either one limb at a time, or the whole body, imagining there was a piece of chalk in the centre of the solar plexus. I discovered that the sensation aroused by this quality of movement was purposeful and therefore quite pleasing, but to some extent it was rather bound or constrained. Although I felt quite confident, it wasn't a very liberating experience.

Finally we explored the ego-state of the *Child*, which was visualised as the *Train of a Dress*. The inner Child is capricious and often acts before it thinks, and so its consciousness is always *behind* the action, following after the impulse like a chiffon train. You can see this with real children: they'll be attracted to the flame for its colour and shape, and then they'll discover that it hurts to touch it. However, in its higher form, the Child ego-state is very 'intuitive', 'creative', 'spontaneous' and carries the core of 'enjoyment'.[59] In fact, the Child is the artist's ally: if an actor can harness the energy of the Child, that Child quality can become the accessory to vital creativity on the stage. Psychologist Arthur Wagner offers the theory that the creative state for the actor when he or she is in *actual* performance is 'the *natural* child ego state defined by Berne. The *adapted* child is controlled and inhibited by the *influencing* parent, while the *natural* child is free of parental restraint and is exploding with archeopsychic (archaic, instinctual, perverse) behaviour.'[60] In other words, if we want to find the true joy of spontaneous creativity on the stage, we need to get back to our natural Child (a state which often lies hidden beneath layers of socialisation and adult inhibition). Through his work at the Moscow Theatre of Clowns, Ananyev tried to make immediate contact with the Child energy. As Michael Chekhov points out, clowning 'will awaken within you that eternal *Child* which bespeaks the trust and utter simplicity of all great artists.'[61] In Ananyev's physical manifestation of the Child ego-state, we explored movements from space to point, as if our consciousness was always behind the impulse of the movement, trailing after it like a scarf. When I've used this exercise with student-actors, the atmosphere instantly transforms into one of sheer delight and abandonment; the sensation is pretty uncontrolled, but exhilarating because of that liberation. There's a sense that the body 'knows' something which the mind doesn't, and a feeling of unexpectedness dominates the experience. It's great!

In exploring these levels of consciousness, Ananyev particularly examined the interplay between *peripheral* and *central* movement. The impulse behind the Adult movement was from point to space, in other words from central to peripheral; therefore, the energy radiated out from the body beyond the point at which the movement stopped. The impulse behind the Parent movement was from point to point, in other words from a central starting point through the periphery back to a central finishing point: all very contained and controlled, with a very strong sense of form. The impulse behind the Child movement was from space to point; in other words, the energy came from the periphery and was brought to a halt at the centre.

As I've already suggested, the exchange of energies between central and peripheral movement was important to Ananyev's understanding of human interaction in terms of giving and receiving information. The movement from peripheral to central reflects our receipt of information from the world; we take that information and we assimilate it within us. The movement from central to peripheral is the way in which we give information back to the world, the way we express our personalities, and the way we as actors express the characters that we're manifesting on stage. Through experimenting with the various ego-states, the actor could note the psycho-physical sensations of halting the energy (bringing it to a point – Child) or radiating the energy beyond the end of the gesture (out into space – Adult), or a combination of the two (Parent), with the accompanying sense of completing the action or continuing the action. But how does all this relate to the actor's work on a role?

Dual consciousness: from technique to inspiration

At the start of this chapter, I discussed the idea of actors 'transcending' themselves in order to step beyond their everyday mannerisms into the characters that the playwright has created. This was really what much of the work on ego-states and psychology was about. It's a question of needing to 'know thyself' before you can step forth into the character, and this bold step forward was the final stage in Ananyev's psycho-physical technique as we experienced it at VGIK. The notion of 'character' is a topic of great debate amongst many practitioners. Do I 'become' the character? *Can* I 'become' the character? Do I simply adapt the information that the playwright gives me about the character to fit my own personality? Many would argue, David Mamet included, that the whole concept of character is in itself an illusion, that there's no such thing as character; it's just you, the actor, doing those actions on the stage. My training at VGIK convinced me otherwise, and I would suggest that the concept of characterisation is what differentiates between actors who see their craft as a *job* and actors who see their craft as an *art*.

Many practitioners are afraid of intellectualising or talking about the process of acting, maybe in the fear that if you talk about it, you won't be able to do it. There's an inverted snobbery that analysis destroys creativity. To some extent I would agree, in the sense that you can't *rely* on analysis as the only inroad to creativity. However, I would contend that those actors who don't spend much time investigating their art and investing in their craft are those who take shortcuts. Either they reduce every character to the limits of their own everyday personalities or, at the other extreme, they consciously adopt physical or vocal characteristics to take the character as far from their own self as possible, and in the process we can admire their range and versatility. But there is a third way, one that *combines* personality with character to create something entirely new. Of course, as actors we have to remain grounded in our own concept of who we are: we can't get away from the fact that we're using our own bodies, our own voices, our own emotions and imaginations. However, at the same time, we have to develop the tools to transform ourselves into the creation provided by the playwright and director, and that creation is *not* ourselves. Unless a part has been specifically written for us, we're *not* in the playwright's head as he or she writes the play. So we're short-changing the writer, the audience and ourselves if we reduce his or her creation to our own personalities.

In order to assist in the strange but exciting transformation into character, Ananyev divided the actor into three working aspects: the Person – the Actor – the Character. *The Person* (the Russian word *lichnost* can also be translated as 'personality') represented the connection between the individual and his or her 'higher self'. What's 'higher self'? It's the elusive, hyper-creative part of us, through which we can tap into inspiration and spontaneity. *The Actor* represented the craftsman or technician, and the ability to juggle points of attention between what's going on on-stage, what's going on in the auditorium and what the demands of the role are. The Person remained constant, unchanged by the variables of audience and performance, as a kind of holistic, centred being. The Actor, on the other hand, responded effortlessly to the influences of the performance, changing and adapting according to unexpected circumstances or opportunities. The combination of Person and Actor 'held in its hand' *the Character* (*obraz* – often translated as 'image'). The Character was separate from, but connected to, real life – like a diamond on a ring. In other words, it had its own parameters but it wasn't entirely independent. It couldn't exist without the Person and the Actor, and so it would be completely impossible to be 'taken over' by the Character in some unhealthy schizophrenic way. It was a *creative* existence, not a *psychotic* one. These three components – Person, Actor and Character – worked together in unison, creating an organic whole during the performance. This union demanded an element of the *naïveté*, mentioned by Stanislavsky to overcome 'carping criticism'.[62] For as Ananyev stressed, and as I reiterate now, you cannot play and judge at the same time. Ananyev was insistent that if you judge yourself critically while you're performing, you take yourself away from the character's words and you fill your head 'with thoughts and feelings of self. Judgement demonstrates conflict inside the performer which breaks the union of Person, Actor, Character.' (I fell victim to this in a big, big way, as we'll see in the following chapters.)

The Person–Actor–Character combination can be seen to correspond to Berne's ego-states of Adult–Parent–Child. In effect, the Person is the 'higher consciousness', or 'superconscious' as Stanislavsky puts it, and it corresponds to 'the Adult' (the overseer of the creative process). It enables the Actor as craftsman and technician to manipulate (with the cunning of the Parent) the vitality of the spontaneous Child – the Character. The Person is a crucial part of the creative process on stage. It binds the *technical part* of the acting process as patrolled by the Actor (things like being heard by the audience, not upstaging or blocking your fellow actors, allowing for the coughing fit on the fifth row) with the *vitality and improvisatory nature* of the on-stage action as expressed by the Child/Character. While the Actor directs the techniques of breathing, diction, gesture and staging *out* towards the spectator, the Character can direct all its life and energy *in* towards what's happening on the stage. The rather holistic *Person* harmonises the two – the Actor and the Character.

This kind of 'dual consciousness' is no new thing: Diderot debates it in *The Paradox of the Actor* and Coquelin analyses it in *The Art of the Actor*. While perhaps the two Frenchmen address it from a rather clinical, technical angle, the Russian approach is more united in its inclusion of 'spirit' or 'higher consciousness' or 'inspiration', or whatever you want to call it according to how threatening or otherwise these terms may sound. Michael Chekhov prefers the idea of 'creative individuality', which he describes as being capable of 'straddling both sides of the foot-lights. It is not only a creator of the character but also its spectator . . . More than that, it has the ability to foretell the audience reaction, an instant before it takes place.'[63] It's a state of existence which is completely *in* the moment and *alongside* the moment at the same time. Many actors do it instinctively, but there are also actors who either stay well within the realm of the technical Actor, or who fly dangerously close to complete consummation by the Character. In order to live as healthy human beings, as well as inspired and inspiring artists, we have to develop the ability to nurture and listen to both, and in that way we will develop the Person.

Ananyev's training work addressed the trinity of Person, Actor and Character through the free improvisation work. During these improvisations, the Actor-technician monitored the work of isolations, co-ordinations, rhythm, impulses and the activity of the inner motive forces. At the same time, the Character–artist could express him or her self freely through the abstract dialogue with the music. Since much of Ananyev's work appealed to the 'spirit' (as was experienced in his exercises involving intangible energies and powers of 'irradiation') each actor's Person was encouraged to develop in such a way that we could begin to acquire the maturity to contain the Actor and the Character within one harmonious unit.

If we were to trace a link between contemporary Russian actor-training and the legacy of Stanislavsky and Michael Chekhov, it would lie in the concept of divided consciousness. Stanislavsky acknowledged that his own dual consciousness as an actor 'lent impetus' to his work, describing how he divided himself, as it were, 'into two personalities. One continued as the actor, the other was the observer. Strangely enough this duality not only did not impede, it actually promoted and lent impetus to [creativity].'[64] Contrary to the popular belief that Stanislavsky was primarily concerned with creating a fourth wall and sub-merging himself in the on-stage action, he actually came to see that a kind of divided consciousness was essential for the creative process. Curiously, his beliefs are not so different from those of the French man, Constant Coquelin, an actor who came from quite a different school of performance. Coquelin divided the actor into Persons One and Two.[65] Person One existed within the actor as an *impassive observer*, who, even in the most emotional moments, was observing, taking notes and understanding how he or she could use that experience in future creations. (I've met actors who do this in everyday life: one actress described how even when she was in the depths of grief following her partner's death, she had one eye on how she could use the emotion to inform future creations.) Coquelin goes on to describe Person Two as that part of the *actor* which does all the loving, hating, grieving and so on. Person One must be completely in control of Person Two, especially during the performance of a play. Even in those moments where the public is carried away by the performer's acting, and thinks him 'most absolutely distracted', he must '*see* what he is doing, judge himself, and retain his self-possession.' Coquelin didn't want the actor to experience even a shadow of the sentiments he's expressing, 'however great the truth and power of his expression may be.'

It's assumed that Stanislavsky held a diametrically-opposed belief, when he argued that 'if the actor is to be emotionally involved and pushed into action on the stage by the imaginary world he builds on the basis of what the playwright has created, it is necessary that he believe in it as thoroughly as he does in the real world which surrounds him.'[66] *But* – and the 'but' is big! – he goes on to say that this doesn't mean that while he's on the stage 'the actor must be subject to some kind of hallucination, that he must lose, while he is acting, the consciousness of surrounding reality.' On the contrary, 'a part of his consciousness must remain free from the trammels of the play, in order that it can exercise some supervision over whatever he is feeling and doing as he plays out the part of his character.' This mutual existence of technical supervision on the one hand and utter belief in the reality of the stage circumstances on the other requires the nurturing of the Person or 'higher consciousness'.

And this nurturing strikes me as being the key to psycho-physical training.

Ananyev likened the developing actor to a rose with strong petals, stem, bud and stamen, and with the actor's Person forming the flower's 'fragrance'. Without strong physical components, the rose can't survive, and yet it lacks its ultimate beauty if it has no scent. Higher consciousness is the 'fragrance' of the performer: if we can tap into it, it has the capacity to inform our work on stage with qualities beyond our own everyday consciousness. Ananyev started with simple technical exercises and gradually worked towards a physical expression of psychological ideas such as Person, Actor and Character. In this way, he sought to develop our higher consciousness through remarkably tangible means. We endeavoured to work in a state of dynamic meditation, allowing our sensation of movements to awaken our inner motive forces. At the same time, we listened to our psycho-physical activity through constant moments of silence, or pauses. This was no mean feat, and it wasn't always successful. Nonetheless, bit by bit the journey from technique to psycho-physicality was unfolding.

The ten-month Scenic Movement course culminated in an Open Class, to which all our tutors and any other interested parties were invited. Since the emphasis in the work was on process, not result, this was less of an examination and more of a demonstration of work-in-progress. The Open Class was to follow a specific format: it would start with the whole group demonstrating the regular exercises and *études*, and after that we were each to choose an aspect of the work through which we could explore our elementary psycho-physical technique. I wanted to have a go at what appeared to me to be a rather elusive aspect of the work: I wanted to try and unite the Person, Actor and Character and to discover the 'fragrance' of a role. And so I decided to conclude my year's training with Ananyev by working on a piece of text. To this end, I chose the speech from Oscar Wilde's *Salome*, in which Salome addresses the decapitated head of Iokanaan (Wilde's name for John the Baptist). Since my first

Eureka! moment of psycho-physical understanding had arisen when my sweater 'transformed' into the head of John the Baptist, this seemed an appropriate place to finish my journey.

Summary of Exercises

Following the Psycho-Physical Warm-up, a series of exercises expand and develop psycho-physical awareness by harnessing the imagination with the body. These need not follow a particular sequence or be seen as at all prescriptive; they are suggestions as to how psycho-physical technique may work towards the ultimate integration with a text. Ananyev himself is constantly changing and inventing exercises, and any actor or teacher is invited – if not encouraged – to do the same.

All preceding exercises are combined at the actors' discretion.

* **The Object Exercise**
Using any inanimate object, the actors are presented with the contra-dictory objectives, 'I *want* to touch it, but I *cannot* touch it.' (One actor to one object.) Without consciously imposing reasons behind the objectives, the actors explore (through the body as much as the brain) their relationship with the object, by approaching, retreating, observing, all the time paying attention to the changing inner (emotional) responses that arise according to the body's physical relationship to the object. The exercise usually lasts fifteen to twenty minutes, at which point the teacher/workshop leader informs the actors that they can now touch their individual objects. If the actors have truly engaged with the exercise, it's not uncommon for them to take several minutes to reach the point where they can or want to pick the object up.

This exercise benefits from *little* discussion. If too much preamble takes place, the actors begin to ask too many cerebral questions ('Do I imagine the object is something other than it is?' 'Do I have to know why I can't touch it?' 'What do you mean exactly?') Once they begin the exercise, all those questions are answered much more satisfactorily through the experience of *doing* the exercise, than through any amount of discussion. NB. It is not necessary to preconceive what the object might be: if it's a red textbook, it may remain a red textbook throughout the whole exercise, or it might become a magic tome, or a legal document, or a huge slab of chocolate, or a bar of gold. It doesn't matter. By *doing* the exercise, the combination of body and imagination will feed the actors in any way they need. As with most Active Analysis and psycho-physical preparation, it's experiential, not intellectual. The technical elements of joints, curves, waves, opening/closing, and central/peripheral serve as a backdrop to the exercise, albeit an unconscious backdrop.

• Free Improvisations

Usually accompanied by music to enhance a state of dynamic meditation, the actors simply move around the space. At the risk of sounding like a primary school movement-and-music class, it's a question of the physical exploration of the space and the actors' own bodies provoking a growing awareness of inner/outer co-ordination. Michael Chekhov's Psychological Gestures can be incorporated, in that the actors imagine a dynamic, physical position; they get into it; whilst in it, they think up the next position; they get into it. As they do so, they take note of the sensations aroused by the body's movement from one physical shape to the next, so that the movement *between* statics becomes as important and informative as the static positions themselves. The process is sped up, so that the time between each static is reduced to the extent that the body is eventually in a state of almost constant motion. However, there must be pauses (however momentary) between the movements in order that the actors may sense the psycho-physical experience. Free improvisations can last from a couple of minutes to half an hour, depending on what key element is being explored – straight lines, curves, waves, opening and closing, central/peripheral. Actors usually work individually, though encounters with other actors will also expand psycho-physical adaptability. NB. It's important that there is an imaginative objective behind the movements, otherwise it ends up with a group of actors wafting round to a bit of music. No doubt, concentration will come and go within a free improvisation, but it is during extended free improvisations that major experiential break-throughs are most likely to occur, when the brain shuts up and the psycho-physical integration of body/imagination/emotions/spirit takes over.

• Application to Text

The actors work with dramatic monologues (usually worked through in their heads rather than spoken aloud).

One part of the body leads the movement as the text is internally 'spoken'. The chosen part corresponds to the governing centre in the speech – Thought, Feeling or Action.

Through the speech, *different parts of the body* take over leadership of the movement, as the changing centres in the speech are explored; e.g. where the character is thoughtful, a finger might lead; as the character becomes emotional, the shoulders might lead; where the character becomes active, the groin might lead.

Sitting/walking/turning are the only actions to be used, the actors using 'their own' bodies, but the motivations and decisions of the character.

Sitting/walking/turning actions are led by particular body parts in relation to the matrix of inner motive forces. In other words, does the character 'sit thoughtfully', 'turn actively', or 'walk emotionally'? If so, is it the toes, the elbows or the eyes leading the physical action.

• Objects and Text

This is simply a question of how, in rehearsal, the actors may pay particular attention to their relationship with props and furniture, noting how inanimate objects are significant 'partners' in psycho-physical awareness. In this way, subtle physical nuances may convey important dramatic information to an audience. Does an actor (or character?) throw a letter on the floor, or fold it neatly and put it in a bureau, or rip it up, or discard it and move on to other business? All these 'dialogues' with objects texture and inform the audience's understanding of the dramatic action.

• Levels of Consciousness

These exercises should be treated with ease and as experimental.

Leading the Blind: Actor I leads Actor 2 (whose eyes are closed) round the room, with the palm of Actor I's hand c. 10-15 centimetres from Actor 2's body

Silent Commands: Actor I and 2 sit opposite each other, Actor 2 has closed eyes. Actor I pictures a simple command ('lie on the floor', 'stand up', 'roll over', etc). When Actor 2 gets a sense of what the command may be, he or she executes the action. (According to Ananyev, men are more obedient than women! Women often distrust the image they have received, not believing in their instinctive reaction. The actors should be encouraged not to think too much about the exercise, but just go with gut feeling. It doesn't matter if they're wrong – and they'll be surprised at how often they're very close to what the silent command actually was.)

• **Adult-Parent-Child**

Through a series of imaginative pictures, the actors move around the space, exploring the psychological effect created by the particular movement qualities:

Adult: standing on a mountain top with rays of light streaming from all extremities (Point to Space – consciousness ahead of the action)

Parent: a piece of chalk on a blackboard (Point to Point – consciously manipulating the action)

Child: the train of a dress (Space to Point – consciousness behind the action)

Salome

When it came to the final Open Class, my decision to work on (1) a piece of text and (2) *this* piece of text was quite specific. My ambitions with the exercise were high: I wanted to combine the truth of everyday naturalism with the passion and extremes of expressionism. I felt that I'd reached a certain degree of physical liberation, and so now was the time to test how far my body had acquired its psycho-physical knowledge by focusing on a concrete text. I was curious: could I connect the body's knowledge of Thought, Feeling and Will to the heights of physical expression and the depths of inner feeling? Just how far had I tuned myself to the nuances of the inner/outer continuum? I was prepared to face a certain amount of hard work, and in all probability, defeat . . .

It struck me that *Salome* was a great piece for testing the extremes of physical expression on the one hand, and inner feeling on the other. The writing is wonderfully musical, and yet at the same time, it rings true psychologically. The play presents us with a young woman (really still a wilful child) who has demanded an obscenity – a beheading – because, in her heart of hearts, she understands her erotic power over Herod, and she wants to put that power to the test. Iokanaan's (John the Baptist's) rejection of her budding sexuality, and the pain caused by her unrequited love, have incited her to try and 'possess' him through murder. The flamboyance of the material provided an intriguing combination of operatic language, potent emotions and truthful psychology, which could be explored and expressed through non-naturalistic, expressionistic movement. I decided to perform the speech in Russian to explore another dimension of the dialogue between text and body. Although that might sound horrendously pretentious, it was in fact more of a cop-out than a pretension. The Russian language is extremely lyrical and onomatopoeic, so much so that it's much easier to find the confidence and reverberations in the language to make the hyperbole of Salome's words feel convincing. Of course it complicated matters to some degree, as I'm hardly bi-lingual. But what it did do was challenge my dependence on my thought-centre. Because the text was alien, I wouldn't be able to rely on the cerebral appeal of familiar English, and so my mind would have to work in closer collaboration with my emotion- and action-centres.

The structure of the text itself was dynamic and compelling. The movement of the speech through desires, passions and the inner motive forces was clear and articulate. Salome begins with fantasies as to what she'll do with Iokanaan's head, followed by reminiscences of his beauty when he was alive. She goes on to express her wilful desire to throw his head to the dogs, and finally she mourns for lost love. It was an exciting journey to explore as an actor. Added to the detailed structure, the speech also provided an opportunity to explore a dialogue with an *object* – the head of Iokanaan. As we have already seen with the work on *Uncle Vanya* and the 'transformation' of my sweater into the head of John the Baptist, Ananyev had explored the process of endowing objects with an inner life of their own, so that they can awaken new sensations in the actor. So selecting the object, which would represent the head of Iokanaan, became a key question. From the start of the speech, Salome's objective is 'to kiss Iokanaan'. The head is a treasure for her, a trophy. Yet as much as she wants it, she's afraid of it; as much as it's beautiful, it's loathsome. As much as she loves it and wants to kiss it, she delights in exploiting the power she has over it, relishing the knowledge that she can mercilessly abuse it if she wants to. In a variety of ways, Iokanaan has aroused six of Salome's deadly sins. She feels lust for his body, anger at his rejection of her, vanity because all men should love her, pride that he dared to reject her, greed to have whatever she wants, and envy that his God was more important to him than she was. The fact that one object can be invested with so many properties is a potent springboard for any actor playing Salome. What served as a vital image for *my* connection with the object was Salome's desire to bite the head 'with my teeth as one bites a ripe fruit'. These delicious words conjured up images of devouring the head, juice dripping vampire-like, as Salome sucks dry Iokanaan's life-force. The relevance of central and peripheral impulses also came into play here: Salome's impulse to action comes from *space/periphery* (with her fantasy of what she'll do with the head) to *point/centre* (with the physical presence of the head itself). The provocation for her action – the head – is outside her, and she takes that information and assimilates what it means for her, coming out with a series of physical responses.

Finding the appropriate head took various twists. In the first rehearsal, I improvised freely – both vocally and physically in a kind of Active Analysis – with a fabric *mannequin*. The result of this was far too baroque and all my energy became focused towards the doll. The mannequin attracted my attention so compellingly throughout the speech that I didn't really explore the stage space, and the dramatic dynamics were limited. To try and expand the spatial relations and to decrease the (embarrassing) literalness of my improvisations, Ananyev suggested that I act out the speech in front of an imaginary mirror, as if the mirror were hanging right at the back of the auditorium. We didn't get rid of the mannequin, but in the improvisation that followed, it remained on the stage as the corpse of Iokanaan, while my main focus was on the imaginary mirror in front of me. What this meant was that I could keep an awareness of the corpse's presence, without feeling obliged to look at it all the time or relate to it directly. I could sense it through different parts of my body: spine, head, side, calf, with the result that the relationship with the object developed and became more complex. The lure between the mannequin and my self-absorption in the mirror created an inner conflict between the centres, and an outer conflict between the physical objects (mirror and mannequin). Through this process of Active Analysis, we made discoveries about Salome which might have eluded us otherwise. She became coquettish, self-aware, vain through the split-focus with the imaginary mirror. The movement seemed to become more sinuous, with a prevalence of wave motions through the body and in particular through the arms and back. The combination of the Iokanaan-mannequin behind me and the imaginary mirror in front of me created a complex dynamic of space-object relationships, encompassing the entire theatre area. In a curious way, I felt my sense of Salome expand: I felt bolder, more confident, almost gargantuan, because my focus had been shifted from the limitations of the stage-space and expanded to the whole of the auditorium. It was as if my Salome could conquer not only Herod and Iokanaan, but anyone else who dared to watch her macabre emotional tango with the corpseless head.

At the second rehearsal, Ananyev presented me with Iokanaan's head in the form of an *orange*. The decisions I'd taken and the attitudes I'd adopted in the previous rehearsal with the mannequin were instantly challenged and transformed by the change in the object. Mainly because it was smaller and didn't look anything like a human being! Because Ananyev's training had developed a sense of constant inner adaptation, I actually became quite excited by the orange and that in turn enhanced the spontaneity. I embarked on an improvisation with it, making some further intriguing discoveries. The fruit was instantly more sensuous than the mannequin – it could be smelt and tasted, it squelched when I squashed it, it oozed when I scratched it. An original concept I'd had of enacting the speech with a living actor as a supine Iokanaan now seemed horribly naïve, as once the orange was introduced many more options arose. I could now throw the head, kick the head, or place it on a pedestal. In the course of the improvisation, I squeezed the orange and a split appeared. It looked like a mouth, so I stuck my tongue in. While I was rather pleased with my sensual improvisation, Ananyev wasn't quite so impressed: for him, that kind of explicit action wasn't necessary. He reminded me that the power of the stage lies in its *metaphor*. What the audience sees in their imaginations can be far more graphic than anything the actor may actually be doing.

The metamorphosis of the head didn't stop there. At the third rehearsal, Ananyev presented me with Iokanaan's head in the form of an *apple*, partly because he couldn't find an orange and partly to remind me that each new object brings with it new sensations. This time, we abandoned all text, which to some extent was getting in the way. Learning the speech in a foreign language meant that at a certain stage in rehearsals, my exploratory work was in danger of becoming too cerebral, as the Russian text was complex. Instead, a free improvisation with music ensued, during which I moved how, when and where I wished in response to the music, the space and the apple. Again, I was quite pleased with my Isadora Duncan show. However . . . Ananyev's observation was that my dialogue always seemed to begin with the *external* object, rather than the *inner* voice. In other words, the impulse to move always seemed to be from periphery to centre, as if I was waiting to get information from the outside world and then responding to it. I acknowledged that usually the dialogue with a partner – whether that partner was the space, music or object – helped me to contact deeper feelings within myself. I wasn't good at trusting my own inner life. Limitless attention to the outside partner was easier than limitless attention to the internal voice. The trouble with this, in Ananyev's opinion, was that it can lead to externalised, 'needy' acting, which is often less interesting, both to watch and to do, than in combination with more reflexive, central-to-peripheral action.

Not one to let an actor get away with anything, Ananyev insisted that I embark on a second free improvisation, this time allowing myself time (through the pauses) to listen to what was really going on inside me, rather than letting the external

influences dictate to me all the time. I instantly felt rather
vulnerable and exposed, although I gradually found that if I
allowed myself to be inwardly open during this exercise, the
physical sensations of *doing the scene* aroused new emotions in the
character. After all, this is the premise of Active Analysis: *doing*
the scene teaches you what the scene is about, and one action
feeds and inspires the next in an endless chain of spontaneous
moments. I followed Ananyev's directive to respond to inner
impulse not outer object, and the result was that Salome's complex inner life emerged. How much love there is inside her, and
yet how great is her grief at destroying the one thing she loved,
Iokanaan! But she has no choice. The pain that she suffers when
Iokanaan rejects her is so profound that she has to have him
destroyed. She has to obliterate any chance of disappointment
that their future love won't be consummated. It was by allowing
the inner dialogue to *exist between* – and to *be heard by* – my inner
motive forces, that I genuinely and effortlessly understood
Salome's pain. The relationship with the object also flourished:
when I got to the end of the speech, I dashed the apple onto the
floor of the auditorium, without thought, just impulse, and the
flesh shot in all directions. It was my Salome's way of destroying
the spirit of Iokanaan.

All the work to date had been on my own with Ananyev's
direction. To some extent, the object became a partner, but you
don't get too much feed-back from an apple! In the fourth
rehearsal, Ananyev combined my *Salome* project with a fellow
actor who was looking at Peter Weiss's *Marat/Sade*. We were to
work together in a free improvisation with music, but my partner
was to relate to me as if I were Marat, while he was my Iokanaan.
Ananyev provoked us by saying that, if an actor was uninhibited
in his or her inner life and precise in his or her attention to the
partner, the addition of any given circumstances, however
strange, could lead to insight into and discovery of the character's soul. In other words, if you're in a constant state of inner
improvisation, you can go with anything and react to anything
and learn everything. And he was right. What happened was that

being released from the text, as well as from any logical given circumstances, allowed the characters to develop their own inner tempo-rhythm. Salome became a cocktail of contradictory and spontaneous responses, full of bright coquettishness and deep-felt anger. But the overriding sensation was that she was actually very scared of the powerful emotions stirring up inside her, emotions aroused by Iokanaan's responses to her initial provocations. She's a virgin; she doesn't understand the promptings of her own femininity. She's confused and tantalised, attracted and repelled, open and closed, aroused and defensive, all at the same time. These interesting contradictions arose from the freedom of the strange dialogue between Salome/Marat and Iokanaan/Sade. Here was a flesh-and-blood living man, so Salome now had the possibility to explore in reality what she could only fantasise about before. A strange *mélange* of responses arose for both my partner and myself, sparked by our differing objectives and the various obstacles that we were unwittingly throwing in each other's way. It's through this kind of free improvisation that a character's 'creative individuality' has the chance to unfold – without force and with nothing but 'limitless attention to the partner'.[67] And as we'll see in the following chapter, an improvisation like this can involve a whole host of different characters from a number of different plays, all exploring their relationships in a sort of limbo-land of given circumstances.

The fifth rehearsal combined various exercises: the dance with the apple, the interplay between the fruit and the imaginary mirror, and the text of the speech. I'd decided to extend the opening *Ah!* to three half-sung vowel sounds to give a sense of ritual: I thought this would be an original and mysterious way of beginning the speech. Once again, however, Ananyev stopped me. 'Why was I trying to find emotion through text and *voice*, when his discipline was concerned with the interplay of text and *body*?' He could see that I was so concerned with giving a good performance that I wasn't so much *experimenting*, as *pre-determining*. To help me connect more directly with my body, he suggested that, at any point in the text in any way that seemed appropriate, I should try and find a physical position which expressed Salome's solitude. He reminded me that I'd find this moment if I just allowed the *pause* (physical and inward) to inform the subsequent action. I felt full of trepidation: I knew I had to 'get rid of my head', to stop my brain getting in the way, and at first I was pretty sure that I wouldn't be able to do it. Then I suddenly thought, 'Stop *caring* so much – just get up and do it!' And in fact, through free improvisation of the speech, I did spontaneously find the moment when suddenly my body needed to close in on itself. Embryonically, protectively, almost like in the torch-beam exercise. At this point, with a painful sense of utter loss, the words tumbled out:

> *Ah! wherefore didst thou not look at me, Iokanaan? . . .*
> *Well, thou hast seen thy God, Iokanaan, but me, me, thou*
> *didst never see. If thou hadst seen me thou hadst loved me.*
> *I saw thee, and I loved thee. Oh, how I loved thee! I love*
> *thee yet, Iokanaan. I love only thee . . .* [68]

My *body* discovered a position, which then inspired the *thoughts* (as expressed in the concrete form of writer's words), which then fed back an appropriate *emotion* to me, the performer. At last I was beginning to understand that the body has a superior intelligence.

Summary of the application to text

Of course, every text will demand a different approach; however, a quick outline of the improvisations undertaken with *Salome* will give an idea of the kind of structure that may be used in applying psychophysical techniques to text.

- **Free improvisation using body and spoken word**
  (In this instance, with a mannequin as the prone Iokanaan.) Such freedom in the very first stage of rehearsals allows the actors and director to explore what happens when attention is shifted around the physical space. This enables the actors to find a means of

expanding 'inner life' to fill the outer theatre space, maintaining an 'inner' connection at the same time as building effective dramatic pictures. It's very important that the actors feel that anything goes at this stage, that creative freedom is the order of the day. A workshop leader or director must allow and encourage such liberation, so that the actors can activate their creative 'Child-state', without worrying that they have to come up with the ultimate performance/interpretation.

- **Constantly changing the given circumstances**
(In this instance, by changing the head of Iokanaan from a mannequin to an orange to an apple.) Through exploring the physical and vocal connections with various stage objects, the actors can allow their bodies, not their brains, to feed the imagination and awaken artistic emotions.

- **Free improvisation with unexpected given circumstances**
(In this instance, the dialogue between Marat/Salome and Sade/Iokanaan.) All these exercises are concerned with continually changing circumstances, so that the actors develop a state of constant inner adaptation, so that once the *mise-en-scène* is determined, there will remain a sense of inner play and improvisation within a set structure.

From the actor to the ensemble

The Open Class in itself revealed a few problems. However much I believed that if a process is correct, you can show it at any moment and *that* will be a result in itself, I still felt the need to *perform*, to illustrate how far we'd come in the process. I had yet to mature in my psycho–physical awareness to feel the confidence simply to let go and to allow the audience to be part of the dramatic experience, rather than spectators of a finished product. This feeling was endorsed by Ananyev's comments following my presentation of *Salome*; too frequently in my performing, he saw the *actress at work*, the craftswoman sharpening her tools, to the detriment of the character's free expression. He had hoped to see the quality of rapid change in Salome's character that I'd spontaneously found in the free improvisation with the

Marat/Sade. During that particular improvisation, I'd organically discovered the fluctuation of emotion from scorn to love to
fear, whilst in performance, according to Ananyev, I seemed to dis-
play the cleverness of the actress. I still had a very long way to go.

At the end of the day, the re-education of the body requires a
period of study far more intensive than a brief ten months could
allow. Ananyev's work had set in motion a process of re-
encountering and fine-tuning the actor's physical instrument.
This began with a Psycho-Physical Warm-up incorporating isolations and co-ordinations; physical wave movements; opening
and closing physically and imaginatively; and an understanding
of the inner waves between the thought-, emotion- and will-
centres using a matrix of body parts. Once the actors' bodies had
been individually prepared, exercises incorporated the complexity
of dialogues with stage objects, music, the space and the fellow-
performer; free improvisations based on Michael Chekhov's
Psychological Gestures; application of these exercises to inner
monologues; development of levels of consciousness, through
the potent and intangible 'irradiation' of energies; and exploration of psychological states of Adult, Parent and Child, through
imaginative pictures and physical expressions. All this led towards the development of an actor's 'creative individuality'.
These components comprised the psycho-physical technique
underlying the contemporary Russian training, and connected
directly to Active Analysis. What became clear to me was that a
real state of constant inner improvisation was truly accessible
through the element of *play*. Although the solo work on Salome
was incredibly challenging and immensely rewarding, the best
way of expanding your sense of play is by *working in an ensemble*.

ACT 3
Working in the Ensemble

Seizing 'the passionate kiss'

Most actors yearn to be spontaneous in performance. By that I mean, they yearn to give the appearance that every word they utter, every movement, glance, pause, chuckle, tear has sprung immediately from that moment in response to that partner, whether it be on the stage or in front of the camera. It depends on the style of the piece, of course, but in terms of realistic drama or television, the illusion of spontaneity is probably most actors' dream. While in many ways this illusion may seem to be an impossible expectation, it needn't be so difficult or remote. As I discussed in Chapter 1, William James proposed that the most important part of our environment is our fellow-man. And, in fact, we only have to turn to Stanislavsky to discover that the secret of spontaneous reaction on the stage is simply to pay 'limitless attention to your partner.'[69] If you give absolute attention to every gesture and intonation made by the person you're on-stage with, you can't help but locate your action directly in what Stanislavsky called the 'transient now'.[70] You're not thinking about your next line, you're not thinking about why the audience didn't laugh tonight, you're not thinking about why your agent took ten per cent of your holiday pay. You are here and now listening to the person you're performing with, and in this way, you can begin to hold a vital and truthful dialogue.

In most acting set-ups, we don't often have the privilege of creating a strong ensemble. Companies such as the Royal Shakespeare Company, Steppenwolf or Theatre de Complicité do place a great deal of emphasis on ensemble collaboration. But in your average theatre environment where rehearsal time is limited to three, four or – if you're very lucky – six weeks, or in much television filming where rehearsals are more for the camera crew than the actors, there just isn't the opportunity to develop group interaction. But for Stanislavsky, the importance of collaborative creativity was so great that anyone who marred the ensemble was committing a crime against the very art that he or she served.[71] A strong ensemble can provide the most delicious of working environments. And it's actually very sexy, in the sense that when the creative energy is really racing between a company of players, then the spontaneous communication can be exhilarating and exciting. This 'sexiness' was something that Stanislavsky was clearly very aware of, describing ensemble interaction as 'even more powerful than physical attraction. This unity is of tremendous importance to actors. It gives them great creative joy. It is stronger than the most passionate kiss.'[72]

This makes it all sound very desirable and very easy. And yet, most of us know – whether we're actors, directors or teachers – that the 'passionate kiss' can be very elusive. After all, an ensemble can only comprise the sum of its parts, and if it's going to be successful, there has to be an inherent complicity between the individual actors. Since actors are only human beings and since (as we all know) human beings have a certain chemistry which either works between them or doesn't, it's hardly surprising that complicity within a company of actors can be rather inhibited at first. Or even non-existent. So how can we go about finding this 'passionate kiss' and creating an interactive ensemble? Again, for me, the answer seemed to lie in the psycho-physical training as I experienced it in Moscow. If the work of Vladimir Ananyev (see Chapter 2) developed the actor's ability to listen to *personal* creative impulses, the work of Katya Kamotskaya extended this sensitivity to the impulses of *fellow actors*. Kamotskaya was responsible for a class called Actor-Training, and the great potential of this training lay in its simplicity and in the directness of its penetration into the problems of on-stage interaction.

Much as we may desire it, there's no infallible formula for creating a collaborative ensemble, but that doesn't stop us investigating the possibilities. And Kamotskaya's work was very much 'active research'. She had devised her Actor-Training programme in co-ordination with the text-based classes of Albert Filozov, a celebrated actor with whom she worked as a tutor over the course of seven years (see Chapter 4). According to the make-up of each new student-group and along with the plays being staged by Filozov, Kamotskaya changed and developed the structure and content of every training programme. This enabled her directly to address the problems presented by each new group through permutations of the various core exercises that she'd devised. Because her course design was constantly changing, this chapter can in no way offer a hard-and-fast A–Z of Ensemble Building, although it does contain a number of key exercises, which probe certain generic problems. As I've discovered through my own use of these exercises, they can unlock a number of the basic inhibitions, which beset a growing ensemble whatever the age or experience of its composite members. In fact, the underlying principles behind the exercises arose from the struggles that Kamotskaya herself had met as an actor, particularly those she'd experienced as a drama student.

Convention versus Innovation

In her teens, Kamotskaya had attended Vakhtangov's Shchukin Theatre Institute in Moscow, and she vividly described the experience of traditional Soviet training in the late 1980s: 'After my third year at the Institute, I was very inhibited. I desperately wanted to be an actress, but when I went out on the stage I was empty and frightened. In my drama school, every exercise inhibited me more and more, because they used the components of Stanislavsky's system *separately*. For example, the teacher would say, "Relax your hands. Your legs are very tense. We are having a Relaxation class, so please! Relax!" '

During her time as a student, Kamotskaya undertook other classes involving deeply emotional or involuntary responses which were conducted under similar orders. One of these classes was called *Otzenkofaktor*, which roughly translates as 'Appraisal of a Situation'. Each week, the students, including Kamotskaya, were asked to set up a true-to-life situation involving an ordinary activity. It might be preparing a meal for a sweetheart, for example, and all the students would bring the relevant props, foods and costumes they needed to recreate a naturalistic environment. During the improvisation, an unexpected event would suddenly take place: perhaps the telephone might ring, and the student would hear a voice claiming that some terrible disaster had befallen the awaited sweetheart. At that precise moment, the student was expected to react to the situation 'truthfully and spontaneously' – which really meant 'emotionally'. Kamotskaya described how over the three-month period of the course, the on-going demand for instantaneous reactions seemed to rob both herself and the other student-actors of any chance of spontaneity. As far as the class-tutor was concerned, it was essential that the students registered their reaction on *immediate* receipt of the bad or shocking news. But Kamotskaya struggled against this. She felt that instant reaction wasn't necessarily true to human nature: we often find, especially in extreme situations, that delayed reactions or diverted angers manifest themselves some time *after* a particular event. And for Kamotskaya, the reverberation of *natural* human responses was surely the raw material of actor-training. Handling the nuances of natural responses requires a tutor to pay particular attention to the individuality of each student. At the Shchukin School, however, they seemed to be more concerned with every student being perfect in the exercise. As Kamotskaya put it, her tutors' expectation was that 'Two and two has to be four. Please, show me this four!' But emotions aren't arithmetic: what if it's five? 'No, that's wrong. You've made a mistake. Show me four!'

At last, with the final year at drama school pending, Kamotskaya decided she had to do something to unravel the psychological mesh which her formal training was weaving. So she travelled to Poland to Jerzy Grotowski's Teatr Laboratorium . . .

Given the Teatr Laboratorium's infamous reputation for physical and emotional extremism, this might sound like a case of 'out of the frying pan, into the fire'. But no. After three years at the Shchukin Theatre Institute, Kamotskaya spent only twenty-four hours at the Teatr Laboratorium, but her response to the work there was profound. She took part in *The Tree of People* workshop, under the guidance of actors Ryszard Cieslak, Rena Mirecka and Antoni Jaholkowski.[73] This workshop was part of a project established in 1978 by Zbigniew Cynkutis (one of the first members of Grotowski's troupe) and each event involved up to four hundred people at a time. Any division between leader and participant, between work and rest, was eliminated so that the whole experience became a living event, or what Grotowski called a 'work-flow'; in Kamotskaya's case, it lasted for twenty-four hours. All activities, be they domestic or training periods, became part of the same 'work-flow', and every couple of hours, two new leaders came into the work-space and began fresh activities. The participants could join in whenever they felt like it, whatever the time of day or night and, although there were rest hours, it wasn't uncommon for participants to stay awake for the duration, so keen was their hunger to try each new experience.

The various groups involved in *The Tree of People* project consisted of actors, theatre researchers, and members of the public who were simply there to experience Grotowski's approach to life as much as to acting. Because of the range of experiences and backgrounds, the group leaders engaged with the participants in a very professional, but very emotionally open, way. Kamotskaya described how the leaders worked with them almost as if they were untamed animals: 'If you have a wild dog or fox and you want to befriend it, you take very slow, very small steps. You pause, because you're afraid of causing it pain, or frightening it. And the same rules were applied to our work.' Over the twenty-four hour period, there was a series of exercises, beginning with simple eye-contact with one other person and building up to complex and extended improvisations involving the whole group. (The nature of these will become clearer as I discuss Kamotskaya's own Actor-Training programme). Through these exercises, the experiences at *The Tree of People* workshop combined to form the first step in awakening each individual to the power of the ensemble.

Although Kamotskaya's time at the Teatr Laboratorium was incredibly brief, it revolutionised her approach to her own acting and formed the cornerstone of her future training technique. All the physical and psychological tensions she'd accumulated during her formal training in Moscow were replaced by an immediate physical and inner relaxation. It was as if the processes that she'd been somewhat 'force-fed' at drama school were presented in an utterly simple and totally practical way during that one day at the Teatr Laboratorium. Armed with this new knowledge, she returned to Moscow to begin her final year at the Shchukin Institute.

Collaboration with Filozov

Kamotskaya's intention was to incorporate this simple, direct and liberating training into her own performance practice. It wasn't long, however, before she realised it was almost impossible: she now had one kind of approach inside her, while her fellow students were in another system. She graduated, and spent the next few years as an actress at the Moscow Philharmonic Dramatic Theatre, the theatre at which Vladimir Nemirovich-Danchenko (Stanislavsky's co-founder at the Moscow Art Theatre) had done a great deal of pioneering work in the late nineteenth century. During her time there, Kamotskaya struggled to absorb the new Polish training into her acting work, but with little satisfaction. It was during this time that she was cast in the Soviet music-drama *Ekspromt Fantasy* by Vitoria Tokareva, in a production which was to be staged at the Stanislavsky Dramatic Theatre. Suddenly Kamotskaya found herself playing opposite the leading Russian actor, Albert Filozov, and she soon realised that at last she was working alongside a kindred spirit.

Filozov took considerable interest in Kamotskaya's description of her work in Poland, and he was intrigued by the difficulties she'd had in introducing these simple, yet rather esoteric ideas into what was still a fairly staunch Soviet environment. Some time after *Ekspromt Fantasy*, Filozov was invited to take up an acting 'mastership' at the famous State Institute of Cinematography (VGIK). VGIK was steeped in the history of filmmaking and acting. Founded in 1919, it had been the artistic 'home' of the early pioneering cinematographers Eisenstein, Kuleshov, Gardin and Kozintsev. Here Pudovkin had established his laboratory into screen acting for movies including *Mother* (1926) and *The End of St Petersburg* (1927), and delivered some of the first ever lectures on Film Acting, later published in Britain in 1935. And it was here that Filozov came in the late 1980s to be responsible for the practical training of undergraduate students on both the four-year Acting and the five-year Directing courses. Having discussed the Polish experience extensively with Kamotskaya, Filozov knew that she passionately wanted to explore the potential of this training. And so he invited her to become his assistant. In this way, he could provide her with an environment in which to experiment and explore, and with a group of talented young students eager for new experiences. So in 1989, Kamotskaya joined Filozov as a fellow pedagogue at VGIK. While Filozov worked on playtexts, Kamotskaya started to form a training system based on simple, organic exercises and rooted in direct contact with an ensemble as she'd experienced it at the Teatr Laboratorium.

During the first year, Filozov and Kamotskaya worked with a group of eighteen-year-old Russian acting students, trying to draw out their *individuality*. The main focus was on inner process rather than external result: what was going on inside the students rather than well-executed theatre presentations. We have to remember that this was Moscow in the late 1980s and the early 1990s: it was still very uncomfortable for the 'establishment' to deal with ideas of individuality, spirituality, personality. The powers-that-be in VGIK considered the unconventional methods adopted by Filozov and Kamotskaya to be extremely *hooliganski*. VGIK's Acting Department endorsed traditional Soviet interpretations of Stanislavsky, and fellow acting 'masters' still approached student-work with the aim of producing a formal result on the stage, a schematic production. In stark contrast, Filozov and Kamotskaya wanted to release the *personality* of their students, enabling them to explore their human freedom, their human truth, their individuality. They consciously sought to break down the formal barriers between master and pupil, encouraging their students to feel a sense of creative freedom within the classroom, the like of which the young adults had never really known before. The intentions were brave, and Filozov and Kamotskaya pursued what they were doing, despite their colleagues' antipathy, doubt and sometimes blatant disapproval.

In the autumn of 1993, Kamotskaya and Filozov met the eclectic troupe of English-speaking actors (myself included) who had begun a one-year study at VGIK: a motley crew of British and Irish practitioners, strangers to each other and totally alien to the culture in which they had suddenly placed themselves. Out of this unlikely band, using the techniques which she'd developed with her Russian students and based on her own discoveries in Poland, Kamotskaya would attempt to form a collaborative creative ensemble.

Finding yourself:
circles of attention, five-minute recollection

The first few stages of Kamotskaya's approach were nothing terribly new. Her main aim was to create an environment in which each actor could begin to listen to him or her self and be comfortable with that feeling. (This is where the Work in the Ensemble is clearly connected with the Work on Your Self.) To do this, Kamotskaya began each session with an exercise based on Stanislavsky's 'circles of attention', or 'stage attention' as it's more accurately translated. The exercise is very straightforward: it's quite simply a matter of sitting with your eyes closed and distilling your attention down to yourself at first, your own body, your own thoughts, your own breathing and how you're feeling here and now. Slowly you start to widen this circle of attention to take in other stimuli: the people in the room, the noises outside the room, the noises in the rest of the building, the noises outside in the street, the noises in the rest of the town and so on. In this way, the exercise begins by focusing on a very definite sense – sound – and gradually expands to an exercise about imagination. Can you hear the cashier at the local supermarket? Can you hear the child in the school playground? Can you hear the conversation in the call-box on the corner? Although the exercise is very basic, it's actually a wonderfully focused way of beginning ensemble work: it engages everybody in the same activity, while allowing each individual to explore his or her own frame of mind each day.

Grotowski refers to this as 'creative passivity': 'The artist must begin by doing nothing. Silence. Full silence. This includes his thoughts. External silence works as a stimulus. If there is absolute silence and if, for several moments, the actor does absolutely nothing, this internal silence begins and it turns his entire nature towards its sources'.[74] For Kamotskaya's work, this starting point of tranquillity and attention was paramount, as it instantly focuses the actor *inwards* on him or her self. It then allows the actors to take their attention *outwards* to the present moment, 'the transient now' – what's happening here and now with these people in this space?

This permutation of Circles of Attention was then followed with an imaginative memory exercise. Again this was very simple: each actor remembered as accurately as possible the first five minutes of the day, including all the sensory experiences such as the sound of the alarm clock, the feel of the pillow, the smell of the coffee, the first look in the mirror, the taste of the toothpaste. Every time the mind wandered, which inevitably it did as the brain is very tricksy, it was quickly coaxed back into the exercise by simply recalling the vividness of the senses. (We like sensual things – it's not a big problem to ask the brain to conjure up sensory memories.) The exercise needn't focus on the first five minutes of the day: it could be the first five minutes in this particular room, or the journey to the rehearsal or the class. Whatever the task, it should be something fairly straightforward, with no huge emotional connotations, unless they arise spontaneously from the recollection of simple sensory details.

A combination of these exercises – *Circles of Attention* and *Five-Minute Recollection* – was repeated at the beginning of most of Kamotskaya's sessions. The result was that each actor's powers of concentration and imaginative recall began to gain in strength. Even on the occasions when it was difficult to get the mind to focus, something new was revealed. The exercises became a kind of touchstone for preoccupations or excitement or anxiety or some other psychological area which made each individual day particularly special or troubling.

At first, the time taken for the two exercises was about fifteen minutes. Gradually the time was reduced to about five. The more the exercises were practised, the less effort was involved in silencing the mind, and eventually it was possible to reach a state of deep relaxation and intense concentration within a few moments. It was a kind of 'Pavlov's dog' effect. In turn, *creative passivity* was strengthened: the ideal state to begin creative work is one in which you, the actor, are so psychologically relaxed, but imaginatively active, that anything is possible and you can turn your emotions on a dime. Whatever your director suggests to you is accessible and easy, because your inner life is putty in your hands. And no matter which emotion is asked of you – be it laughter, tears, anger, hatred, ecstasy or even equilibrium – the sensation of playing with your inner life is both pleasurable and fun. (This, of course, is the perfect state for working with Active Analysis.)

Finding the others – sound over sight

So that was the first step in Kamotskaya's Actor-Training. Taking the time – be it fifteen minutes or thirty seconds – to find yourself, to listen to what's going on inside you today, and to relax yourself into a state of creative passivity to prepare your inner instrument. The aim of the exercises which followed was to bring you (in your highly prepared state of being) into contact with other members of the group.

Acting is about play. One of our first means of human socialisation is play. But we find it hard to play as adults: we're so worried about what others will think of us in terms of how we look, what we say, how we move. We're vain. So the first stage in creating a responsive ensemble is to liberate its participants somehow from the social constraints which, in the course of time, have inhibited and stifled our innate sense of play. The most simple and direct ways of addressing this challenge are (1) to remove sight, (2) to remove speech and (3) to free the actors from certain physical boundaries. Over the years, Kamotskaya had observed the difficulty actors have – whether they be first-year drama students or experienced thesps – in establishing and maintaining direct eye-contact with strangers in an unfamiliar ensemble. During the early exercises, this inhibition was side-stepped by encouraging the participants to keep their eyes closed. In this way, she could begin to release them from critically observing each other and feeling embarrassed about themselves in the first stages of getting to know one another.

By taking away speech as a means of communication, Kamotskaya could release the participants from any kind of cerebral association with the spoken word. One such exercise was introduced very early on in our course. One day, we happened to be working with some of the third-year Russian students, and as we spoke practically no Russian and as their English was minimal, Kamotskaya suggested that we only use sounds to communicate with the others in the group. As usual, we all sat with our eyes shut, each in his or her own space scattered round the studio.

Then we took ourselves individually through the Circles of Attention and the Five-Minute Recollection exercises. When we were ready (every actor taking as much or as little time as he or she needed to reach this point), we each began to emit a sound expressing how we felt that day. The sound could be anything – a wail, a whistle, a hiss, a murmur, a shriek, a sigh. But it had to be a sound that could be repeated. All the time that we created our own particular sound, we listened to the noises being emitted by other group-members who were scattered all around the room. Once we each heard a sound that attracted us, we were to begin to move towards it as if towards a magnet or a sonar signal (don't forget, eyes closed all the time). Having found the emitter, we were to make some kind of basic physical contact with our selected partner, maybe something as simple as just touching fingers or faces. This was a canny way of taking a critical step towards developing an ensemble with very little effort. The usual inhibitions of visual, vocal and physical intimacy were side-stepped because we were all directly pursuing a simple objective. That objective was: to make physical contact through basic oral communication. Unlike the vibrant theatre games proposed by practitioners such as Clive Barker and Augusto Boal[75], the Russian approach was surreptitious. It released the actors slowly from the inside out, to connect them freely with others in the group.

Removing sight and sound is comparatively easy. The biggest challenge is finding a way of changing everybody's physicality, so that they're not stuck in their formal behaviour and etiquette. To do this, Kamotskaya explored with us 'the animal within'.

The animal within

I'd participated in 'Animal Exercises' during my British training, and never really taken much pleasure in them. It always seemed to be a case of who could portray the best dung beetle or wildebeest, so in Moscow I was rather resistant to the idea. I was surprised, then, to discover just how quickly my whole perspective on the exercise was changed. The task was simple. Following the Circles of Attention and Five-Minute Recollection, we were to imagine waking up on the planet as if for the first time (again, eyes closed throughout). We were to discover what our personal body felt like, how it moved and how it experienced the environment in a non-human way. The invitation to embody animals – or rather, non-human 'creatures' – released us from our individual physical limitations and from social human etiquette. It wasn't a problem what you touched or who you came into contact with, as it was all a voyage of discovery for these strange new beings. For me, this was an important and exciting departure from previous animal exercises. It didn't matter what the creature was. We didn't even have to decide: we could simply allow our imaginations to respond to the various movements that our bodies were researching. We were as free as children to move how we wanted and to do what we wanted, and if we made physical contact with another 'creature', we were to understand our relationship with it. Were we attracted to it, were we repelled? Were we intimidated? Were we affectionate? To use Ananyev's terms, did we open to this creature or close from it? The result of being so wonderfully liberated from polite human etiquette was that straight away we could build a far stronger, far deeper and far more trusting ensemble, than the boundaries of social intercourse might otherwise allow. Taboos were removed, because the freedom of play was incorporated along with the excitement of exploring the unknown. Creatures intimidated at this stage by physical contact simply retreated from the others until the point at which they wanted to engage more actively in the environment. This activity essentially incorporated Ananyev's notion of central-to-peripheral movement (giving information to the world) and peripheral-to-central (taking information from the world) (see Chapter 2). Those creatures who were more confident or extravert were possibly exploring central-to-peripheral co-ordination, while those more timid individuals were peripherally taking information (from the environment and/or other 'creatures') and assimilating how that information affected them centrally.

The impact of keeping your eyes closed during this exercise is potent from two perspectives, the more obvious being the removal of certain inhibitions. The second is that it quickly deepens your connection with your own self, and in so doing it develops and enhances your psycho-physical connection with the exercise. In other words, the *physical sensation* of being earthbound by four limbs for example, or slithering on your belly, or balancing on one leg, permeates the whole body and that in turn arouses *emotional reactions*. Having your eyes closed seems to intensify the experience, just as we'd found with the Ananyev's early work. My own discovery was that the 'animal' released the body from its usual habits and clichés, enabling it to find new physical expressions and strange new sensations. It was a bit like experiencing the physical freedom of a cat – the way it lies on the floor and stretches and twists and contorts and hangs head-first off chairs, taking pleasure in finding unusual positions, however uncomfortable those shapes may look.

I repeat: much of this work was familiar to me, as no doubt it is to many other practitioners, but the *emphasis* was new. It wasn't primarily about using an animal to find new aspects of a character's physicality, although in later modifications of the exercise we did work on characterisations. It was about using 'creature-contact' to develop an ensemble. It also cross-referenced with Ananyev's work on the Self, as it was using non-human movement to explore rhythms and gestures that were new and unexpected to the individual actors, so that they found themselves breaking free from the bounds of habits and clichés.

From I to eye

Exercises involving closed eyes, sound and non-human movement can be extremely liberating, as well as being jolly good fun and creating powerful collaborative energy. But ultimately, of course, the work has to develop. Having initially side-stepped the difficulty of establishing intimate eye-contact, Kamotskaya's second task was to address this very problem. For an interactive ensemble to grow, you have to feel safe. You have to find the collective state where, as Kamotskaya put it, 'We can look at each other and we're not afraid of each other, and any reaction is good. If I laugh, or cry, or remain silent, it doesn't matter. I'm not afraid of my feelings, and I'm ready to express whatever feelings I have to my partner.'

Once again, it was a question of psycho-physical awareness. In Ananyev's work, we were each independently discovering that the greater our sense of physical freedom, the more our psycho-physical sensitivity grew. As that psycho-physicality grew, our emotions were more readily accessible. The result of this chain-reaction was that it gradually became easier to express whatever feeling arose from the inner 'dialogue' going on between our own bodies and our own psyches. Kamotskaya now shifted the emphasis from self to partner, from inner dialogue to outer connection. There were three key phases in the early ensemble training. The first phase, as we've seen, involved Circles of Attention and Five-Minute Recollection to try and create a state of creative passivity. The second phase involved 'blind' encounters between different animals or creatures, responding to sound and touch. It was now time for the third phase – for the actors to open their eyes! While 'opening your eyes' sounds like a fairly simple instruction, the speed at which the 'inner life' is disrupted is quite startling, and the third phase can take some time to settle into. The safety of exploring the world and a group of strangers from a darkened cocoon is suddenly exploded, and it's not uncommon to feel a peculiar sense of vulnerability. And that's in spite of the fact that we spend most of our waking lives walking around with our eyes open anyway.

According to the nature of the group, these three phases can follow on from each other fairly quickly, even within the same day's workshop. But it's important to be aware of the significant shift that happens psycho-physically when you do open your eyes. A whole new nest of vipers is unleashed once you start to invite one or more partners into a game or dialogue. What I've termed the 'third phase' was in fact used during our very first class with Kamotskaya in an exercise which had as its back-drop an extract from Antoine de Saint-Exupéry's classic French tale, *The Little Prince*.

The Prince and the Fox

During this first class, we worked with a group of third-year Russian acting students. So there was a curious combination of students who already had two years' collaboration and a sense of their own ensemble, and then ten of us foreign actors, unknown to all, having only just arrived in this strange Russian culture. We were working in one of the myriad of small acting studios at VGIK, each of which is equipped with a performance area and an 'auditorium'; each studio has enough lanterns to light the stage and create a powerful atmosphere for even the most basic of exercises. This was a wonderful facility, as it strengthened the Circle of Attention for every task, as well as giving the actor-students a sense that any work in training was using *creative* energy and *artistic* emotions, not reaching into personal history (something to which I'll return in Chapter 4). The first exercise involved the Russians sitting scattered around the floor of the half-lit stage, while the English-speaking actors remained in the darkened auditorium. When we were ready, we were each to enter the Russians' space and find a partner with whom we would begin a non-verbal dialogue, much in the same way that Kamotskaya had experienced it at the Teatr Laboratorium.

What exactly does that mean, 'a non-verbal dialogue'? Well, it's actually very straightforward. Once we'd approached our chosen Russian, we were to start off just observing one another, establishing eye-contact. If we wanted to, we could touch the other person, simply exploring hands or faces. And if eventually sufficient contact was established between us, we could try and find a common game. A 'game' – what does that mean? Again, it's as simple as possible. A game might be winking or tagging – an activity so effortless that it could transcend the language barrier, which at this stage obviously existed between the

English-speakers and the Russians. But it could be even simpler: an empathy, a complicity, some simple understanding, without the slightest gesture or indication, would be powerful enough to know that there was a genuine communication.

The idea which formed the backdrop for this exercise was the episode in *The Little Prince*, in which the Prince befriends a Fox. The Fox says to the Prince, 'If you want a friend, tame me!' to which the Little Prince replies, 'What do I have to do?'. The Fox then describes what the Prince must do to gain a friend: 'You have to be very patient. First, you will sit down a short distance away from me, on the grass. I shall watch you out of the corner of my eye and you will say nothing; words are the source of misunderstandings. But each day you may sit a little closer to me . . . If you tame me, then we shall need each other. To me, you shall be unique in the world. To you, I shall be unique in the world.'[76] This image harks back to Kamotskaya's description of the work at the Teatr Laboratorium, and it was also the essence of the dialogue between the Russians and the English-speakers on that very first day in Moscow. We, the Princes, were seeking some simple point of contact with our Russian Foxes, beginning with observation, slowly building up towards trust, and finally developing a connection or non-verbal dialogue which (if it was truthful and honest) would of course be unique. Because we'd only just arrived in Russia, because we had no language and no points of contact, because we were seeking 'to find our place in their territory', the image of the Fox and the Little Prince was not only pertinent, it was also very poignant. The curiosity, doubt, possible fear, but ultimate friendship that existed in the fictional relationship between the Fox and the Prince filled the real-life encounters in the studio that day. What the story also did was illustrate how every exercise the Russian tutors gave us, however technical it might be, had an imaginative or even allegorical backdrop. Nothing was purely technique. In this way, even the simplest task formed a significant component in psycho-physical development.

And so the exercise began. At first, we were disorientated. The Russian students were restless and seemed to be laughing at us.

Perhaps it was because we didn't know the language, perhaps because we didn't understand the culture, but somehow everything looked different, smelt different, sounded different. The atmosphere in the room seemed to be more conducive to doubt and fear than to trust and friendship. It was hardly surprising then that it took some time to establish open, direct contact: we flinched from their overt laughter, we loitered against the walls, the gap between the darkened auditorium and the lit space seemed too far, too revealing. However, with this kind of exercise (although I didn't understand it at the time), every expression or reaction informs the ensemble activity. The Russians' laughter was simply a manifestation of their own awkwardness at encountering us as an alien culture. While it was unsettling to be at the receiving end, I realised in retrospect that it illustrated how open they were to their inner feelings; they felt like laughing, so they laughed. There was no obstacle, no apology, no block, no justification.

My own journey through this exercise was revealing in terms of the balance between process and result. My 'fox' was a young Russian male, and right from the start our connection was fairly immediate. We were cautious and attentive, but before long we'd found a simple physical contact which developed into a basic 'mirroring' game. But at the back of my mind, I felt it wasn't entirely successful. A small voice kept whispering in my head, 'What's the aim of this exercise? Are we all supposed to find a point at which the whole Anglo-Russian group is joined in some united welcome?' In other words, almost as soon as we'd started the exercise, I'd begun thinking about the objective, the result, where we were heading. So the contact with my fox became a means to an end, instead of the process of connection being the end in itself. Having decided that the point of the exercise was to unite us all, I tried to make similar close, unaffected links with several other people at the same time. And I wasn't very successful. It soon became clear that I wasn't the only one: there were a number of us in the group who were trying to impose a narrative or scenario on the exercise. Little pockets of people were linking arms, trying to form circles or start collaborative games. And it just wasn't working. We were wading through treacle.

After a while, Kamotskaya stopped us. Watching from the outside, she could see how our collective instinct was to superimpose a result on the games, as a consequence of which we were forcing the activity rather than allowing it to develop its own narrative. The general impulse within this group at this stage of its infancy was that concrete decisions had to be taken: 'Now we'll play tag. Now I'll hide from you. Now we'll link arms. Now we'll clap hands'. We were consciously navigating the game, rather than letting its course emerge through limitless attention to our partners. Given that it was only the very first day of work, this was in fact quite a major discovery for me. I suddenly realised that I'd spent much of my career as an actor trying to identify what the aim of a certain game or exercise was, or what result a director wanted me to achieve. In a strange way, I'd spent my creative life trying to please other people, trying to do the right thing. Which was probably why I wasn't such a great actor: I wasn't really listening to my own creative voice. I didn't realise that the real answer, the real activity, the honest truth, is in *this* moment, with *these* actors, in *this* space. It was very difficult for me – as with many of the others in the group that day – to trust the inner process, whereby a game or an activity would inevitably arise if the simple direct contact with a partner was open and responsive.

This illustrates the complexity of forming an ensemble: you have to be very precise in your contact with *one* partner first. Once you know you can maintain that degree of attention and honesty, only then can you open it out to include two, three, four and finally a multitude of other partners without the real contact being broken. In many ways, it'd be idealistic to think that something as delicate and complex as a truly unified ensemble could have been achieved in the very first session. Nonetheless, it was useful to experience the trial so early on, and to understand just how far we had to go and how many obstacles there were to remove.

Summary of early ensemble exercises

- **Finding Yourself:**

Circles of Attention: With eyes closed, listening to the sounds in yourself, the room, the building, the street, the town.

Five-Minute Recollection: With eyes closed, recalling all the sensory details of the first five minutes of the day, the class, the rehearsal.

- **Building an Ensemble:**

Sound Contacts: With eyes closed, emitting a simple sound, and gradually making physical contact with the person emitting a sound to which you are drawn.

Animal Exercises: With eyes closed, imagining that you are a 'creature', awaking for the first time on this planet; exploring movement, environment, other creatures with whom you come into contact. When you wish, open your eyes and continue explorations.

The Prince and the Fox: Half the group are Princes, half are Foxes. The Princes gradually 'befriend' the Foxes, finding a simple point of contact which may develop into a basic game. Once true contact has been formed with one partner, connections with other partners may be developed, gradually and attentively opening up the possibility for the whole group to participate in a collective game or interaction.

Walking the *via negativa*

Removing obstacles is at the heart of creating a vibrant ensemble, and The Prince and the Fox Exercise provided the first step in understanding what Grotowski called the *via negativa*.[77] The *via negativa* was a process of simplification, in which the actor was not required 'to *do* something, but to *refrain* from doing something.'[78] For Grotowski, the inner journey on which an actor goes is almost sacred in its asceticism. He referred to it as the technique of the 'holy' actor: it's an *inductive* one, in other words a process of eliminating blocks. Whereas that of the 'courtesan' actor is a *deductive* technique, concerned with the accumulation of skills. The idea behind this inductive process is similar to the psycho-physical technique that Stanislavsky proposed, as

Grotowski believed that an inductive process would reduce the time-lapse between the inner impulse we experience and the outer reaction we express, so that 'the impulse is already an outer reaction. Impulse and action are concurrent.'[79] This is what the Prince and the Fox was all about: the elimination of blocks, rather than the acquisition of skills. In other words, there was no preconceived result being sought; it was just a question of letting go, of submitting to whatever was really going on in each moment, of allowing impulse and action to be concurrent, and of walking the *via negativa*.

As I've touched on in reference to Scenic Movement, this proved to be one of the most significant and problematic lessons for those of us who had worked in British theatre, where short rehearsal periods often preclude ensemble collaboration and invite swift results. As far as the Russian actor-training was concerned (and as we've already seen with Ananyev's work), engaging in the process *was* the result. Yet in spite of its apparent simplicity, I found this an incredibly difficult concept to grasp. It's a dichotomy that's summed up by Grotowski, when he says, 'You must not think of the result. But, at the same time, finally, you can't ignore the result because from the objective point of view, the deciding factor in art is the result.'[80] Because of the significance of the 'end product' in the creative arts, Grotowski goes on to say that Art 'is immoral. He is right who has the result. That's the way it is. But in order to get the result – and this is the paradox – you must not look for it. If you look for it, you will block the natural creative process. In looking, only the brain works; the mind imposes solutions it already knows and you begin juggling known things.' So what Grotowski is saying is that we have to engage in our artistic endeavours without becoming preoccupied with the outcome: that's the only way we can begin to provoke ourselves into finding creatively new and unexpected things. Wise words indeed, but so hard to implement.

One of the most refreshing aspects of Katya Kamotskaya's work was that there was no right or wrong beyond the elimination of blocks – when you feel that you're responding to the reality of living here and now, then that's right! It's as simple as that. If here and now you feel uncertain, work with that apprehension; if here and now you feel tired, work with that fatigue. And yet the paradox of this simplicity is that it illustrates the degree of *complexity* involved in truthful on-stage dialogue. What quickly becomes apparent – if you work attentively in developing an ensemble – is that it's not just your partner who affects your psycho-physicality: the acting space *itself* gives you a huge amount of information.

Two People in the Empty Space

Ananyev's premise in Scenic Movement was that the space through which the body moves is just as important as the physical position itself. So if I raise my arms in a desperate plea to God, the sensation I experience as my hands move from the sides of my body to above my head is just as significant as the final gesture of prayer. Exactly the same relationship between space and body exists when you're working in an ensemble. Usually, we're so preoccupied with the 'blocking' of a scene, that we don't even think about the sensation of moving round the stage and negotiating our partners. And it's our loss: because that movement and those physical negotiations can actually give us far more psycho-physical information than the final position itself. With this in mind, it comes as no surprise that the early stages of Kamotskaya's work were concerned with the simplest encounters between actors in an empty space. The first of these exercises I've unimaginatively called *Two People in the Empty Space*. But in fact, this is a misnomer. When a true sense of what Michael Chekhov calls 'radiating and receiving energy' exists between two or more people, the space between them is far from empty – it's actually very full.

In Two People in the Empty Space, two actors entered from opposite sides of the stage. No word was spoken. The only communication came through their eyes, through radiating and receiving the energy between them (as communicated from solar plexus to solar plexus), and through 'reading' the space that existed between them. So, it was a matter of being attentive to the way in which the space expanded and contracted as they approached and retreated from each other, and how that changing distance informed the communication between them. Through paying limitless attention to each other, they were to determine their relative status and dynamics, and to move anywhere in the space according to their inner impulses. It might well be that neither person would feel the desire or the need to move at all, in which case they could simply stand still. Nonetheless, this stillness should be active and receptive, alert to any changing energy which might then inspire either party to move. In other words, it was to be a 'creative passivity'. Sometimes they might find that they come very close, that they touch, embrace, slap, retreat, circle each other. One partner might move a lot. One partner might move very slowly. It was all dependent on the two participants' attention to each other and to the space, and to the tiniest of changes which they might perceive. Each encounter usually lasted between five and fifteen minutes.

While the exercise may sound rather esoteric, there's actually nothing very new about it. This kind of non-verbal, minimalist communication was referred to by Stanislavsky as 'communion' or 'irradiation', and Kamotskaya's exercises were essentially using the same kind of energies that I've described in Ananyev's work. As far as both Stanislavsky and Michael Chekhov were concerned, these intangible means of communication were intrinsic to the acting process and to the development of a co-operative ensemble. Chekhov believed that to 'radiate on the stage means to *give*, to send out. And its counterpart is to *receive*. True acting is a constant exchange of the two.'[81]

With Two People in the Empty Space, it was clear to see how powerful narratives effortlessly arose out of the changing spatial dynamics between two partners. All they were doing was giving out and receiving psycho-physical information through their eyes, their bodies and their energy centres (located more or less in the solar plexus). The reason why these exchanges were so powerful both to experience and to watch was that the actor had to be so simple. It's back to Grotowski's idea of the *via negativa* – the elimination of blocks. It's a question of the actors surrendering their desire to demonstrate or act the externals and, instead, releasing themselves to what's really going on inside the relationship. When participants tried to short-cut the process by overtly gesturing, nudging, winking and generally sign-posting what they wanted their partner to do, the whole encounter was rendered void and boring. Radiating and receiving energies required a naïve trust in unseen forces. Not that there was anything particularly Darth Vader about this: we're all engaged every day in intangible communication – picking up on bad atmospheres, sensing when our personal space is invaded, being affected by someone else's good humour. But it's not often that we focus so intensively on these energies. And trusting in them was no mean feat, particularly with those actors who were still firmly entrenched in the need to present a 'result'.

It proved to be extremely difficult for one participant, Claire, for whom these exercises weren't always very successful. One day, there was a particularly frustrating experience when Claire and I took part in Two People in the Empty Space. The basic problem was that she didn't give herself time to locate her 'creative passivity', or (to put it more simply) to start from neutral. Instead, she entered the space very quickly and, straight away, she made a decision and sought a result. Her decision was: to befriend me. She walked right up to me and offered me her hand. When I didn't respond to her invitation, she sat on the ground and patted the floor, letting me know that she wanted me to sit down next to her. Intransigently, I still didn't respond. The problem was that she hadn't allowed what Stanislavsky calls a 'moment of orientation'. This is a moment of observing your partner and sussing out what's actually going on, here and now. (I'll talk about it more in Chapter 4.) Because we'd rushed the moment of orientation, we couldn't find the direct inner contact between us, and so truthful communication couldn't exist.

After the exercise, Kamotskaya's observation was that Claire's 'signposting' had been 'cold' and 'empty'. This unsettled Claire, since she felt that she'd been open and warm with me, and it was me who had been cold and empty towards her, as I rejected her invitations and generally greeted her with hostility. In some ways, she was right. The point of the exercise is that you pay limitless attention to your partner and respond to whatever he or she does in an open and spontaneous way. I certainly hadn't been open to what Claire was doing. In many ways, I was as guilty as she was. I had gone into the exercise expecting a certain quality of response: when that didn't happen, I felt myself starting to judge the connection (or lack of it). Instead of going with what she was doing and working with her, I began to have this conversation in my head, saying, 'You stupid woman, why are you being so phoney? Don't think I'm going to come and sit down next to you, just because you're patting the floor telling me that that's what you want me to do.' I was resisting what *she* considered to be serious attempts at communication, because *I* believed they were superimposed and insincere.

And herein lies a major lesson about acting, one which was to take me some time to really learn. And that is: *you can never make your on-stage partner act in the way you want them to.* I'm sure many actors have had the experience of thinking their partners are making a complete pig's ear of the parts they're playing. Instead of truly responding to the reality of what's happening on the stage, the tendency is to start acting *as if* they were relating to you in the way in which you wanted them to. And this is when on-stage communication becomes formal and fake. Each actor starts working in a bubble, as if his or her partner is doing one thing, when in fact something completely different is going on. If we want to develop a true ensemble, we have to work with our partners here and now in the present tense. (Again, this is something I'll come back to in Chapter 4.)

Claire's experience to date had encouraged her to work in a way where each individual takes care of his or her own work (particularly in television), and truthful interaction with a partner is a happy (if occasional) by-product. This was confirmed the next day when she tried the exercise with actor-student, Danny. Once again, Claire entered the space with pre-determined choices, as if (understandably) she was *afraid* to enter the stage in neutral and just see where the dialogue took her. She started slapping her arms to indicate imaginary cold and banging an oil drum in the corner of the room to initiate some kind of game. In other words, she was looking for the root of the dialogue in the *environment*, whether real (the oil drum) or imaginary (the cold), rather than in the simple connection with her on-stage *partner*. These activities rendered it difficult for Danny to strike up any dialogue with her beyond joining in her superimposed games, which indeed he did. But because the games weren't rooted in a dynamic connection between the on-stage partners, they quickly became dull, both for the participants and for the observers.

The exercise demands nothing more than paying simple attention to your partner. I know from experience that that degree of simplicity can be very daunting, in that it heads straight for the unknown, or as David Mamet wonderfully puts it, 'the terrifying unforeseen'.[82] At the same time, it can be hugely liberating for exactly the same reason – *because* it heads straight for the unknown. You don't have to be clever, you don't have to be funny, you don't have to think up anything wonderfully original. You just have to plunge into the empty space, pay attention to your partner and respond with the lightness of a child.

Three People in the Empty Space

Like Claire, I had many problems with the work in the early stages of the Russian training. At the time, of course, I didn't understand the strands that would later become so obvious with 20:20 hindsight. Suffering under my own preconceptions of what the exercises should be about, they weren't always successful for me, as was the case with *Three People in the Empty Space*. This was basically an extension of the previous exercise; once a relationship was established between the first two participants, a third person entered the space. Instantly and inevitably, the dynamic between the first two people was affected. It was very important at this point that all three participants were fully attentive to the shifting inner connections, otherwise it was very easy to begin *superimposing* a narrative of alliances and conflicts within the triad. That's not to say that narratives were invalid; in fact, as I've described in Ananyev's work, they were inevitable. But it was important to be aware of when these shifting alliances were spontaneous and when they were contrived.

As a *spectator*, it was very easy to see the difference between *conscious decisions* being made within a group, and *spontaneous reactions* to the given moment. This distinction was particularly clear with one trio, who interacted as if they were in a game of chess: one moved, waited for the others' assessment of that move; the second moved, waited; the third moved and waited, and so on. Each participant was pre-determining his or her next move, as a result of which everything was rather generalised. The moments when they weren't precisely absorbing the 'radiated' information were frighteningly evident. It'd be wrong to dismiss their interaction completely, as in fact this trio was certainly involved in a kind of *game* with each other. But the quality of their play remained formal and formulaic, locked in the brain, rather than integrated between themselves and the space.

When actors were really radiating and receiving between each other, Three People in the Empty Space – just like the previous exercise with Two People – had the potential to be an extremely liberating exercise. To have the freedom just to enter a space with no preconceived relationships or formulated story, to allow your 'inner ear' simply to listen and to respond was very exciting, both to experience and to observe. If you entered the space in a state of 'creative passivity' whereby you were ready for anything to happen, then the subtle changes in mood could be quite profound, according to the spatial dynamics established between first two participants and then shifted by the third.

Where's the fun in it?

Despite the freedom of the Empty Space encounters, there was another lesson I found ridiculously difficult to learn: that acting could be *fun*. These exercises weren't necessarily august and earnest; there was plenty of room for humour. It was the third week of the course and up until now, the atmosphere had been rather austere. After all, this was Russia, this was the land of Stanislavsky and 'serious acting'. Or so I thought. Until I tried the exercise with a wonderfully playful actor, the aforementioned Danny, who on this occasion entered the space with a provocative sense of mischief-making. At this point in the training programme, I was still rather *result*-orientated, still too intellectual in my approach. It was difficult at the beginning of each encounter not to think in terms of 'What are the parameters of this exercise? What are we allowed to do? Can we laugh? Can we touch?' What I hadn't yet appreciated was that there was only one parameter with all these exercises: honesty of communication. There was no right or wrong. If you felt the impulse to do something, you did it: that was the sole criterion of communication.

This brought into focus even more sharply the fine line between spontaneity and imposition. In working towards the *via negativa*, I'd become so cautious about not imposing anything on any encounter that, paradoxically, I was beginning to block everything. That in turn was killing any sense of play. Danny, on the other hand, wasn't forcing a narrative, but he was certainly encouraging a quality of playfulness. So anxious was I to start from neutral and not superimpose anything on the encounter, I impeded any natural flow of communication and I completely failed to respond to the light and mischief in his eyes. It was as if he'd said, 'Let's play cricket,' and I'd said, 'Ah no, we can't, because we're not wearing cricket whites.' He was offering a game, and I was looking for the rules. This rendered it impossible for him to develop any true dialogue with me, so that when the third person, Bex, entered the space to join the encounter, she couldn't understand what on earth was going on. I was blocking all the channels of communication between us. At the end of the exercise, Kamotskaya reminded us that 'Every exercise is a game, it's fun. Please don't be so serious! You're not in a serious profession!'

How can you apply these exercises to text?

Taking things too seriously could certainly have its draw-backs ... It's important to remember that, right from the start, Kamotskaya's programme ran in conjunction with Albert Filozov's text-based work. Therefore, while we were exploring various non-verbal exercises in Actor-Training, we were also allying them to the plays being staged in the parallel class. To this end, we were asked in the first week of term to select scenes from Shakespeare. That evening, Bex and I diligently selected our scene, opting for the meeting between Viola and Olivia in *Twelfth Night* (Act One, Scene Five, when Viola arrives to press Count Orsino's suit). Determined to take the work seriously and get our homework done, we speedily began learning the words of the text in preparation for the following day's class. This was more or less in accord with the result-orientated background from which most of us in the English-speaking group had come: learn the text, and plan a bit of 'blocking'. Next day in the Actor-Training class, we proudly volunteered ourselves for the presentation of our scene. What followed was an outpouring of rapidly-learnt text with a hastily pre-determined *mise-en-scène*: it was little more than an empty rattling of words with no inner content and a gaping chasm between action, emotion, text and partner. Nonetheless, we felt assured that we'd taken the assignment seriously.

In response to the empty 'result' of our approach, Kamotskaya suggested that we try the Two People in the Empty Space exercise. In other words, we were to take the minimal given circumstances and the relationship between the two women, and explore the meeting without the scripted text. Bex would start off on her own in the empty space (as Olivia is already in her court) and I was to enter that space (just as Viola enters the court); by simply paying attention to each other, we were to allow the relationship to unfold. Before any action began, we were to take a moment of stillness to eliminate our preconceptions of what might happen, and to free ourselves up to respond to whatever unfolded following the first 'moment of orientation'. Strangely, the challenge was far more daunting than trying to remember the rapidly-learnt text. Nonetheless, by removing mental obstacles and 'clearing' the space between us, we discovered that, as the simple spatial dynamics changed, the status fluctuated between Viola and Olivia. No effort was involved in experiencing the shifting emphases of curiosity, suspicion, fear and attraction: real sensations and emotions arose purely from concentrating on the radiation of energy between us. It didn't call for any heavy-weight emotion memory: the action – both inner action and physical action – stemmed from just paying limitless attention to the partner. These were the early stages of Active Analysis.

Out of this apparent shapelessness, a very clear form emerged. The point of the exercise wasn't to play out the dramatic action silently in our heads, but we discovered that by attending to each other's faces and eyes, it was fairly obvious which part of the scene was unfurling. Sometimes it was almost as if our thought-processes were plastered across our foreheads for the other actor to read like a text. Once again, there was nothing new about this exercise. The process was clearly rooted in the kind of experiments undertaken by Stanislavsky in 1926, when he was working on *The Sisters Gérard* by D'Ennery and Corman. He instructed his cast to 'Speak the text . . . only with your eyes. Don't speak aloud one word, but say your lines to yourself.' At this point, one of the actors, Luzhsky, quizzed Stanislavsky, saying, 'I think, Konstantin Sergevich, what is not clear is how one would know that his partner had finished a sentence if he only speaks to himself?' To which Stanislavsky confidently replied, 'The whole question depends on extreme attention to one another . . . Observe each other constantly and you will always guess when one finishes a sentence or completes a thought, although he never speaks it aloud.'[83] And this is exactly what Bex and I discovered and the freedom was exhilarating.

Of course, this was only the start of the work. It's all well and good feeling the intensity of Shakespeare's text without the worry of having to speak any of the poetry, but there has to be a way of keeping that dynamic inner connection once the words start to form the ideas. In fact, our intense observation during the first exercise was a huge help when it came to the second task proposed by Kamotskaya. This time, we stood about two metres apart and simply spoke the text in half-tones, with very little physical movement. (Once again, this echoed Stanislavsky's practices during his early exploration of psychological action in 1907 when he was rehearsing *The Drama of Life*.) Now the text did all the work. By stilling the body and responding to the impulses behind the words, a multitude of rapidly-changing emotions were released, each of which might flash, recede and come to prominence if we just paid attention to each other and lived in the 'transient now'. Bex's face seemed to transform, sometimes almost beyond recognition, as I became intrigued by her, bewitched by her, envious of her, hateful of her, suspicious of her. And in this way, we took the first steps towards finding the psycho-physical connection between the space, the on-stage partner and the emotions *as inspired by the script*. During this slow journey into the text, we both experienced an intense inner activity, which was so pronounced that it didn't take me long to recognise the hollowness of our initial 'presentation'.

Silent partners

It was now a question of integrating text, body and radiation. To this end, we applied the Three People in the Empty Space exercise to the *Twelfth Night* scene, with a third actor as a mute Orsino. During the improvisation, all three of us could move anywhere we wanted, meaning that Bex and I could both relate to the silent Orsino as and when it seemed appropriate. She and I could also use any words from the text if we felt like it. The presence of the non-speaking Orsino served two particular purposes, the first of which was that it extended the dialogue into an ensemble. Since Orsino could also move whenever he wanted, the tensions and pain within the scene soon became clear, as invariably his attention was focused on Olivia/Bex when, of course, I (as Viola) wanted it turned towards me. The second effect of the third person was that the integration of the three centres (thought, feeling and action) came to light. Sometimes the emotion-centre was predominant, when the energy was being radiated between partners. Other times the action-centre dominated, as each of us felt physically drawn *away* from one person and *towards* another. And sometimes, through the use of the text, the thought-centre predominated. We rarely spoke complete sentences, but just uttered isolated words if they seemed necessary in a given moment. Except Orsino, of course, who was silent throughout.

Although there's nothing revolutionary about working through a scene using only the occasional word, the result of doing it as part of a sequence of exercises had two striking effects. The first of these was that the process of selecting the specific words led us to uncovering the *subtext* of the scene. The words we each chose at any given moment illuminated for the other actors what we (through our characters) considered to be at the heart of the encounter. It was a sensational – or experiential – response to the situation, rather than a cerebral one. And ultimately it's the information you receive from 'experiencing' a scene that underlies Active Analysis.

The second important factor with this exercise is that you have to pay absolute attention to your partner. Not only do you have to hear the chosen word, but you really have to understand how that word affects you emotionally, intellectually and viscerally. There were times when we found ourselves repeating the same word several times, as if we were striving to underline an emotion or thought, to try and persuade or impress upon the other character just how significant that word was for us. There was one moment in particular which struck me with unexpected force, and that was the point at which Olivia finally began to raise her veil. Throughout the scene, I'd had a burning desire to see Olivia/Bex's face and yet, at the last moment, I simply couldn't watch as she lifted up the veil: all I wanted to see was Orsino's reaction. When I did look at Bex's face, it had completely changed; there was a bizarre neediness, as if she wanted to be seduced by Viola/Cesario. And all I wanted to do was to yell repeatedly the single word 'Olivia!'. I was starting to understand the psycho-physical nature of *words* themselves, and with that understanding came an awareness of how phoney and shallow my acting to date had been. How many short-cuts I'd taken. How often I'd put beautiful empty form before rough real content. After four years' training and five years in the business, I was beginning to realise how extraordinarily complex the *art* (as opposed to the *job*) of acting is. And it was a painful realisation.

Summary of exercises towards Dramatic Action

These exercises may be used in the abstract, or with a play-text forming the dramatic backdrop. While the nature of these improvisations is still fairly free, the contact is definitely human.

- ### Two People in the Empty Space
Two actors enter the space, moving as much or as little as required, inventing nothing, denying nothing, and allowing the contraction and expansion of the space to give them as much psycho-physical information as the maintained eye contact provides. It's important not to indicate or 'telegraph' anything through overt gestures, winking, beckoning, etc. As long as eye contact is maintained and the arms aren't crossed in front of the body or shoved in pockets, the energy centres will connect and all the 'dialogue' needed by the actors will be apparent.

- ### Three People in the Empty Space
Two actors set up a non-verbal dialogue, shortly after which they are joined by a third person. Throughout the non-verbal 'conversation', the actors note the way in which the expanding and contracting

space between them affects the changing relationships and status between the three. Spectators' observations are always interesting, as inevitably different 'narratives' form in the minds of different observers.

- **Silent Partners**

Two People in the Empty Space go through the scene silently just with eye contact.

Two People in the Empty Space go through the scene very quietly standing 2m apart.

A Third Person is introduced where appropriate, using as much or as little text as is desired.

Laughter-Tears

As I've mentioned, many of the Actor-Training exercises were reminiscent of various practices pioneered by Stanislavsky throughout the course of his life. To a large extent, we were using Active Analysis as a means of developing our *individual* and our *collective* psycho-physicality. The diversity of responses which arose from these improvisations illustrated just how many facets of our psyche we can tap into through *experiential learning*. However, this was only the first building block. It was all very slow and precarious, this business of developing an ensemble and awakening a psycho-physical process. It required constant nurturing during the ten-month programme, if we were really going to prepare our inner 'creative state' for performance. And it was to this end that Kamotskaya had developed her *Laughter-Tears* exercise. The parameters of the Laughter-Tears exercise couldn't have been simpler. You all laugh together, then you each cry on your own. Once you're crying, you halt that solitary emotion and turn your attention back to the group.

So how do you do that, and more importantly, what's the point?

At the start of the exercise, the group sat in a circle and observed one another very carefully, as if it was the first time they'd ever seen each other. It's funny how strange the human physiognomy is, particularly if you really study everyone's face, and especially if the group comprises people you've known for a long time. Noses are suddenly crooked, eyebrows meet in the middle, ears seem to stick out, eyes are totally asymmetrical. Faces you thought you knew so well are suddenly misshapen and comical. This was the starting-point for Laughter-Tears. Just by looking at everybody with a new curiosity, each participant was to find a quality of joy, until the point was reached when everyone in the group was collectively laughing. It's difficult for a new ensemble to find the peak of laughter simultaneously, and so it was important that everyone knew that they didn't have to *wait*, trying to sustain their laughter at an optimum, until the whole group was laughing uproariously. One person's guffaw will be another person's giggle. The *ideal* is that the whole group finds a common height of laughter: *in practice*, each individual reaches his or her own personal peak and then moves on to the second stage. What most ensembles find, though, is that the more they work together, the easier it is to find a level they all share. (It's also interesting to note how easy it is to laugh one day and how hard it is the next, or vice versa.)

The second stage of the exercise was as follows. When each individual felt that they had reached their peak of laughter for that day, he or she was to turn out of the circle and begin to find a quality, or depth, of despair. 'Depth of despair' may sound rather intimidating, but it's not a question of dredging up some deep-rooted childhood fear. Tears can come from a number of sources that exist here and now: the physical position you're sitting in, the coldness of your hands or the curve of your foot. Even the immediate environment can provoke a sense of sorrow: during one exercise, I saw a grimy black patch on the floor where the roof had leaked, and this in itself conjured up a feeling of despair which, within minutes, converted itself into tears. Hearing or sensing the sorrow of other people in the room can arouse an empathic grief within you. Maybe the despair will come from a recent memory such as the flash of an image on the news that morning. But perhaps the most evocative source is imagination: there was one rather melancholy day, when it suddenly struck me that I was too old to play Juliet, and I felt this bizarre sense of loss for the germinating Juliet who would never come to fruition. So, it needn't involve a deep plunging into personal history. If you have an active imagination and an open heart, anything happening in *this* room in *this* moment can inspire a quality of tears. But 'depth of despair' needn't be tears – it can just be an inner sense of heaviness, darkness, emptiness, even nothingness. You don't have to weep and wail.

Once this 'depth of despair' had been contacted, it was very important that the individual stopped the emotion at its nadir. This was the third stage in the exercise. By consciously focusing the mind on the Circles of Attention or the Five-Minute Recollection, it was possible to shift from the emotion-centre to the thought-centre by means of a concrete rational challenge which was simple and sensory. Laughter-Tears is not psycho-drama: it's psycho-*physical* training. Ananyev's work was geared towards tuning up the actor's body like an instrument. The aim of this exercise is to tune up the actor's inner life, so that the highest harmonic or the deepest bass note can be sounded effortlessly and (most importantly) *artistically*. Michael Chekhov talks about 'stage emotions', as opposed to personal emotions. If you imagine that your real emotions are located inside you in your solar plexus, your stage emotions are held out in front of you in the palm of your hand. There you can offer them up to the world and retrieve them at your will. They're connected to you as if through the umbilical cord of your arm, but they're separate from you, in just the same way that you can look at your hand, put it in a glove, close it in a fist, or smother it with lotion. Stage emotions are separate, but attached; *we* harness *them*, they *don't* control us. There is, of course, a strong therapeutic element to hearty laughter and deep sobs, and sometimes we need to experience that kind of cathartic process in a nurturing environment. But we have to be sure that the *artist* within us is guiding us. We need to feel safe and healthy with what we're prepared to show and share with the ensemble and what we'd rather keep for the priest or the counsellor. I repeat: this is psycho-physical acting, not psycho-therapy drama.

Then comes the fourth stage. Having stopped the Laughter-Tears through Circles of Attention or Five-Minute Recollection, each individual then began to turn the focus outwards again by making contact with other members of the group. This usually involved a kind of free improvisation similar to Ananyev's work on the Self, and I'll describe it in more detail shortly. In a nutshell, the *height of group laughter* was followed by the *depths of personal despair*, which in turn was brought to a halt and then followed by the outward reconnection with the group. The premise is actually very simple, the practice is really much harder. But through its simplicity, the exercise can act as a kind of barometer, illustrating the ease or difficulty with which any given ensemble is prepared to interconnect during its various stages of development.

Kamotskaya had devised this exercise during her early attempts to develop a concentrated ensemble. She had observed how difficult it was for her Russian students to maintain eye-contact with each other without dissolving into embarrassed giggles. So she cannily incorporated their spontaneous laughter into the parameters of the exercise: she invited them to laugh together as the first stage of their ensemble interaction. What happened, of course, was that once they were allowed to laugh, the students no longer needed to laugh. The irony of this was that finding a point of communal laughter became a challenge in itself. Addressing this new difficulty –'I can't laugh any more now you've told me I've got to' – Kamotskaya suggested that they take the stimulus for their mirth from each other. Once you start observing familiar faces closely, suddenly nearly everybody looks extremely funny, and it doesn't take long for the whole group to be laughing, without necessarily knowing what it is they're laughing at.

Exploring the extremes of emotions: 'legitimate over-acting'

To follow intense laughter with deep despair demanded that the actor's inner instrument was finely-tuned and versatile, to be able to move rapidly between the extremes of emotion. As far as Michael Chekhov was concerned, it's just a matter of concentration. If your powers of concentration are developed, 'then the ability to laugh, to cry, to be influenced by one's own imagination will come more quickly and easily. It is only a question of developing and training.'[84] Kamotskaya encouraged actors to experience the extremes of emotion (as aroused by Laughter-Tears) throughout all her Actor-Training sessions. This gave us the chance to do two specific things: one was to expand the range and freedom of our own emotional repertoires. The other was to understand the various levels of emotional *energy* required for different characters. There's a subtle difference between over-acting and being over-emotional, and training provides the opportunity to explore those boundaries. Sometimes we have to 'give it large' to know where we've got to bring it back to.

The opposite is true as well: sometimes we underestimate the difference in energy-levels between everyday emotions and creative emotions. Stanislavsky argued that a degree of *over-acting* in rehearsals can increase the 'density' of our creative emotions, and reveal the amount of energy required. Talking about his own work on the character of Famusov, Stanislavsky described how in one rehearsal, 'We all tried too hard. We pressed the pedal of emotion at the expense of thoughts and relationships. We were over-playing. But for what purpose? We learnt what are the limits of our own feelings; for me, how far can I go in a state of rage; for Sophie and Lisa, how far in a state of fright; how far you can go in bitterness and disillusion, Zadavsky. As far as the plot of the play and the characters are concerned, our feelings went out in the right direction. But I can say for myself that my anger was not organised. I forced myself too much. I shouted more than Famusov would have in the given circumstances. In other words, I too was over-acting. Now I know that such wrath is too much for Famusov. But I also learned that the energy I have been using in rehearsals and performances is not enough. My Famusov was too soft.'[85] In a similar way, Kamotskaya's Actor-Training sessions provided us with an environment for making these discoveries – for testing the limits of our own emotions, for defining the threshold of over-playing. We could then take our discoveries into our text-work with Filozov.

Learning extremes of emotion in the safe environment of Actor-Training is essential for understanding the fine balance between stimulating an under-energised emotional life and harnessing an over-active emotional life. It harks back to Chekhov's idea of developing *stage* emotions as opposed to ploughing up *personal* emotions. As Kamotskaya said, 'If your feelings in life are strong, you have to learn to lead them. If you can't lead them, then it's an illness, it's hysteria. For stage work, you mustn't be afraid of strong emotion. Quite the opposite: you have to enjoy it. Having said that, you have to adopt the perspective that "I am the actor; here is the character." It's fine to be crazy, even hysterical, as the character. But as the actor, you just have to say, "It's wonderful to have the chance to play so madly!" and that's all. You are an actor: you have to hold the character beneath you, otherwise you'll lose your head.'

This one exercise – Laughter-Tears – had the potential to set in motion these two very complex areas of acting practice: first of all, to open an actor up to his or her own emotional life, and, secondly, to develop the actor's awareness of the difference between personal emotion and stage emotions. Along with the second, came an understanding of the different level of emotional energy needed on the stage. But it gradually became clear to me that the Laughter-Tears exercise was also an indication of another kind of emotional 'liberation'. While it revealed the ease or difficulty with which the *individuals* could express their inner lives, it also revealed the *ensemble's* willingness to expose those extremes of emotion among itself. For Grotowski, the feeling of security within a group was paramount. For him, 'this element of warm openness is technically tangible. This alone, if reciprocal, can enable the actor to undertake the most extreme efforts without any feeling of being laughed at or humiliated.'[86]

The 'total act'

The unity of an ensemble, however, can't be taken as read. In many ways, the contents of this chapter have been the hardest to articulate, because my recent experiences as an actor, workshop leader and director have illustrated to me that there's no fail-safe recipe for building an integrated working ensemble. It would be wonderful to promise, if you take a group of strangers with different training and experience, and follow the series of exercises – with eyes closed, with eyes open, the Animals, the Prince and the Fox, the Empty Space – that after a few sessions a wonderfully collaborative environment will unfold. Those who work a good deal in trying to develop ensembles will know that simply isn't the case. Suffice to say, that as much as the Actor-Training exercises are profound and attentive, they can't lead infallibly to a harmonious working unit: they can only prepare the terrain. Over the course of the year in Moscow – for reasons both financial and personal – the size of the group fell from ten participants to four. What became clear was the degree of responsibility demanded of all parties involved in handling an ensemble, especially one which suffers from an acute fall-out rate. Despite the odds, the nature of the psycho-physical work was strong enough to reconnect those who did stay, as we endeavoured to immerse ourselves in 'the total act' of acting.

What exactly is 'the total act'? Well, along with the *via negativa*, the 'total act' of creativity was one of Grotowski's ideas which clearly informed the work at the Teatr Laboratorium.[87] The total act demands that every actor gives one hundred per cent to his or her own work, and to the combined identity of the ensemble as a whole. For Grotowski, the concept of the total act was essential for the performer as it was the very crux of the actor's art: 'He does whatever he does with his entire being, and not just one mechanical (and therefore rigid) gesture of arm or leg, nor any grimace helped by a logical inflection and a thought.'[88] This commitment to the total act could also be very revelatory. In the same way that Michael Chekhov incited the actor to discover new things by appealing to his or her 'creative individuality', Grotowski believed that through total submersion in the creative work, actors could discover those very elements of their personalities which were unexpected and surprising. But more than that, Grotowski implied that there's no point even thinking of being an actor unless you can commit yourself to the idea of the total act. He described it as the very essence of the actor's calling, 'allowing him to reveal one after the other the different layers of his personality, from the biological-instinctive source via the channel of consciousness and thought, to that summit . . . in which all becomes unity. This act of the total un-veiling of one's being becomes a gift of the self which borders on the transgression of barriers and love. I call this a total act.'[89] Far from being anything damaging or distorting, Grotowski actually maintained that the outcome of this kind of commitment to creative performance could be remarkably holistic: 'The actor who, in this special process of discipline and self-sacrifice, self-penetration and moulding is not afraid to go beyond all normally acceptable limits, attains a kind of inner harmony and peace of mind.'[90] This was the kind of holistic integration that psycho-physical acting was about and that Active Analysis demanded. By committing to the total act, you quickly realise that acting has to be an ensemble venture. You can't act in isolation, any more than you can live in isolation. And through that commitment to the ensemble comes a sense of play inextricably woven into the experience of *free improvisation*, which lay at the core of Kamot-skaya's work.

Free improvisation

Kamotskaya's free improvisation involved setting up an extended psycho-physical exercise, which might last anything from twenty minutes to two hours. Before the exercise began, she explained the sequence of steps, and it was then up to each individual to moderate his or her own way through that sequence. At first this degree of self-moderation can be quite daunting, especially among young student-actors, who are afraid that they're going too quickly or too slowly through the sequence, as they don't want to get out of synch with their peers. It only takes a few attempts to trust that there is no *right* way of doing the exercise, there is no *right* time scale for reaching the various 'milestones'. The pace that you adopt today is the right one for you today – tomorrow your rhythm may be different.

The joy of extended free improvisations is that it gives each actor's psycho-physical instrument an opportunity to 'integrate itself'. There are, of course, times when the brain is working too hard, thinking, 'Am I doing this right? Has everybody else got their eyes closed? Do I look stupid?' But then there are wonderful moments when the body abandons itself to its own physicality, like a toddler at play, and the movement itself inspires the imagination and the emotions. There are other times when the emotions lead the actor either to make connections with others in the space, or retreat into individual experiences. What's important to remember in these exercises is that there can never be *inactivity* or *passivity*. The psycho-physical instrument is very sophisticated in the number of ways in which it can be stimulated and provoked, be it through the body, the imagination, the emotions or the spirit. Even if the body is still, there'll always be some kind of inner activity. As Kamotskaya said, 'You can't just wait for something to inspire you. A powerful experience can be found in sitting in the warmth, the sun through the window, the dog sleeping, children playing. We have to wake up in every moment. So in Actor-Training, there are many things happening in a room with just five people – you should be able to find real contact in every moment.'

The essence of free improvisations was very simple. As Grotowski puts it, 'Something stimulates you and you react: that is the whole secret. Stimulations, impulses and reactions.'[91] The objective during these sessions was usually to find some kind of very simple game, or contact or non-verbal dialogue, just like The Prince and the Fox. Nothing was forced upon these games; they might only last for a few minutes before going on to a different interaction with another partner. The only parameter of the exercise was that each actor should observe and respond to his or her partner in accordance with *stimulations, impulses* and *reactions*. All this really meant was that the actors engaged with each other attentively and playfully, without judging the activity or superimposing a narrative. If the contact became boring, they should be brave enough to leave that connection and go off and find a new source of interaction. The only limitations on free improvisations were those imposed by the participants' own imaginations.

What these free improvisations did was combine each actor's psycho-physical experience with the ensemble's freedom to play. As Michael Chekhov puts it, 'Let each successive moment of your improvisation be a *psychological* (not logical!) result of the moment preceding it.'[92] You didn't have to have any previously thought-out theme, you could just move from the start to the conclusion, improvising all the way. By doing so, Chekhov maintained that 'You will go through the whole gamut of different sensations, emotions, moods, desires, inner impulses and business, all of which will be found by you spontaneously.' It was really very exciting, as you suddenly realised how endlessly interesting any situation could be if you just opened up to all the psycho-physical information around you. In the words of Michael Chekhov, 'A small hint from a partner – a glance, a pause, a new or unexpected intonation, a move, a sigh, or even a barely perceptible change of tempo – can become a creative impulse, an invitation to the other to improvise.'[93] This process can be exhilarating and liberating, and it's a great antidote to being self-conscious in rehearsal or class. By taking the attention off yourself and diverting it to your environment, it's possible to silence the emotional chaos in your head. Then you can start to relish and enjoy the exchange of information between you and your on-stage partner. Of course, it's a bit harder with a monologue, but that's another discussion entirely!

Testing out a text: Miranda and Caliban

As with the Empty Space exercises, free improvisations weren't restricted to non-verbal, non-specific scenarios. As the ten-month programme developed, they were used to investigate the characters, which we were exploring in Filozov's rehearsals. What this really meant was that the contacts made between us during the free improvisations were no longer completely free: the relationships from the text now formed a kind of gauze or backdrop. We still responded, moment by moment, to stimulations, impulses and reactions; it's just that specific given circumstances could now influence our choices. The first piece we looked at was Shakespeare's *The Tempest*, the casting of which included myself as Miranda and an actress called Vivien as Caliban.

Because free improvisations frequently led straight out of the Laughter-Tears exercise, direct and spontaneous links could often be made between our responses in the exercise and the characters in the play. I noticed this especially during one Laughter-Tears experience, in which Vivien was laughing heartily. She hadn't found the psycho-physical approach particularly easy, and the way she was really chuckling that day gave me a real sense of joy. That in turn provoked in my imagination a possible history behind Miranda and Caliban's relationship. After all, Caliban had been Miranda's 'pet' prior to his attack on her, so it was quite natural that Vivien's laughter could stimulate a sense of the camaraderie which might have existed at some point between the two characters. This camaraderie, or rather empathy, was developed further in another free improvisation, during which there was an exchange between Danny (as Antonio) and a wonderful Irish actor, Tom, (as Sebastian) in relation to Vivien (as Caliban). In the course of this encounter, I noticed how Danny/Antonio and Tom/Sebastian were taunting Vivien/Caliban. As their taunting grew, I began to get truly worked up. I tried to put an end to their aggressive teasing of the 'dumb' Caliban, by pushing Danny/Antonio away. Quite unexpectedly, he reacted so violently towards me that, for a split-second, I thought he was going to hit me, and so I backed off. The two men carried on jibing and goading Vivien/Caliban, who simply joined in with them, apparently oblivious to the irony of their game. Overcome with a sense of helplessness and powerlessness, I found that all I could do was to watch and weep.

What was happening in these free improvisations was that character and actor were surreptitiously interweaving. In other words, although they were *my* tears (after all you can't escape the fact that you only have your own body, your own imagination and your own emotions), the *reasons* behind the tears were those of the character. In this way, there was an effortless merger of *my* actual response to the *real* situation with *Miranda's* response to the *imaginative* situation. These extended free improvisations provided us with a useful environment in which to experience encounters which don't necessarily take place in the script. These encounters could illuminate various – and often very unexpected – aspects of the characters by allowing them to 'live' within a vast and free range of given circumstances. The result of the two responses to Vivien's Caliban, for example, was that in my imagination a concrete, emotional history to the Caliban/Miranda relationship had been established. I could then use that history to inform my playing of the actual scenes. The emotional stakes between Miranda and Caliban had been raised in a way that we might never have discovered through a purely text-based approach.

The crime of judgement

Despite the discoveries made during these free improvisations – individually and collectively – the evolution of the ensemble was still not without its problems. This was primarily because the ongoing development of our *individual psycho-physical technique* was also very tricky. Kamotskaya had striven to nurture an environment in which the actors could feel safe within the ensemble and, therefore, free to try anything. Ideally, this should be an environment where individuals aren't criticised or judged by their peers, but where everyone is invited to consider alternative options if the original choices for a scene turn out to be inappropriate. For Kamotskaya, creativity is impossible in an atmosphere where an actor feels unable to trust partners, directors or teachers: creativity demands openness and trust. Of course, constructive criticism is a necessary part of growth, but the actors within an ensemble have to feel that their colleagues are collaborative. Michael Chekhov is unequivocal about what he describes as Ensemble Feeling: 'Indifference is bad enough. Criticism is a crime.'[94] Once that 'crime' has been committed, the consequences become self-perpetuating. I found that I (maybe more than anyone) was horrendously guilty of the crime of judgement, and it was inhibiting my own artistic development, as well as that of the particular partner with whom I was working.

We were staging Act III, Scene I of *The Tempest*, in which Ferdinand is carrying logs and Miranda is trying to stop him from doing the tasks that her father has set him. My main problem was that I was continually judging the actor (an interesting individual named Khan) who was playing Ferdinand. The fundamental difficulty was that I felt he was presenting me with a *demonstrated* emotion and a string of words based on the text but not quite going places, and I just didn't buy it. This was supposed to be a love scene, in which Miranda should be overwhelmed by Ferdinand's beautiful words. All the time, my inner judge was saying, 'I don't believe anything this fool is saying. He's just spouting words, words, words. The words don't even make any sense! So how am I supposed to listen to them and then be overwhelmed with love for him??' I was getting seriously annoyed, and the voice in my head was getting in the way of my connection with the scene. The biggest problem – one which I didn't know how to avoid – was that the more I paid 'limitless attention' to my partner, the more clearly I saw his lack of true connection with himself, the text and me. The more I listened to him and attended to his every gesture – which is, after all, the root of psycho-physical interaction – the more utterly phoney he seemed to me, and the less inclined I felt to love him. No doubt my partner was watching me, thinking, 'Why's the silly cow so angry all the time? I'm offering her words of love and she's looking at me with a face like a wet Sunday.' The chemistry just wasn't working.

The 'crime' of judgement lies in its misplaced capacity to turn the acting process into one of success or failure. (It's important to note that this relates to a *training or rehearsal process*, not to whether a final production works or doesn't work. That kind of success or failure does, of course, need serious attention from the director and the creative team. In training, it's actually of no consequence whether the actors succeed or not.) As Michael Chekhov puts it, the real value of an exercise lies in the actors' *effort* to open themselves up to the others in the exercise and to intensify their ability to observe their partners at all times, 'thus strengthening sensitivity towards the entire ensemble'.[95] As far as this Miranda and Ferdinand were concerned, it was obvious that the 'effort to open our selves up to each other' was *not* taking place. We weren't working for each other, we were working for ourselves, and it illustrated unequivocally that we simply weren't committing to the 'total act'. As Grotowski points out, 'The principle is that the actor, in order to fulfil himself, must not work for himself. Through penetrating his relationship *with others* – studying the elements of contact – the actor will discover what is in him. He must give himself totally.'[96] We seemed unable to give ourselves totally, and it was difficult to see how work on this scene could progress.

To be honest, I was terribly confused. The whole principle of the training to date hadn't really addressed the idea of *character*. We had always been using our own bodies, our own imaginations, our own emotions as the springboard into non-verbal points of contact. Now, given the words of Shakespeare – which, let's face it, weren't exactly contemporary chat-up lines – Khan and I were floundering, because suddenly the notion of character was very prominent. But even that was an excuse, because when we were improvising the scene using our own words, we still couldn't connect with each other, let alone when the complexity of the poetic language was added. The point of psycho-physical connection is (in the words of Kamotskaya) that 'Every moment must be born on the stage – *without* judgement.' Yet I didn't know how to switch my brain off. I didn't know how to stop myself hearing the literal nonsense of Khan's half-learnt lines. That was until Kamotskaya offered what seemed like very simple, yet very wise advice. The important element that I'd underestimated in my understanding of 'psycho-physical' is *the imagination*. It was perfectly possible to accept everything that my partner was doing, if I just added a sprinkling of imagination. Or as Kamotskaya put it, 'If he forgets his lines or speaks nonsense, you must simply imagine he's speaking a foreign language or he's very nervous! You must only accept *him* – as Khan and as Ferdinand. It doesn't matter if you don't believe every word, but you mustn't judge.'

This advice cannot be underestimated. I'm sure most actors at some point in their lives have acted opposite someone who simply isn't pressing the right buttons for them. And it doesn't have to be in a love-scene, of course. An interpretation of any character can often seem ill-judged, or off-kilter, or just plain stupid, and yet it's not our business to preside over our fellow-actors. The more we hear the voice in our heads saying, 'If only they emphasised that word . . . if only they played that action . . . if only they pursued that objective . . . if only they looked into my eyes', the more we alienate ourselves from the task in hand. We start playing the *form* of the scene as we think it should be played, rather than the *actuality* of the scene as it is here and now between these two actors on this very stage.

In this respect, the free improvisations of Kamotskaya's Actor-Training proved to be a very beneficial complement to text-based classes. They provided a fairly uninhibited opportunity for me and Khan to try and relax the tensions which seemed to arise when, in rehearsals, we were script-bound to the scene. There was one particular occasion when Khan and I seemed to have a major break-through with regard to Ferdinand and Miranda. As usual, everyone was simultaneously involved in the free improvisation; therefore, the room was full of a number of people, each exploring different relationships and different aspects of their characterisations. Suddenly Khan and I made direct eye-contact across the stage. I hadn't been looking for him, but it was as if he'd shot a dart at me, and I found my attention drawn instantaneously across the space to where he was sitting in a half-lit corner. We both felt the potency of this connection, and within seconds we were oblivious to the other actors who were exploring their own dialogues in the expanse of space between us. For some time we didn't move, but gradually – by paying limitless attention to each other – we discovered that the eye-contact alone was powerful enough to draw us very slowly together, until at last we were physically close to each other. It took some time to make any actual bodily contact, but once we did, it was a matter of simply touching finger-tips, then cautiously entwining hands. Up until now, I'd found that I had a great deal of personal resistance to my partner: I couldn't fathom it, as Khan was a good-looking chap, therefore, easy to fancy! But until this point, I hadn't been able to make any attempt at intimacy or closeness with him. Now, all of a sudden, as if responding to Miranda's spontaneous reactions, I closed my eyes and found myself submitting to the touch of Khan/Ferdinand's hands. It was as if all my personal resistance was ebbing away, and some 'quality of Miranda' was inhabiting my body and connecting with my partner. The contact of our hands became more erotic, but there was still a strong feeling of innocence, as if we were exploring the first awakening of sexual responses. The skin was soft. The fingers long. The finger-nails like almonds. After some time, I opened my eyes, and I discovered that Khan/Ferdinand was watching me. Straight away, I was drowned in a sea of self-consciousness, and the sensation I had was similar to when I was observing Vivien/Caliban: I couldn't tell if what I was experiencing was *my* embarrassment or *Miranda's* shyness. Self and character were one.

There was no doubt that both Khan and I discovered a great deal of new information about our characters from this extended free improvisation. We were able to invest the intimacy, which we'd found through this encounter, into our subsequent exploration of the scene in rehearsals. If I'm completely honest, though, the Miranda/Ferdinand scene was never wholly successful. Having allowed myself to judge both my own work and Khan's, I'd undoubtedly inhibited any truly organic interaction between us. I'd walked on dangerous ground: I'd judged the creative process, and in some ways the damage could never be fully repaired. Grotowski emphasises that the 'total act' is required of all members in a creative ensemble; he goes on to advise 'Intimate and drastic elements in the work of others are untouchable and should not be commented upon even in their absence . . . We are obliged to open ourselves up even towards an enemy.'[97] A lot of repair work has to be done once the crime of judgement has been committed.

Summary of exercises towards Dramatic Text

Through these exercises, the group may strengthen its creative identity and progress into exploration of the characters in a text. The exercises provide the opportunity for exploring legitimate over-acting and under-acting to find the appropriate level at which to play artistic emotions in text-based rehearsals and performance. There is also the opportunity in free improvisations for characters who never meet in a play to investigate some kind of interaction, or for scenes not included in a play to be investigated in a kind of Active Research.

• **Laughter-Tears**
To enable the ensemble to 'tune' themselves psycho-physical, everyone sits in a circle facing into the centre. Through simple attention to each other, individuals and the group as a whole try to find the peak of laughter. As the actors find their peak, they each turn out of the circle and find their personal 'depth of despair'. This may simply be a feeling of heaviness; it need not be heart-felt sobs. This state is then arrested through Circles of Attention or the Five-Minute Recollection. Each individual undertakes this series of stages in his or her own time, though as an ensemble works together more

frequently, it may well be that the peak of laughter becomes more collective and the transition to despair becomes more of a shared experience.

- **Extended Free Improvisations**

Following Laughter-Tears, and Circles of Attention or the Five-Minute Recollection, each individual gradually starts to take attention back to the ensemble and, in their own time, begins to make contact with one or more group members by finding a simple game or complicity. Little by little, the actors develop from their own personae into the characters on which they are working in rehearsal.

It should be noted that while the exercises are intended to develop ensemble interaction, each individual actor progresses through the stages of Laughter-Tears and Extended Free Improvisations at his or her own pace. Extended Free Improvisations can involve any number of stages and permutations: these stages are simply outlined by the director or workshop leader before the sequence begins, and then, as and when they wish, the actors move from one stage to the next. There is no 'right' length of time.

Rising to the personal challenge

Creating an ensemble is never easy, and the process can never be fully anticipated. I realise that far more acutely now, with the hindsight gained from leading group-work myself, than I did during my time at VGIK. This particular ensemble was perhaps one of the most precarious: we were all adults with some degree of experience and training. We weren't working towards a production which would ultimately combine us. We weren't working towards a degree or certificate which would ultimately validate our training. We were simply a motley collection of individuals, hungry for experiences and with different expectations. The odds were stacked against us. Nonetheless, the group survived various disruptions – not least of which was the threatened outbreak of civil war in Moscow during October 1993, when the tanks stormed the White House, and we found ourselves under curfew, spending a night watching tracer bullets light up the sky like fireworks. All this goes to show the strength that an ensemble can develop when it ultimately commits to the 'total act'. The fact that group identity is intrinsic to the development of psycho-physical technique became particularly evident during Kamotskaya's Actor-Training sessions at a series of Summer Schools held in Britain in the 1990s. On each occasion, an international group of between twelve and sixteen participants formed an exciting and collaborative ensemble, producing collective activity of an unquestionably open and dynamic nature.

My own difficulty with the ensemble work in Russia revealed that my fundamental problem as a performer was one that I suspect I share with other actors. It was the inability to open myself up to the ultimate enemy – *myself*. It was through the interaction of Kamotskaya's Actor-Training and Filozov's work on character that this frightening truth was brought to light and the demon was confronted. In fact, the correlation of ensemble work and text-based disciplines became increasingly profound over the ten months, and the basic principles of Kamotskaya's work began to bear fruits in rehearsals. Through 'finding yourself' in free improvisations towards dramatic action and towards dramatic text, psycho-physical ensemble-training developed elements of play, spontaneity and attention to our partners. This enabled Filozov to elicit from his actors some exciting and unusual choices for characters through the use of Active Analysis. But this was only achieved after many daunting challenges, as we began the ultimate implementation of a psycho-physical technique – the actor's *work on a role*.

ACT 4
Working on Your Role

Putting it all together

The picture I've been trying to paint so far is that acting cannot help but be psycho-physical. We can't help but recruit our bodies, imaginations, spirit and emotions into an art form which is essentially experiential. In Chapter 2, I looked at this from the perspective of physical training and how our bodies constantly inform our imaginations and our 'inner lives'. In Chapter 3, I looked at it in terms of building an ensemble and how the information we glean from our partners (and the actual space between us) provokes our imaginations and our bodies. And now I want to illustrate how all this can be applied to formal work on a script and a character. Psycho-physical acting isn't just an exciting kind of training; it's a vital and energising approach to text and performance.

At the start of the book, I outlined the legacy left by Stanislavsky known as The Method of Physical Actions and Active Analysis. Many actors and directors are wary of systems or methods or any kind of formal analysis of what is essentially a subjective and ephemeral activity: acting. But the joy of Active Analysis, as described by Stanislavsky and quoted in Chapter 1, is that it's carried out simultaneously by all the intellectual, emotional, spiritual, and physical forces of our nature. It's not theoretical, it's 'practical research for the sake of a genuine objective, which we attain through physical actions.'[98] The notion of 'practical research' is an important issue in current educational thinking. The idea behind it is that the best researchers are those

who are putting their research into practice, and the best practitioners are those who in some way research whatever their
practical field may be. In other words, they're not just doing it,
they're exploring it, challenging themselves and pushing forward
the frontiers of their crafts. It's this hands-on interaction of
practice and theory that can take us deeper into our specialities
and help us develop into richer, more adventurous practitioners.

   In terms of acting, it means that we don't just 'do our thing',
we evolve a kind of dual consciousness: we're observing what
we're doing as we're doing it, so that we're developing as we
practise. Dual consciousness doesn't impede our intuitive processes, but rather it links technique and inspiration in a way in
which we can harness one to serve the other throughout all our
creative work. Having said all that, I'm going (seemingly) to
contradict myself by saying that the heart of Active Analysis is
that you *do* just get up and do it – because it's *practical research*.
The actor discovers the inner life of the character not through
theoretical analysis, but through actively pursuing his or her
objective by simply 'doing' the scene. 'Don't think about it: go
for it!' The experience itself will give you the information you
need to uncover the character; experience involves the simultaneous and collaborative work of body, mind and spirit.

Finding the Russian spirit – where action meets emotion

In terms of a contemporary approach to acting, it's the work of
the spirit which is pertinent. But 'spirit' hasn't always been an
acceptable part of Russian vocabulary. Far from it. The relevance
of various developments in Russian actor-training became clear
to me when working under Albert Filozov, the film- and stage-
performer, who served as acting 'master' to our eclectic troupe in
Moscow. Through him, I came to see the power that politics can
have over art and how that power has been an essential component in our own interpretation of Stanislavsky. Let's turn back
the clock to get a perspective on how it all came about . . .

In terms of a psycho-physical technique, the year 1934 marked the beginning of stagnation in Russian actor-training. This was the year that Stanislavsky's 'system' was officially proclaimed by Stalin as the gospel of Socialist Realism. Socialist Realism was a curious phenomenon in the way it interpreted life. Early literary definitions of Naturalism had explored the effects of both environment *and* heredity on a human's personality, but the Soviet ethic behind Socialist Realism dismissed the idea of personal psychological circumstances. Why should man think he's a victim of his genes? Oh, no – heredity was removed from the equation, and only things that could be changed by man (e.g. his environment) was of any relevance to a Socialist society. Anything that might be beyond our control, such as genetic structuring and personality were blasphemies against the Soviet doctrine. Conjectures about airy-fairy nonsense such as 'spirit' or 'soul' were even less welcome.[99]

It was actually very canny of Stalin to legitimise Stanislavsky's 'system'. After government vetting, Stanislavsky's first book, *The Actor: Work on Himself* (translated as *An Actor Prepares*), was officially formalised, ensuring that ideas of personality and 'higher consciousness' were defined in terms of nice scientific labels such as 'objectives', 'through-lines of action' and 'inner motive forces'. (Even the term 'affective memory' slipped from common actor-parlance during much of the twentieth century in the USSR.) From 1934 onwards, every student-actor was to set in stone the processes suggested by Comrade Konstantin. Of course, this officialisation instantly and ironically robbed Stanislavsky's 'system' of the very spontaneity that it was designed to inspire.

The three inner motive forces of intellect, emotion-centre and action-centre became acceptable currency. But the fourth motive force – the spirit – was completely taboo. This meant that concrete physical action was stressed, and intangible inner action was conveniently ignored. For Filozov, this was extremely frustrating. Just as Katya Kamotskaya had struggled with her restrictive training at the Shchukin Theatre Institute in the 1970s, Albert Filozov also suffered a lack of artistic fulfilment at the

Moscow Art Theatre's training Studio some twenty years earlier. He studied at the Studio for four years, during which time he discovered that the tutors were only concerned with one thing: Action, the struggle always to find Action, Action, Action. Following his graduation, Filozov struggled for ten years to 'unlearn' all this action, because he found that when he acted it was utterly boring. 'I knew *everything*. I knew I had to do this action here, that action there, and going onto the stage wasn't interesting for me. But really – I knew nothing at all.'

The person chiefly responsible for the emphasis on action at the training Studio was the director-teacher, Mikhail Kedrov. Immediately following Stanislavsky's death in 1938, Kedrov took over directing Molière's *Tartuffe* which, until he died, Stanislavsky had been exploring with a small group of young actors from the Moscow Art Theatre. Writing about Stanislavsky's particular interest at the time, one of the actors – Vasily Toporkov – described the process they adopted with *Tartuffe* as being not so much work on a play, but 'work on perfecting the technique of actors engaged in a play'.[100] In other words, it was a method of rehearsal rather than a system of actor-training or a desire to create a polished production of *Tartuffe*. It came to be known as the Method of Physical Actions, and Kedrov was at the heart of this – Stanislavsky's final research.

Kedrov's own definition of the process illustrates its psycho-physicality: 'Konstantin Sergeyevich used to say that when we say "physical actions", we are fooling the actor. They are *psycho-physical* actions, but we call them physical in order to avoid any unnecessary philosophising.'[101] (This fits in with the Soviet ethos.) He goes on to describe the nature of these physical actions as being 'concrete and easily understood. Precision of action . . . this is the foundation of our art. If I know the exact action and its logic, then it becomes for me a score; how I carry out the action according to the score, here, before the audience – that is creativity.' Although in theory he was clearly anxious to highlight the 'psycho' part of 'psycho-physical', in practice, Kedrov emphasised the 'logic' of action and its concreteness.

But he had to: that's what the regime endorsed. And so, creating a 'score' of actions – that is, a moment-by-moment listing of 'turning a handle', 'opening a door', 'switching on a light switch', 'arresting the burglar', etc. – became the actor's chief rehearsal preoccupation. During his time at the Moscow Art Theatre training Studio, Kedrov delivered many lectures about action, and in class he criticised his students' work, saying, 'No! You're not *doing* anything!'. In every moment, he wanted to see an overt action, believing that the art of acting was like riding a bicycle: you can't stay still, you can't go backwards, all the time you can only go forwards. As an actor you always have to be doing something, as if you're in a maze, always looking for where you're going. Action was Kedrov's lodestar, to the extent that the young student Filozov was left with the impression that, 'Without action, an actor is not an artist.'

Kedrov wasn't the only Action Man: the majority of tutors at the Studio perpetuated this dependence on continuous external action. Except one: Filozov's own acting 'master' (or 'mistress'), Evgenia Maryes. In contrast to her colleagues, Maryes focused on the more emotion-based aspects of Stanislavsky's system. When she herself was an acolyte actress, she had studied under Stanislavsky, taking the role of Mytyl in Maeterlinck's *The Blue Bird*. So, while Kedrov seemed to assess Stanislavsky's work from a *director's* perspective, Maryes's approach to training stemmed from her direct experience of Stanislavsky's work on the *acting* process. She recalled how Stanislavsky never dismantled individual terminologies from his 'system' and never talked about any rules. He talked only of things which would arouse the actors' emotions and artistic feelings. He sought out analogous events or objects from their lives which would stimulate their fantasies. It might be something lying deep in their subconscious which at first they didn't even fully remember, but it gradually filled out when they started to work with it creatively. In other words, the area of Stanislavsky's work which struck the most profound chord for Maryes was affective memory. Following in her master's footsteps, she got to know each of her students extensively, so that she too could access the most useful affective memories for them. As Filozov described, 'Maryes knew everything about each of us – who was in love with whom, what particular difficulties people had at home, what people's parents were like. And everybody told her everything, because she was such a good person. Then, when she was working with a particular student on a particular role, she would say, "You remember what you told me about your grandmother?" Because she was trying to get them to understand something about that particular role, their connection with it, an analogous situation.' The pay-offs of this personal connection were two-fold. First of all, it contradicted the clinical rule-by-rule 'action' study of Stanislavsky's system as promoted by the Soviet approach. As far as Filozov was concerned, this was a good thing, as you can't start teaching anybody with a *theory*. For him, it was nonsense: a theory could only work if it combined the personality of the person being taught with the personality of the person who is teaching. A theory was only a recipe for a cake, not the cake itself.

Secondly, it highlighted the fact that the laws applying to the *preparation* of a role differ from those applying to the *performance*. And this could be where the distinction lay between Stanislavsky's concept of affective memory and the ideas perpetuated by Lee Strasberg in America. For Stanislavsky, affective memory was a means of triggering an actor's enthusiasm for a role, enabling him or her to connect truthfully with a character's inner life. It's just another part of the homework involved in preparing a part – homework which might also include cerebral analysis of the scene's actions and objectives, as well as other more image-led work. But you don't put your homework on the stage. By the end of the rehearsal period, you have to put this preparatory work to one side so that you can live freely within the part during a show.

In contrast to all this, Strasberg *did* suggest with the American Method that you should use affective memories during the performance itself. In his tape-recorded sessions, Strasberg tackles the problem of how to fuse the actor's personal emotion with the character's existence on stage. He suggests that when you're performing, you listen to the text that your partner is delivering and you answer naturally, but at the same time you try and concentrate on conjuring up your own affective memory. Obviously it's much easier if you don't have many lines to speak, as there are fewer interruptions to your emotion recall. But Strasberg suggests that with practice 'the memory process becomes faster so that the performance of the affective memory actually takes no more than two minutes.'[102] Although this sounds like an extraordinary – if not schizophrenic – activity, Strasberg goes on to describe his own experience in the Group Theatre, where they actually set a definite amount of time for conjuring up an affective memory. 'When an emotional response was needed at a point in the middle of a scene, the actor knew that he had to start the affective memory sixty seconds before and that the emotional reaction would be ready exactly on cue.'

This is not at all the way in which Maryes used affective memory as taught to her by Stanislavsky. Maryes described to her pupils how Stanislavsky sought out analogous events from real life simply to ignite a connection between actor and role. Only when Stanislavsky felt that the actor really understood the depth of a particular part; only when he had awakened that special emotion within the person; only when everything began 'to breathe with humanity'; only then would he begin to talk about the technical elements, such as, 'You have to be faster here, slower there, and here you need to pursue your task more definitely.' Only then did he take the step from personal preparation to performance technique.

The search for inner action

Although all this seemed to make perfect sense, the student Filozov felt there was a missing link between Kedrov's search for forward-moving *external action* in performance, and Maryes's awakening of the *inner emotional mechanism* in preparing a role. In an attempt to bridge the gap between the two, Filozov returned to the words of Stanislavsky himself. As he re-read *The Actor: Work on Himself*, he began to see that there needn't be a conflict between external action and emotion; they actually synthesised to form *inner action*. Although this might sound obvious to us now, we have to remember that the Soviet consciousness couldn't accommodate any kind of reality which was unseen. It was only during a chance trip to Paris that Filozov suddenly understood the nature of psycho-physical action. He saw a woman at the Sacré Coeur, standing quite still, with her head bowed in deep conversation with God. As he stood there watching her, Filozov was captivated by her. The woman wasn't moving, but she was active all the time. She was silently talking to God, and in that silent dialogue was a powerful and fascinating *inner action*.

As he began to search for this inner action in his own work, Filozov found himself wrestling with the limitations of the Method of Physical Actions as taught to him by Kedrov. The conflict between his new understanding of inner action and the Soviet emphasis on outer action was so great that Filozov came to believe that the Method of Physical Actions had 'in effect killed Russian theatre'. (N.B. He's talking about the Method of Physical Actions, and not Active Analysis.) For the ten years following his graduation from drama school, Filozov fought this struggle and saw himself surrounded by 'dead' acting – until he met the actress, Maria Knebel. Knebel had been a member of the Moscow Art Theatre, as well as studying extensively under Michael Chekhov. And just like her teacher, she sought a 'feeling of ease' on stage, to reinvest the acting process with a sense of *play* and a *spirituality*. Filozov discovered that whereas Kedrov had pursued the path of external action and Maryes had sought the resonance of the actor's soul in the author's creation, Knebel invited him to loosen the stranglehold of his training and just have fun.

The actor's 'secret'

This appealed to Filozov: it was something he could work with. So he took the idea of fun (or 'feeling of ease') and translated it into a game or 'secret' – a secret that could exist between *actor and audience*, as much as between *actor and actor*. He described how this secret propelled him onto the stage, to the extent that 'I found that without such a secret, going on the stage wasn't really necessary.' In many ways, a personal secret is at the heart of each actor's creative individuality, and Filozov saw it as the magnet that drew the audience to an individual performer. 'You have to have something mysterious within you, which only you can give the audience. If you don't have this secret, you might just as well say to the audience, "Here's the play. Go away and read it for yourself."' The secret wasn't just a general idea: it could also be used very specifically with characterisations. Which is exactly what Filozov did with the role of Ignati Gatzovich in the 1979 film *The Wild Hunt of King Stakh* directed by V. Ryubinchik. The film told a strange tale set in an ancestral home in which mysterious and violent events take place; it transpired that Ignati Gatzovich was both the perpetrator of the evil deeds and their victim. As Filozov described it, 'Right from the beginning, my hero was dictated to me by the genre of the film. I knew his secret and I had to keep it, and the spectator had to be kept in ignorance almost right up to the end and, at the same time, throughout the film I had to reveal just a bit of this secret. I had to push the spectators into making conjectures: I had to make the spectators follow the behaviour of Gatzovich. I had to make them, as it were, "decipher" him, but then again I had to trick the spectators, because my hero is clever and ironic. In fact, he's not the person that those about him perceive him to be. Gatzovich is constantly playing a part and yet, at the same time, he's very careful to make sure that nobody should guess about his secret life.'[103]

Filozov's need for an inner secret – either for a specific character or for acting in general – wasn't just an artistic hunger; it arose partly out of necessity. The heroes of most Soviet films in the 1950s and '60s were presented as a particular physical type – athletic, strong, almost Aryan in its ideal. Filozov's personal type or acting *emploi* simply didn't fall into this category; he was slim, wiry, with pale skin, sandy hair, and almost icily blue eyes. He was caught between two stools: although he wasn't a typical 'lead', neither was he a typical 'character' actor. What really defined his *emploi* was his inner quality, rather than his physical appearance. This inner quality seemed to be a combination of *emotional truth* and the mysterious *secret*. Yet neither of these elements had a place in the clinical teaching of Stanislavsky's system as promoted by Soviet drama-training; they were qualities which Filozov had to develop through his own understanding of the acting process. And it wasn't long before the success of his 'inner action' led to him being recognised during the 1970s and '80s as an eminent actor in theatre and film. As one Russian critic, V. Sologub, described him, Filozov's talent lay in 'expressing diametrically-opposed sources of psychology in his heroes. Ice and flame, calm and passion, confusion and restraint, cruelty and defencelessness, uncomplaining resignation and determination, a nihilism of the soul and spiritual heights.'[104] (Once again, it's worth noting the emphasis on the spirit.)

Filozov went on to work with some of the most influential and pioneering directors of the modern Soviet and Russian theatre, including Anatoly Vassiliev and Anatoly Efros. He took leads in some of Vassiliev's provocative productions, which rocked the Moscow stage in the '70s and '80, among these the role of Bems in Viktor Slavkin's *A Young Man's Grown-up Daughter* at the Stanislavsky Dramatic Theatre in 1979. When I encountered Filozov in 1993, he was a leading actor at Moscow's Theatre of Contemporary Drama under the directorship of Yosef Raikhelgaus.

Filozov's approach to psycho-physical acting

Filozov's idiosyncratic acting style grew out of a combination of Kedrov's physical action, Maryes's affective memory, and Knebel's relaxation in the acting process along with her exploration of

Active Analysis. To all this was added, of course, his own imaginative understanding of performance practice. By the time he turned to teaching in 1989, Filozov had spent a long time reappraising Stanislavsky's system, including his shift from Physical Actions to Active Analysis. Filozov believed that, unfortunately, many actors who read Stanislavsky's books in drama schools go into the theory without entering the process, but 'working only with the theory doesn't wake up the soul: the soul remains asleep.' According to Filozov, Stanislavsky 'knew that actors spiritually sleep. First you have to *wake up the spirit* and then mould it and then rearrange it.' That, for Filozov, was the difference between the contemporary Russian approaches to acting and those promulgated in the West. 'You have to know that your spirit needs waking. I think that's what defines the real Russian school: it's concerned with awakening the spirit.'

'To awaken the spirit' seemed to be Filozov's super-objective with the English-speaking actors at VGIK in 1993. Although he offered no explicit outline of the programme, he approached the task through four different projects. In retrospect, I realised that each project had presented a different challenge to our group. By facing these challenges and attempting to surmount them, we were able (to a greater or lesser degree) to develop a psycho-physical technique, which was rooted in Active Analysis. It was far from easy, and our success in each project was in no way guaranteed. But what also became clear in retrospect was that the difficulties, mistakes and failures, actually accelerated the process of psycho-physical development far more than those practices which came easily.

Basically, the four stages explored the various layers involved in building a character, beginning by focusing in Stage One on *the actor's own personality*. This was simply a question of bringing the character *into* yourself, finding the most natural and direct means (for you personally) of expressing the lines and exploring the situation. The use of games was integral to this process, and the text we used to do all this was Shakespeare's *The Tempest*.

Stage Two was really about *removing the blocks*. Having found the most 'comfortable' characterisation in Stage One, it was now time to see where our points of resistance lay, in terms of emotional and physical blocks. This was addressed through C. S. Lewis's metaphorical, almost parable-like, novella *The Great Divorce*. It was a question of each actor finding an episode from the book, which appealed to him or her, and translating that episode into a *concrete situation*. At this point in the work, affective memory came to the fore.

Stage Three looked at *finding the physical actions*. This stage was concerned with developing a kind of psycho-physical versatility, whereby you could imaginatively and physically connect with almost any stage situation, whatever the text and whoever the character. While this work demanded a certain degree of bodily and emotional flexibility, the crux of inner adaptation lay in executing physical actions. To develop the necessary sensitivity, as well as a sense of play, we worked on a variety of self-selected extracts – known to the Russians as 'Self-Works'.

Last but by no means least, Stage Four was to do with *releasing the character*. In this final part of the programme, the emphasis subtly shifted towards characterisation. Through a combination of improvisation and technical adjustment, actors were encouraged to go beyond their own selves into the characters' 'creative individuality'. To this ambitious end, we explored a dramatisation of Dostoyevsky's *Crime and Punishment*.

In some respects, the fourth stage was a culmination of the first three: having attempted to awaken the actor's spirit (through Stages 1 – 3), Filozov sought to push the actor beyond his or her own safe haven of personality into an area of deep character-research (Stage 4). Our work in all of these stages used Active Analysis as the main method of making discoveries. And each step along the way was complemented by the inner/outer co-ordination of Ananyev's work on the self and Kamotskaya's Actor-Training. Taking the final step into 'creative individuality' invited us to delve into the kinds of self-analysis proposed by Grotowski. Self-research is unavoidable in the art of acting, and

I'm sure many actors would argue that it's actually a major part of the attraction. After all, as Filozov suggested, 'the work of an actor isn't a profession, it's a diagnosis. If it were just a profession, it wouldn't be interesting.'

It should be noted that Filozov spoke no English and taught purely in Russian; however, all the actors worked with English language texts. During the first months, classes were translated by Kamotskaya, but gradually as our Russian knowledge grew, direct negotiation between us as actors and Filozov as tutor/director became possible. It's curious how an appreciation of good or bad acting can transcend all language barriers; in fact, Filozov's lack of English served as a magnifying glass in his penetration of our work. His acute observation of our rehearsals pinpointed moments when inner and outer actions were not clear or not being played truthfully, or when flashes of great honesty and artistic integrity moved our psycho-physical development forward. There were only a few complications: for example, where a Shakespeare play read, 'How fares my Lady?', the Russian translation was, *Kak dela* – 'How's things?' Sometimes Filozov just couldn't understand why we native English speakers found Shakespearean text so difficult . . .

Stage One: Personality and *The Tempest*

At the risk of over-stating the case, this is *my* retrospective interpretation of Filozov's process. At no point did he overtly propose these four stages as the ideal way to enter deep character-research, just as Kamotskaya never offered an A-Z of building an ensemble. In some ways, it would be absurd for any of the practitioners whom I've discussed to offer a handbook of exercises, as all of them adapt their work to each new set of circumstances. During the ten-month programme, I often wondered whether results might have come more swiftly if we *had* known where we were heading. But I gradually came to realise that with psycho-physical work, you can't pre-empt the outcome. It's your *experience* of the exercise which finds the objective behind it, not your preliminary cerebral understanding of the task. In fact, knowing the objective beforehand could be detrimental to your progress: you might start looking for particular outcomes rather than immersing yourself in the present-tense experience. During an exercise, you sometimes find yourself thinking, 'Why am I doing this? What's it all working towards?' but you have to trust that in the end it'll all become clear. It may not be immediately apparent, but at some point in the future, it *will* all become clear. After all, the combined forces of body, imagination, spirit and emotion are far more intelligent and intuitive than mere reason alone.

I say all this because I actually found the work on *The Tempest* extremely difficult and not necessarily very successful. I didn't realise how simple the task was – just to connect one's own personality to the given circumstances. That's all the first stage of psycho-physical activity is concerned with: awakening your own creative personality, so that you don't just put the character on like an overcoat. The problem was that, at this early stage in the programme, I was still extremely result-orientated; I was always trying to come up with some clever and innovative characterisation, empty form without content. *The Tempest* project proved critical in taking the first tentative steps along the *via negativa*.

For Filozov, the root of spontaneous acting on the stage was a *constant ability to improvise*. This really seemed to be the essence of psycho-physical acting: it corresponded to Ananyev's quality of inner/outer synchronisation and Kamotskaya's extended ensemble exercises. The premise behind Filozov's constant improvisation echoed that of Michael Chekhov, who believed that 'there are no moments on the stage when an actor can be deprived of his right to improvise.'[105] Chekhov maintained that, if you were psycho-physically 'tuned', you could fulfil all the strictures imposed upon you in a production and at the same time preserve your spirit as an improvising actor. It's not a question of making up the text or arbitrarily changing the *mise-en-scène*; the quality of improvisation remains firmly within the director's framework and the playwright's structure. It's 'a finer kind of improvising that can take place anywhere, at any moment during the acting'.[106]

The rehearsal process adopted by Filozov to develop this ability to improvise was heavily influenced by Active Analysis as discussed in Chapter 1. The first step was for the actors to read the text *silently* to themselves. Filozov insisted that they didn't read the script out loud, in case they felt they had to *perform* the scene; that could lead to a very superficial first interpretation, separating the actors from the text, rather than connecting them with it.

Having read the script silently and following a brief discussion of the facts and events implicit and explicit in the text, the second step was to get up and improvise the scene, *without words*, simply to find the essence of the relationship – this was closely linked to Kamotskaya's Two People in the Empty Space.

The third stage was to improvise the scene *with words*. Stanislavsky is quite explicit about this stage in the process: 'If you must use words . . . please do not use the author's exact text, only the ideas embodied in it. Don't *act* anything, just play each action.'[107] It doesn't mean to say that you're absolutely *forbidden* to use the playwright's text; as Michael Chekhov proposes, 'if by chance you've retained some of the author's words in your memory, there's no need to mispronounce them deliberately in order to make them sound "improvised".'[108] The idea is simply that the improvisation shouldn't be a memory test: you're concentrating on your partner and what you're trying to do to your partner, not on struggling to give an accurate delivery of the script. Having said that, of course, if you find you *do* know the text, it's a gift.

Finding the game – Prospero and Caliban

When it comes to playing a scene, Filozov believed there are two 'co-ordinates': 'What do I *feel* here?' and 'What am I *doing*?' The whole thrust of this book is that feelings are important on stage, but, as we discussed in Chapter 1, feelings alone can't drive a scene. An actor relying heavily on emotions, claimed Filozov, is like a samovar or kettle, boiling but not moving, when in fact he or she needs to move those feelings along the path of *action*, the path of doing – more like a steam engine! Any rules suggested by Stanislavsky are only good when they allow the actors to express their *spirit* and direct it towards *action*. Action – or 'What am I doing?' – relates directly to a partner, and in order to ignite a scene, the actors have to get right inside the dynamics of an on-stage relationship. As I've suggested, Kamotskaya's Two People in the Empty Space exercise lay at the heart of much of this work, the difference being that Filozov (building on Knebel's sense of fun) specifically sought a *game* as the starting point for each encounter. Finding a game served three particular functions: (1) It presented the actors with tasks (or physical actions) which were easy to fulfil. (2) Because the tasks were simple, the combination of actor-scene-character could be effortlessly aligned in the pursuit of these physical actions. (3) Finding the appropriate game at the start of an encounter could unlock the rest of the scene's trajectory, as the right game could go straight to the heart of the characters' relationship.

As in Clive Barker's *Theatre Games*, many of the activities suggested by Filozov were variations on children's playground themes. The energy and simplicity of these games had the power to arouse the participants' imagination and spirit, and direct them straight towards action. Very quickly, life could be breathed into the scenes. This was certainly the case with two English actors – Ben and Vivien – who were working on the meeting between Prospero and Caliban in Act One, Scene Two of *The Tempest*. Filozov envisaged this encounter as an oblique variation of 'Grandmother's Footsteps'. So he set up a *mise-en-scène* in which Miranda lay sleeping, while Caliban crept up on her to molest her in some way. Maybe playfully, maybe more sinisterly? That was for Vivien as Caliban to decide. Prospero arrived on the scene, and seeing the imminent danger, arrested Caliban's actions with the words:

Thou poisonous slave, got by the devil himself
Upon thy wicked dam, come forth![109]

The game changed the 'moment of orientation' (i.e. the first
moment of an encounter, when each character assimilates the
other, as discussed in greater detail shortly), although it still
remained faithful to the sense of the text. 'Come forth' was no
longer a summons for Caliban to crawl out from his den; it was
now a command to stop him dead in his attempted molestation
of Miranda.

Before Filozov suggested the game, Ben (Prospero) and Vivien
(Caliban) had tried improvising the scene in their own words, the
result of which was that it was all rather formal and unnatural.
The moment they added the variation of Grandmother's
Footsteps, they broke free from their stilted performances,
instantly raising the stakes and investing their encounter with
real dramatic potential. It was simultaneously and unexpectedly
funny and sinister. Vivien relished the naughtiness of the game,
striking some great comic notes, as well as a strange kind of
empathy. As she crept up on the sleeping Miranda, Caliban's
concoction of risk, fear and desire sprang to life. Because she was
closer to Miranda than Ben was, he was immediately disem-
powered: it would be dead easy for Caliban to harm Miranda
before Prospero could get near enough to stop it. This is where
the variation of Grandmother's Footsteps came to the fore.
Every time Ben approached Vivien, she froze; just when he felt
that she no longer posed a threat, and so moved away again, she
advanced once more on her sleeping victim. She was like a
naughty child who, having been told not to stick her finger in a
cream bun, just has to do it. Sometimes she drew away from
Miranda, as a teasing reassurance to Ben of her innocent obedi-
ence, only to dive straight back towards the 'cream bun'
the minute his attention relaxed. There was a wonderful contrast between the mischief of the game and the abusive language
that Prospero and Caliban hurl at each other; this counterpoint
created a fascinatingly sinister, yet humorously playful, dynamic

between the pair. And there was another pay-off: their absorption in the game eliminated any division between actor and role. Just by playing their objectives – Caliban's 'to provoke' and Prospero's 'to disempower' – each of them blended with their respective characters within the given circumstances of the scene.

These first inroads into the text were extremely successful, but they were *only* inroads. It soon became clear that something was missing. If this encounter was really going to reverberate, Ben felt he needed to experience some degree of anxiety or fear of what Caliban might do to Miranda. Although he found the game provoked a sense of fun and excitement, there was no genuine threat: he knew that Vivien wouldn't inflict any real harm on the sleeping actress, and his imagination wasn't filling in the necessary gaps. Since Filozov's concern at this point in the programme was to connect the actors as truly as possible with the on-stage action, he decided to change the game. The next time they tried the scene, Ben/Prospero came in to find Vivien/Caliban with a notebook, that looked horribly like one of his own. She was tearing it, chewing it, chucking it about – in other words, she had a real object on which real destruction could be wreaked. And it was an object for which Ben felt a genuine anxiety: he didn't want it being torn to shreds. So the game then became one of 'Catch' – a real pursuit with a heartfelt objective – as Vivien taunted him with the book.

By simplifying the conditions of the game and altering the object under threat, the actors found a new and truthful dynamic. Ben's previous concern about feeling a real emotion (fear) was gone; instead, conditions were imposed in which he couldn't help but experience a genuine sense of provocation through active pursuit of a physical task. To make it even harder for Ben to achieve his objective (i.e. 'to retrieve his book'), Filozov handicapped him as much as possible. He was made to start the chase right at the back of the auditorium with chairs, tables, and other heavy obstacles over which he was to clamber before he reached a very high stage onto which he had to climb. All the while, Vivien happily destroyed the book, gleefully chuckling at Ben's physical exertions. Inevitably Ben rattled with a true sense of frustration, as he fought over his assault course and chased Vivien around the stage in the hope of retrieving his much-loved book. In this way, his psycho-physical mechanism was activated by executing *physical actions* in pursuit of a *psychological objective*. The only ingredient, which then had to be added, was (of course) *imagination*: for Prospero, this wasn't just any old note-pad, it was one of his most treasured magic books. And so the tricky transition from Renaissance text to the investment of human content was initiated through simple games and genuine objectives.

Changing the game – Miranda and Ferdinand

We adopted a similar process, working on the first encounter between Miranda and Ferdinand. As Miranda, I was to find a game for my partner, Khan (Ferdinand), with a double-edged motive: to stop him moving logs (the task set for him by Prospero) but, more than that, to provide a means of drawing us together in a moment of forbidden aloneness. The first time we tried the scene, Filozov piled a stack of chairs on the floor to represent the logs. Khan's task was to shift these chairs to another part of the stage and my task was to prevent him doing so. What emerged at first, albeit rather predictably, was a 'tug of war' with the chairs. Nonetheless, it made sense, as it corresponded with Miranda's line:

> If you'll sit down,
> I'll bear your logs the while. Pray, give me that;
> I'll carry it to the pile. [110]

Of course, Khan/Ferdinand refused my help with the log-carrying. So, I sat on one chair that he was trying to move and I hung off another chair that he was trying to carry. And quickly the nature of the game became very robust, and soon we were laughing and tumbling around through the vigorous physical action.

However . . .

As I've already discussed, Filozov's psycho-physical technique was one of constant improvisation. So the next time we tried the scene with the same game, Filozov stopped the exercise within minutes, declaring in no uncertain terms that our game had already become repetitive. He sensed that there was no new spark of spontaneity between me and Khan: we were simply trying to reproduce the previous day's *external* action without unleashing the corresponding emotional *inner* action. It was form without content. After that kind of provocation, we quickly made sure we found a new game: it began by Khan picking up every piece of rubbish and grime off the stage-floor laboriously with his fingers. I suddenly understood how I could join in the task, with the words from the text: 'It would become me / As well as it does you.' It didn't take long before we were scrabbling around on the floor like puppies, picking up bits of filth, in a game which was so very simple, but which provoked a youthful, energised communion between us. Once a real connection had been made, once we were really listening and responding, we were ready to take the encounter beyond the game into the scripted scene. In other words, the game had provided us with an unexpected and truthful avenue directly into the playwright's text. It also uncovered something about Miranda, which I don't think I'd even considered before: just like me, she was ready to muck in and get her hands dirty, she was almost a tom-boy. The more I allowed my own 'action-based' personality into the text, the more I unlocked a vitality in Miranda which I'd never really perceived before. It might not be to everybody's taste, but at this stage in the programme, we weren't concerned with finished, polished characterisations: it was simply a question of connecting truthfully and vitally with a text and investing it with something of ourselves.

The moment of orientation: Antonio and Sebastian

Filozov's work led from the premise that unless the first entrance into the scene is spot-on, the inner process can't truthfully live: if the very first encounter is wrong, then every subsequent physical action will take you further and further off course. It's what Stanislavsky calls 'the moment of orientation', and another reason why the games were so useful was that they clarified this moment. For Stanislavsky, the 'moment of orientation' begins before the first word is spoken and doesn't necessarily end when the partners enter into conversation. If actors rush this moment, 'their first words do not sound really effective because each has not made for himself even a preliminary evaluation of his partner.'[111] By taking that moment of orientation, the actors (and the characters) can understand how important this meeting is to them, how much they want to influence their partners, how high the stakes are – all those elements (discussed in Chapter 1) which inspire human beings to play their actions and achieve their objectives. If the moment of orientation is true, the audience will understand the first step in the line of physical actions: they'll believe in your performance.

Filozov frequently stopped an improvisation even before the actors had spoken a word. If he saw that the moment of orientation was incorrect or if the concrete action for the text was unspecific, there was no point in continuing. It was not dissimilar to Toporkov's description of Stanislavsky: Toporkov complains that on one occasion he didn't even have time to open his mouth before Stanislavsky stopped him, paying attention to some 'trifles' which seemed to have very little relation to the action. 'Well, let me say at least one sentence! Maybe something will come out of it,' begged the frustrated Toporkov. 'Nothing will come out of it if you are not prepared' was Stanislavsky's reply.[112] As far as *The Tempest* was concerned, it was actually very clear to see how an inappropriate game or a rushed moment of orientation presented difficulties to the actors when it came to motivating the subsequent action. Danny and Tom found themselves in this predicament with the dialogue between Antonio and Sebastian in Act Two, Scene One, in which they watch Gonzalo and the other courtiers sleeping, having been overwhelmed by a 'strange drowsiness'.[113] Filozov's image for the scene was that this drowsiness was a source of bemusement and amusement for the two courtiers who, for some reason, hadn't been affected. So great is their confused amusement that Filozov proposed that the actors began the scene with an outburst of vigorous laughter. Out of this laughter, Antonio unexpectedly reverses the dynamic by sowing the seed in Sebastian's ear that they kill the king in his sleep.

To reach this pitch of laughter, Filozov worked on the principle of Kamotskaya's Laughter-Tears exercise. Danny and Tom were to enter the stage and look directly at the audience as if they were the sleeping courtiers; by paying limitless attention to the spectators, the actors were to find the reasons for their amusement, which would bring them both to the peak of laughter. From his many years of experience with some superlative directors in theatre and film, Filozov knew that it's rare for actors to have the liberty of entering a scene at zero and finding the inner stimuli simply from what's going on in the 'transient now'.[114] He therefore believed that if the actors really started with nothing more than observation, which would then lead to laughter, they would actually find the rest of the scene would unfold extremely easily.

In fact, it did prove extremely easy for Danny, who was an open and emotional actor; however, Tom, who was equally skilled but with different talents, found it particularly challenging. Because the moment of orientation was with the audience and not with the on-stage partner, the actors had to allow their powers of observation to generate all their inner activity. The fact that Danny could engage his psycho-physical motor so easily complicated the process still further for Tom, who became increasingly inhibited. The result was that, as Antonio, he began to 'play the baddy', rather than play the action. From the outside, it was clear to see that in our current state of psycho-physical education, we just weren't ready yet, and the game was unhelpful in this particular instance. Perhaps Tom and Danny might have had more success had a more tangible game been found, one which stemmed from the on-stage moment of orientation between the actors and (at the same time) the characters. The long-and-the-short of it was that, in this particular encounter, actor and role became *dislocated*, rather than *synthesised*. The game must be helpful for the actors and appropriate to the scene, otherwise it hinders rather than facilitates the on-stage action.

Here and now, and nothing else

Obviously, the moment of orientation depends upon limitless attention to the partner. Kamotskaya's ensemble work had revealed the extent to which this kind of focus is a corner-stone of psycho-physical activity. As I'd already discovered to my cost, there were difficulties involved in developing psycho-physical sensitivity, difficulties which could sometimes manifest themselves through a kind of 'negative' observation of one's partner. The problems I'd had working with Khan as Ferdinand in Kamotskaya's classes reared up again now in Filozov's parallel rehearsals. The first encounter between Ferdinand and Miranda was a love-scene, and what could be more fundamental to a love-scene than absolute attention to the partner? However, Khan and I eventually acknowledged that there were acute fractures for both of us in that degree of attention. On the one hand, I knew I was being judgmental of my own performance and my partner's, and, on the other hand, Khan admitted racing through parts of the text which he felt weren't very successful. The result of all this was that the game with the logs became a diversion from our own incompatibility as actors, rather than the characters' excited embarrassment at being alone together. This was supposed to be a romantic encounter, in which the characters use physical objects as a means of bringing each other closer together. It's a scene about human relationships and how characters spiral in closer and closer together, until the moment when they can both look each other full in the eye and touch each other.

As Kamotskaya pointed out, the way that *we* were enacting the scene, the logs were now more important to us than each other's presence – it had become a show about shifting furniture! We were impeding our psycho-physical development: because our brains were working over-time (through our mutual judgement of each other and the scene), we were both blocking the creative flow of the encounter. And it was all pretty dull.

On the very first day of the programme, Filozov had given us an introductory talk on the current Russian understanding of Stanislavsky. In this talk, he'd advised us that there's always an inner conflict between *reasoning logic* and the *subconscious mind*. Through his lifetime of practical research, Stanislavsky had striven to unlock the secret of the actor's subconscious mind, the nature of which will, of course, be different for every single actor. He maintained that if we can find *psychological truth*, we can suddenly unblock and unlock the 'undiscovered' aspects within ourselves as creative performers. Since Khan and I were unable to find the 'psychological truth' – either within ourselves or between each other – we were blocking and locking all avenues to subconscious work, and the encounter was very boring. Filozov could see this inhibition, so he tried to find a means of silencing our inner judges. At first he reminded us that the secret of truthful acting is real attention to your partner, in that you can only take from your partner that which your partner is giving you. If you demand something of another actor but you don't get it, you have to work with what you *are* given. Otherwise, it's not a constant state of improvisation that exists, but rather a constant state of distortion or superimposition. If you try to struggle against this distorted on-stage dialogue, you'll end up with an acute inner conflict. Nine times out of ten, this inner conflict will be inappropriate to the scene, since it usually belongs to the *actors*, not to the *characters*; therefore, it can only lead to psychological untruths. It goes back to what Ananyev said about the inner policeman: 'Judgement sits like a sentinel between inner action and outer expression.'

As I suggested in Chapter 3, this problem is not uncommon, and Stanislavsky, Michael Chekhov and Grotowski each had very specific reactions to it. Grotowski categorically stated that 'An actor has no right to mould his partner so as to provide greater possibilities for his own performance.'[115]

Stanislavsky was a little more diplomatic (if idealistic) in his assessment of the problem. He believed that an actor must 'develop an ability to adapt to the conditions of the stage'.[116] This means that you don't see your on-stage partner in terms of the ordinary, everyday, human characteristics that he or she possesses. Instead, you should only see the aspects which are appropriate to the circumstances of the play. This may sound as though you have to filter out your powers of observation in some bizarre way. But Stanislavsky maintained that it's this feeling alone that will be correct, and it's in this feeling that you'll always find that note or that rhythm, in which you can unite with all the other actors taking part in the performance.

For Michael Chekhov, spontaneity and collaboration on stage required all actors to be generous towards one another, 'regardless of personal attitude'.[117] To this end, he invited each member of the ensemble to find 'just one moment, just one little thing which you like' in every performer's acting.

As far as Filozov was concerned, there were three things an actor *must not do* when working with a partner to whom he or she cannot connect. The first major 'no-no' was that the actor mustn't imagine his or her partner to be different from the reality. As Filozov put it, 'You cannot build another construction in your imagination; that will never succeed as it will close you off from your partner.' This position is unequivocally upheld by Stanislavsky, when he describes 'What torture it is to play opposite an actor who looks at you and yet sees someone else, who constantly adjusts himself to that person and not to you. Such actors are separated from the very persons with whom they should be in closest relationship . . . Do avoid this dangerous and deadening method. It eats into you and is so difficult to eradicate.'[118]

Filozov's second prohibition was that the actor mustn't struggle with his or her true feelings concerning the partner, as again 'this will distance you from the truth of your inner life and the truth of your scene.' You have to find a quality of ease.

The third thing, that Filozov declared, was that the actor 'must not build a wall around himself in an attempt to act within his own space, as this will also lead to conflict and thus close the inner life.'

Filozov's solution to this complicated problem was to create an inner monologue which accommodates the situation, such as: 'My partner can't speak the truth to me as he's afraid to admit it to himself.' Or 'He speaks the text so strangely because the language is foreign to him.' Which indeed it was in this case, as Khan had had little classical experience to date. Creating an inner monologue is exactly what I did with the Miranda/Ferdinand scene. In fact, once this troublesome encounter was addressed like this, the solution was comparatively uncomplicated. After all, Ferdinand and Miranda have had completely polar up-bringings. As soon as I'd realised that, it was possible to take genuine delight in the strangeness of some of Khan/Ferdinand's delivery, as if he were from an absurd-sounding culture. This in itself created an element of play, and we found that the new sense of freedom allowed the scene to find its own natural rhythm. Previously we'd rushed certain moments in the text because we knew we weren't doing them very well. (How many actors have been guilty of that at some point in their careers?) Now we actually allowed ourselves to take our time – and, dare I say it, even to pause! Suddenly the whole encounter made sense in its own terms, given these two actors and their particular dynamic. And lo and behold, we could almost *enjoy* the scene.

Out of our new-found relaxation more spontaneous games arose. At the next rehearsal following our break-through, there were no chairs to represent logs, so a new manual task had to be found. Seeing a huge oil drum in a corner of the room, Khan/Ferdinand started manoeuvring this, as if it were the task to which Prospero had set him. So I helped him. We soon dis-covered that our hands were covered in thick disgusting grease from the drum, and what could be more mischievous than to have a game of tag? And what happens when you play tag? – You get to touch people . . . The result of which was that suddenly we realised that we were physically very close. One thing led to another, until we were sufficiently intimate for the scene to progress quite naturally to the point in the text where the characters devise love poems for each other. Introducing the internal monologue in rehearsals had silenced my inner judge and allowed me to take a new perspective on the scene. This in turn released a sense of freedom between us, out of which new and spontaneous games arose. Through these games, we found an intimate connection, both as actors and as characters, from which the scripted scene began to flow. Filozov had addressed the dislocated dialogue between myself and Khan by introducing a 'feeling of ease' and a quality of play, in which whatever happens here and now is valid and creative.

Personality, not character . . . yet

As I've already said, the emphasis of this first project lay in the connection of the actor's own personality with the text: Filozov's concern here was not with the ultimate interpretation of a character. This was the first stage in a psycho-physical *process*, not a final result. This meant that while Ben's own natural, youthful gentleness wouldn't have been appropriate for a final interpretation of Prospero the Magus, he was simply required to connect his gentleness with his fight against Vivien's tricksy Caliban. As a result of their connection with each other, they had some moments of great success. Danny presented a Prospero and an Antonio which were actually very similar in character, but it didn't matter – he was successful in his work because both his Antonio and Prospero were invested with his particular quirky perspective. He had found his own organic assimiliation of the playwright's text, giving rise to colourful and playful interactions.

However . . .

I didn't find it easy to access such openness, due in part to my own background in the short rehearsals of rep theatre, where (as

I've previously suggested) rapid results were a common necessity. Filozov's directive to the actors at this point in the programme had been: 'Don't think about the character, just start from zero. It's only interesting to be yourselves and to play for each other, like children play for each other, and not for the audience.' The argument was that, without starting from zero and working *through* your own personality in the early stages of preparation, characterisation could so easily be superimposed rather than organically discovered. That's not to say that the actor should deliberately avoid characterisations if they naturally manifest themselves. Referring to a similar rehearsal technique, Michael Chekhov's advice was, 'Do not as yet try to develop your characterisation, otherwise your attention will be distracted from that "inner voice" which guides your improvisational activity. However, if *the characteristic features of the role "insist" on coming to the fore* and being incorporated, do not suppress them.'[119]

Ananyev had hinted at the great difficulty of unlearning habits before relearning can begin, and now I knew for sure. My psycho-physical development was being thwarted by my brain doing too much work. I was in the habit of reading a script and making broad decisions about a character before actually getting up on my feet and negotiating either the space or my fellow actors. What had happened with *The Tempest* was that I'd pre-determined Miranda's qualities as innocent and brave-new-worldish. These weren't Chekhov's idea of 'characteristic features of the role which insist on coming to the fore'. They were conscious choices which I'd cerebrally made, and, once I'd made them, I found it difficult to shake them off, despite the fact that I had to contort my own personality to accommodate them in the first place. I don't think I was aware that that's what I was doing, but Filozov seemed to sense my squeezing of personality into part, and so he tried to realign actor and character by altering the beginning of the Miranda–Ferdinand scene. He was really going back to his original premise that if the very first 'moment of orientation' is truthful, the rest of the scene will naturally unfold. Filozov encouraged me to make Miranda very down-to-earth at the start, as he struggled to help me find a Miranda which would work for me. After all, he suggested, she's a very grounded individual. She's walked barefoot on the sand and in the sea, catching fish, moving logs and stones, playing in the woods. She's a wild creature, in contrast to Ferdinand, the refined poet. She simply says that if the log's heavy, then put it down.

This change of direction – from an attempt at unworldly innocence to a harnessing of my own more earthy practicality – was again successful for the first few attempts. By accessing Miranda's sense of humour, stemming directly from my own personality and my own assessment of the given circumstances, we managed to find a sense of intimacy full of teasing and flirtation.

A word of warning!

My success in this part was limited, primarily because the development of a psycho-physical technique is so complex and I was having to fight against my own ingrained bad habits. It's comparatively easy employing isolated aspects of a system, but synthesising the whole is quite another matter. As Stanislavsky admitted, 'It isn't difficult to teach the separate elements of the method, but it is difficult to teach an actor how to link all the elements tightly together for his correct and creative being at rehearsal or in performance. It is difficult to channel the actor's knowledge of the method's principles – plus his own thoughts and feelings and experiences – toward the creation of a role on stage, and finally to the overall problems of the author's ideas.'[120]

This is where a word of warning comes in! On the one hand, experience has taught me that Active Analysis can be a wonderfully liberating and exciting channel into a script. On the other hand, if the actors aren't prepared for such a psycho-physical approach, there are certain traps which they can fall into in the early stages of the process. This was really the case with *The Tempest*. While the work on personality into character was challenging and revealing, taking it into a more structured *mise-en-scène* was very tricky. This 'word of warning' is for those practitioners – actors, directors or teachers – seeking a similar experience-based process. Active Analysis is not a one-minute cure-all. It's difficult, it's challenging, but ultimately it is organic and natural in its implementation of theory and practice. But it needs time . . .

What happened next with *The Tempest* project was that, after Filozov had helped the actors to locate an emotional truth through improvisation, he then tried to convey a theatrical picture by constructing a *mise-en-scène*. This he did by observing how the actors organically dramatised the scene during their improvisations, and he then tailored these movements to create an expressive construction. This was then 'fixed' into a 'score' – although Filozov insisted that 'nothing is law, nothing is literal'. In theory (and as I later discovered in practice), this is actually a great way of turning improvisation into theatrical pictures without disturbing the actors' sense of *inner* improvisation. The trouble was that some of us just weren't open enough so early in the programme to deal with what seemed like a contradiction: 'I thought the point was that we could move anywhere, and now he's telling me I have to go here and then there.' Furthermore, in the final stages of the project we were of course asked to learn the text fully. The comparative complexity of Shakespeare's poetry was now added to the tangled web of developing a technique, in which inner action and outer expression are supposed to be simultaneous. In fact, some of us found that the speedy transition from improvisation to theatrical construct meant that the fixed *mise-en-scène* soon became a straitjacket, not a navigation system.

That certainly didn't negate *The Tempest* project: we were the first English-speaking actors to study at VGIK, and the whole year was in many ways an experiment. It simply illustrated once again how much we needed to unlearn before we could relearn. Truly accessing our own personalities was a big enough lesson at this stage: the real pay-offs of Active Analysis, especially in terms of constructing stage pictures, would come later in our psycho-physical programme. This was particularly true for me: I found the whole process of 'awakening my inner life' painfully slow and difficult. In his end-of-term report to me, Filozov stated quite categorically, 'I have nothing positive to say to you. Until you learn to unblock as an actress, there is nothing I can do with you.' I gulped . . .

It was with a heavy heart that I returned to England for the Christmas vacation.

I had always thought I was rather a good actress. I was trustworthy, imaginative, got good reviews, was re-employed. Now my ego was more than a little bruised. Filozov was basically telling me that I was emotionally inhibited on the stage, and a constant state of improvisation was not a natural one for me from my result-orientated perspective. While this indictment was un-deniably galling, I knew he was right. The truth of the matter was that if I really wanted to embrace a character honestly and artistically, I first of all had to unlock my own individuality. In many ways, I found Grotowski's words strangely reassuring: 'To fulfil this individuality, it is not a matter of learning new things, but rather of ridding oneself of old habits. For each individual actor, it must be clearly established what it is that blocks his intimate associations, thus causing his lack of decision, the chaos of expression, and his lack of discipline; what prevents him from experiencing the feeling of his own freedom, that his organism is completely free and powerful, and that nothing is beyond his capabilities. In other words, how can obstacles be eliminated?'[121]

I returned to snow-bound Moscow in January to seek the answer to this awesome question . . .

Key components in Activating the Actor's Own Personality

• Active Analysis develops in an actor the ability to improvise constantly.

• Learning the words comes through a process of improvisation: (1) Read the text silently to yourself; (2) Discuss the scene with the director in terms of the relationships between characters and the general dramatic structure of the scene; (3) Improvise the scene without words as in Two People and the Empty Space; (4) Improvise the scene using your own words, with as much or as little text as you wish in the early stages. If the playwright's actual text comes to you, use it – don't pretend you don't know it.

• Find the game between the characters.

• Change – or challenge – the game in each future improvisation.

• Experience the 'moment of orientation' between characters. Don't continue the scene if the moment of orientation feels wrong.

• Be yourself. At this stage, don't think in terms of character, unless you find elements of the character coming to the fore, in which case don't suppress them intentionally.

• Find a 'score' of actions through the process of improvisation; an appropriate score of actions will integrate you with the text.

• Once an organic connection with the script has been triggered through games and improvisations, learn the text. This trigger moment might come in the first rehearsal or the twentieth; it doesn't matter. Keep exploring until you find it, and then just learn those lines.

Stage Two: Removing the blocks through *The Great Divorce*

Having acknowledged the difficulty many of us had in connecting ourselves with a text, Filozov seemed to focus the second term on the *elimination of obstacles*. The material he chose for his daunting task was philosophical in nature, which meant that each actor could connect with the subject-matter in his or her own individual way. In many ways, the first stage in eliminating blocks is to access affective memory.

C. S. Lewis's short novel, *The Great Divorce* (subtitled *A Dream*), is an allegorical tale in which the narrator takes a bus trip to Heaven. Once he gets there, he sees a number of translucent beings stumbling through the strange land, and he soon realises that these are dead humans who have yet to pass through a kind of purgatorial waiting-room to higher consciousness. The Solid beings, who also inhabit the land, are the spirits of humans who have reached fulfilment through self-awareness after death. Each episode in the allegory explores an encounter between a Solid spirit and a dead human being struggling to give up his or her earthly desires. Once those desires have been relinquished, the dead human can pass through to the beautiful life of the spirits.

Each actor was to select an episode to work on, but in choosing the scene, Filozov wanted us to go beneath the psychological and philosophical content of the piece and to find simple and concrete situations, which could accommodate the fables. There were two particular reasons for finding tangible circumstances. First of all, it clarified our understanding of Physical Action, as a very specific *external* activity had to be found to inspire *inner* action. Secondly, in locating an appropriate situation, the actor was (albeit subconsciously) appealing to his or her own emotion memory. The idea was to search within your imagination for an analogous situation to fuel your connection with the role; this in turn would trigger those genuine emotions, which Filozov considered to be the actor's raw materials. These two complementary aspects of character research mirrored the parallel influences of Filozov's own training – Kedrov's physical actions and Maryes's affective memory – in the hopes that their synthesis would activate true inner action.

Pam and her brother: 'Don't play the conditions'

It was curious how the episodes we chose seemed to reflect the obstacles which we each needed to overcome in the development of our own psycho-physical technique. This certainly seemed to be the case with Vivien who chose to work on a section between a dead mother, Pam, and her Solid spirit brother. Having died and found herself in Heaven, Pam demands to see her prematurely deceased son, Michael. Her brother denies her all access to Michael until she can learn to experience love, not in terms of possession, but in terms of an all-encompassing altruism attainable through 'God' or higher consciousness. As long as Pam obstinately clings to her belief that 'I want my boy, and I mean to have him. He is mine . . . Mine, mine, mine, for ever and ever,' she's denying the very power within her to reach her precious son. Her brother keeps stressing to her that 'You're treating God only as a means to Michael. But the whole . . . treatment consists of learning to want God for His own sake.'[122] In many respects, this was a poignant analogy for Vivien's reaction to her training at VGIK. She had come to the world-famous State Institute of Cinematography with the express aim of being in movies. Therefore, engaging so deeply in acting processes and self-research didn't always seem to interest her that much. Just as the real point of Pam's journey to Heaven was not to unite her with her son but to develop her own inner self, so too was the training at VGIK intended to develop the actor's inner technique and not simply to produce showreels.

Maybe it was because of the hidden 'home truth' that Vivien actually found the scene extremely challenging. In many ways, the root of the problem went back to Filozov's belief that if the moment of orientation is wrong, the rest of the action will go off at a tangent. Fulfilling her remit to find a concrete situation for the essentially philosophical story, Vivien chose to set the scene on a park bench. The trouble was that each time she entered the scene, she came in playing the *condition* of despondency. Much as Filozov wanted us to fill our creative work with real human content and emotions, he was also adamant that you can't *play* emotion. An affective memory might help you find a trigger into a scene, but when you're playing the scene you have to *play the action*. If the action is played with imagination and commitment, then the by-product of that action will be an emotion, which might be despondency, or frustration, or grief or even joy. The danger of playing conditions is that you end up demonstrating rather than living – it can all too easily become form without content. One of the most telling examples of actors playing conditions is in drunk scenes. The thing about being drunk is that we do everything we can to convince the world we're sober. As Stanislavsky pointed out, each action is played with extreme concentration and attention. It's the accumulation of those actions which will convey to the audience the condition of drunkenness, without the actor having to worry about it. Honest playing of action requires raw human material, not the 'condition' of human emotion.

The Tragedian and The Dwarf: facing the obstacles

Locating the emotional raw material and applying it to the creative process was the challenge presented to me, Tom and Khan with the tale of The Tragedian and the Dwarf. For various reasons, we'd each independently chosen this episode, which told the story of the recently-deceased human, Frank, who encounters the enlightened spirit of his dead wife, Sarah. Frank, however, is represented by two individuals, a shrivelled Dwarf (Tom) and a Tragic Actor (Khan). The Dwarf is basically Frank's true self, who throughout the episode becomes smaller and smaller until he ultimately vanishes, and the Tragedian is in essence his negative ego. The Dwarf is attached to his Tragedian-Ego by a chain and, as the power of the Ego (with its exaggerated and theatrical self-pity) increases, the Dwarf diminishes. Throughout the scene, Sarah (played by me) always addresses her words to the Dwarf, although it's usually the Tragedian who replies on his behalf.

Filozov seemed to be aware that, with this combination of actors, there were three different tasks to be addressed. The role of the Tragedian could provide Khan with the opportunity to explore his own naturally bold acting style. The personality traits which had been contorted by the role of Ferdinand in *The Tempest* were now liberated and granted free expression in the role of the Tragic Actor. Tom had the tendency to be slightly eccentric (if not a little manic) in his acting style, so the role of the Dwarf would challenge him into finding a gentle vulnerability. And Filozov attempted to address my own emotional inhibitions through the character of Sarah.

In the early exercises, Tom was bound to Khan by a rope, and the improvisations proceeded along similar lines to those with *The Tempest*: without any text, we entered the space and tried to find a point of contact between us in a kind of Three People in the Empty Space exercise. When Filozov felt that there was a strong, true connection between us, he prompted us to use our own words to improvise the scene.

Two problems arose in these early improvisations in terms of psycho-physical development. They both stemmed in part from *my* lack of inner freedom, which then exerted its hold over the ensemble. I still didn't really understand the nature of limitless attention to the partner and a constant state of inner improvisation; instead I was far too concerned with being faithful to the author's text and characters. I was familiar enough with the Lewis story to know that the improvised dynamics between the three of us were 'wrong' in terms of the author's intentions. Instead of just getting on with it and responding to the dynamics which were spontaneously emerging, I was trying to steer the improvisation back towards the text. Again, I was committing the heinous crime of judging my fellow actors. I felt that we weren't really getting very far with these early improvisations. I was conscious that Khan was prohibiting Tom from moving very much, to the extent that Tom was left with very little choice about whether the Dwarf wanted the Tragedian to talk for him or not. I could hear this schoolma'am in my head saying, 'The story expressly says that the *Dwarf* is leading the *Tragedian* at the start, not the other way round. Yes, I know that the Dwarf gradually diminishes in size, giving power over to the Tragedian, but that's later! It's not what it's like at the start!' I didn't realise that the position I was putting myself in was untenable: you cannot judge and act at the same time, and you can only respond to what your partner gives you.

There was a further complication in that Filozov seemed to be propelling me towards a particularly emotional state, which something inside me was resisting. Without him actually saying it, he was driving Sarah towards tears, and I was afraid – not of the emotion, but of the very fact that I'd never been emotional in performance. I was one of those actors who would read the stage direction, 'She cries' and instantly dry up with terror, knowing that I would never be able to achieve that state to order, so I might as well fake it – and badly at that. I was also one of those people who thought that actors who could cry on cue must be brilliant, and that there was no way I could ever be that good. just didn't understand that acting is about *actions*, not conditions. Play the actions with imagination and commitment, and the emotion will follow, like day follows night.

I was aware that I was blocking the natural flow of the improvisations, both in terms of narrative and emotional content – and this was frustrating the hell out of Filozov. Following Stanislavsky's premise that 'Without experiencing a role there can be no art in it',[123] Filozov reiterated that the only materials with which he was interested in working were 'human emotions, real feelings'. That's not to say either he or Stanislavsky believed that to play Macbeth you have to murder, or that he wanted pain and suffering, as he was also an advocate of Michael Chekhov's quality of ease and the love of the work. He just abhorred intellectual performances or cheap imitations when human truth was infinitely easier and so much more artistic.

My resistance to engage with the necessary emotions created a conflict inside me, and that conflict was in itself psychologically uncomfortable and deeply frustrating. The most frustrating thing was that the given circumstances of the episode and my imaginative connection with Sarah actually *did* arouse genuine feelings, but some perverse part of my psyche kept pushing those emotions away from me. This doubled my self-criticism and frustration. The contorted inner conflict was crippling. I read Stanislavsky's words: 'Our deep spiritual wellsprings open wide *only* when the inner and outer feelings of an actor flow in accordance with the laws fixed for them, when there is absolutely no forcing, *no deviation from the norm*, when there is no cliché or conventional acting of any kind.'[124] And I began to realise what I was doing. I had always abhorred actors who squeezed emotions out of themselves like tubes of toothpaste: now I seemed to be doing an equally unnatural thing, but from the other end of the spectrum. There were big emotions welling up inside me and I was forcing them away, but by striving to block them, *I* was 'deviating from the norm'. I was preventing the natural flow of my own inner and outer feelings, and the knock-on effect was that I was chronically inhibiting the creative process for all of us in the scene. I was becoming scared of the very process of rehearsal: I didn't want to turn it into an emotional trash-can.

Rehearsal as laboratory

Charles Marowitz summarises the rehearsal process, saying that 'it is only through the actor that any experience can be conveyed to an audience, and unless he has created *his own experience in rehearsal*, there is, literally, nothing to be conveyed – except the empty shell of the writer's experience: a second-hand experience.'[125] Filozov didn't want to work with second-hand experiences. He wanted brand-new sensations, born out of true Active Analysis. In order to access those kinds of raw material, he adopted a similar approach in the rehearsal room to the one employed by his own acting teacher, Evgenia Maryes. If an actor was struggling with a particular character or scene, Filozov tried to locate an analogous sensation from the actor's own life in order to release the scene from the limitations of demonstrated acting.

Aspects of emotion recall demand deep self-analysis. For Grotowski, 'Self-research is simply the right of our profession, our first duty' to the extent that 'if during our creation we hide the things that function in our personal lives, you may be sure that our creativity will fail.'[126] Grotowski described the acting craft as 'the surpassing of the limits, of a confrontation, of a process of self-knowledge and, in a certain sense, *of a therapy*.'[127] Words like this – especially from the mouth of Grotowski! – can strike fear into some practitioners. While I in no way advocate that the rehearsal space is a hospital, where childhood psychoses are dredged up and prodded, I do believe that we should be able to consider it as a laboratory. If acting involves all aspects of the human being (imagination, body, reason, spirit and emotions) we have to be sure that we are healthy human beings – physically, mentally and emotionally. If we have creative blocks – just as if we have physical blocks – they'll confront us at some point in our work, and as creative artists we have to ease ourselves through those blocks in an artistic and healthy environment. The given circumstances of the tale of the Tragedian and the Dwarf involved a personality (the Dwarf) being swallowed by an addictive behaviour pattern (the Tragedian). I suddenly realised that the root of my creative block in this scene was that a potent affective memory from my own life (when I'd lived with an alcoholic partner) was resisting direct contact for fear of transforming a rehearsal situation into that very therapy advocated by Grotowski. I wasn't afraid of what reliving the memory would do, I was afraid of 'what others would think'. Yet the basis of the Russian approach embraced the awakening of the spirit. Therefore, a *liberation* or *diffusion* of the particular affective memory, not its *avoidance*, was paramount if I was going to unblock my own creativity. Once that emotion was aroused, it could be converted into artistic raw materials by applying it to the text of The Dwarf and the Tragedian.

Sure enough, as soon as I'd silenced my self-censorship and allowed a degree of artistic 'therapy' to exist, the emotions were released by diffusing the affective memory. This diffusion took place partly during Kamotskaya's Actor-Training sessions (in particular through the Laughter-Tears exercise) and partly through committing myself to Grotowski's 'total act'[128] during the rehearsals of the Lewis scene. Once those repressed emotions were released, it was like the pressure off a stop-cock: it was exhilarating. It felt almost as if all my acting to date had been done by a bloodless phantom. In rehearsal I suddenly felt alive. My mind was relaxed, I could see my partners, hear their text and allow their words to reverberate in my heart. I could begin to integrate my emotion-centre with my body and my brain. It was all part of the self-research intrinsic to psycho-physical acting.

Getting technical

As soon as actors were working with their personal raw materials, Filozov could guide them through dramatic texts, in this case the C. S. Lewis scene. He encouraged them to pay precise attention to each other, and he created an environment in which the parameters were unlimited, but the ensemble was safe. It also meant that he could start to introduce more technical aspects. During our subsequent improvisations of the scene, Filozov coaxed the actors from the sidelines, giving directions, such as, 'Now touch him', 'Now restrain her', 'Now smile at him', 'Now turn away', as if drawing out inner sensations and transmuting them into concrete actions. Through these actions poured emotions. By means of a strange understanding that Filozov seemed to develop for each of us, he was able to combine raw materials with technical directions. Through this combination, he took us even deeper into our own character research, all the while keeping the triad of Ananyev's Actor, Self and Character (as discussed in Chapter 2) in harmonious balance.

The emphasis was still on personality rather than characterisation, which meant that certain 'facts' from the text didn't have to be held as gospel; they could be manipulated to suit the exercise. After all, this was still project-work on psycho–physical development, not rehearsal towards a polished performance. This adaptation of text to personality became particular evident with Filozov's direction of the character I was playing – Sarah. While C. S. Lewis's Sarah was continually soothing and loving, reassuring the Dwarf that 'There are no miseries here', Filozov anticipated a more potent way of connecting *my* individuality with the text. He gave me a very specific instruction: when I was talking to the Dwarf, I was to smile and when I was talking to the Tragedian, I was to look serious. This was actually the opposite of the original text, in which it's the Tragic Actor's ridiculousness that makes Sarah smile. However, the result of Filozov's direction of my *inner sensation* through the *outer act* of smiling was that there was a very powerful build-up of energies. I began to feel more and more frustrated with Khan's body! As the Tragedian, he was physically blocking me from getting to Tom's Dwarf and I had an overwhelming desire to heave Khan out of my way so that I could make direct physical contact with the gibbering Tom-Dwarf cowering pathetically behind him. Filozov could see my irritation mounting. The more frustrated I became, the more he coaxed me to smile, as I uttered the words, 'Don't you look lovely today?' to the cowering Tom, who in turn became increasingly diminished and deformed. The contrast of external action (to smile) and inner action (to pity) aroused powerful sensations, and the more I smiled, the faster the tears streamed down my face. I wasn't looking for emotion, in fact I was trying to do the opposite: cover my emotion by playing action. The result was that the emotional conduit was well and truly opened.

During this project, Filozov had insisted that we try and connect ourselves openly and honestly with what each scene was really about. Our connection with the text was fuelled with affective memory and spurred by Filozov's 'side-line' promptings. The result of this research was that several of us in the English-speaking group were able to take a significant step forward in the development of psycho-physical activity. Once the psycho-physical valve had been opened, there was a flow between inner action and outer expression, along with a concurrent emotional unblocking. Having aroused this kind of active state, the next hurdle for each of us was to understand how it could be applied to a diversity of plays. The work on *The Great Divorce* had been a laboratory exploration of a philosophical text. Now Filozov wanted to encourage a constant state of improvisation and versatility in each actor, so his next project involved the staging of various extracts individually selected by the group. We were all involved in several different scenes: this was a deliberate challenge to see if we could respond freely within a number of contrasting given circumstances by finding the appropriate lines or 'scores' of physical action.

Summary of Key Components in Removing the Blocks

• Play action, not condition of emotion.

• In rehearsals, face the obstacles, be they physical or emotional, and find a way of working through them creatively.

• Don't judge yourself or your fellow actors.

• Allow artistic 'therapy' a legitimate, but balanced, place in the rehearsal laboratory. Rehearsal is *rehearsal* – raw emotion will be refined to artistic emotion if, in rehearsal, there is a working atmosphere of freedom, so that performance can be emotionally expressive, but technically controlled. To that end, appropriate affective memory should be allowed its place in expanding your psycho-physical expression and in informing your artistic emotions.

• Don't force anything, but don't suppress anything. 'Invent nothing, deny nothing.'

• Allow a quality of ease in all you do in rehearsal – laughing, crying, loving or hating. Enjoy your emotions.

- In the early exploratory stages of Active Analysis, don't cling to the 'facts' of the text if other actors aren't adhering to them. Listen, accept and build. Herein lies the pathway to inner improvisation.

- You will then be able to preserve this quality of inner improvisation (as it will become second nature) once the director shapes the *mise-en-scène*.

Stage Three:
Finding the Fun and the Physical Actions: Self-works

In retrospect, the first two projects had very clear objectives. Through his work on *The Tempest*, Filozov had connected the actor's personality with the script by engaging in a game. With *The Great Divorce*, Filozov had located and unblocked the actor's raw materials through awakening affective memory and finding tangible situations for philosophical fables. In this third project, Filozov focused primarily on concrete *physical actions*. He defined these as 'very definite actions executed in such a way that there is essentially a dual dialogue between words and actions, where sometimes the actions might almost contradict the words.' This was still the first component of Filozov's programme – the actor's work on *him or her self in a role* – before the journey would continue beyond personality into the *character's* individuality. The nature of this work went hand in hand with Ananyev's invitation to re-negotiate even the most simple movements in our bodies before striving to find the 'fragrance' of the role. We had to remember how to be ourselves before we could transform that re-negotiated self into other characters. To this end, Filozov asked each actor to choose a short extract from a play with which he or she felt a vibrant affinity.

Work on self-selected pieces (Self-Works) was practised throughout all the acting courses at VGIK, the reason for which was summed up by the Institute's Pro-Rector, Tatiana Storchak. She said, 'You are asked to examine Self-Works in rehearsal in order that you can construct and perform the piece of your choice and use elements of Stanislavsky's system in your rehearsals, without opposing or invading your spiritual state and your logical, individual understanding of a role. To help you, your pedagogue gives you certain elements of the method, which will be a tool, a device for your acting later on.' (It's interesting to note how this academic historian, allegedly ex-KGB, again emphasised the significance of the actor's 'spiritual state' without any coyness in using the term. It's also interesting how 'spiritual state' and 'logical understanding' were seen as two necessary halves of a whole.)

Although it wasn't clearly defined at the time, I could see in retrospect that the tool which Filozov explored through Self-Works was the Method of Physical Actions. Filozov's rehearsal practice was precisely that of Stanislavsky, when he said, 'Here is my approach to a new role . . . Without any reading, without any conferences on the play, the actors are asked to come to a rehearsal of it.'[129] As I mentioned in Chapter 1, there had been a huge outcry at the Moscow Art Theatre, when Stanislavsky had first introduced this instantaneous approach to text. Nemirovich-Danchenko had written to him in despair, declaring, 'You wanted actors to go on the stage and act bits of the play *when neither they nor the director had any kind of images*!! You wanted to draw the material for the production from what they acted without any knowledge of the characters or of the overall tone. So that out of this weird acting by actors, whose gifts and natures you know down to the last detail, you can draw a new original tone for the production!'[130]

This was exactly what Filozov intended with the Self-Works.

All actors chose one or two pieces (mine being Pinter's *The Lover* and Wilde's *Salome*) as well as acting in those selected by others. Because the extracts came from a variety of sources – including Tennessee Williams' *A Streetcar Named Desire*, Howard Barker's *Seven Lears*, Chekhov's *Uncle Vanya*, Sebastian Barry's *Boss Grady's Boys* – many of them were unknown to the others in the group, and particularly to Filozov. Before we started rehearsals, he simply asked the actor who had chosen a particular piece to describe it, in as much or as little detail as he or she wanted. At first this struck me as incredibly blasé: how on earth could he rehearse extracts in a language that was foreign to him without knowing the material he was working with? In fact, his approach was strongly reminiscent of Michael Chekhov's method in 1950s' America, as described by film star, Mala Powers: 'Chekhov never read my scripts. He would say to me, "Now, tell me about the script". And I would describe my character and tell him the plot of the play. I wasn't aware until much later that as I quite simply and spontaneously described my character and the story, I was showing him exactly how I was going to play the part. Later still, I realized that an artist's creative imagination goes into high gear when he or she describes the play and the character before having had a chance to "think" about it, before forming intellectual preconceptions.'[131]

After I'd struggled in my pidgin Russian to describe the convolutions of Pinter's *The Lover*, Filozov intuitively grasped the through-line of the play. He provided me with imaginative insights and ingenious directions arising purely from the cursory knowledge that I'd sketched in my outline. By taking the basic given circumstances of each scene, with minimal reference to the play *in toto*, Filozov invited each actor to discover the appropriate actions which would propel him or her through the chosen scene and motivate the on-stage relationship. At first, this process went completely against the grain of my over-conscientious need to analyse an entire script before I could possibly discuss a character's motivations. In practice, it proved to be remarkably freeing: all you had to do was to listen to your partner. You had no choice but to pay attention to the moment-by-moment unfolding of the action, as there was absolutely no cerebral knowledge-base to fall back on, there was no safety-net of cosy homework. If you were acting in somebody else's extract, you might know nothing but the five pages of dialogue that you'd read for the first time five minutes earlier. It was thrilling to swim in the 'terrifying unforeseen', and a complicity on stage inevitably arose as the actors sounded out each other's physical actions.

Action or activity? *Salome* and *Boss Grady's Boys*

At first it wasn't absolutely clear to be honest what was meant by physical action (often translated by Kamotskaya as 'concrete action'). At no point did Filozov give this rehearsal approach a name and, as I've said, I knew nothing about the Method of Physical Actions or Active Analysis until I came back home to England and retrospectively investigated Stanislavsky's techniques. The result of our uncertainty was that our interpretation of concrete action was rather literal. We did lots of smoking cigarettes, making cups of tea, applying lipstick and powder, and other fairly naturalistic details. In effect, however, these were closer to *activities* than to physical actions. This confusion became clear with the 'concrete action' I'd chosen for the episode from Wilde's *Salome*, in which Herod inveigles Salome to dance. I suggested that we staged the scene on a long banquet table, beneath which Iokanaan sat playing a pipe. The table was strewn with vegetable debris from a feast and, out of this garbage, I – as Salome – picked up a cabbage and a knife. Throughout the speeches in which Herod pleads with Salome to dance for him, I carved a face out of the cabbage, pushing a carrot in for a nose, two segments of cucumber into its eye sockets and a sliver of apple peel as ruby red lips. Not until Salome's line, 'I am ready, Tetrarch', did I turn the cabbage round to reveal what my concrete action had been. Although Filozov enjoyed the theatricality of the image, I realised in retrospect that it wasn't entirely what was meant by 'concrete physical action'. My activity had very little connection with the ensemble or the real inner tensions of the piece. I enjoyed doing it and it happily served the purpose of occupying me during Herod's long speeches. But I hadn't considered any psychological investment in the activity, in terms of what I was doing to my on-stage partner. In fact, to be perfectly honest, I wasn't really interested in what Herod was saying, I was having far too much fun with my cabbage head. Nonetheless, the parallel classes with Ananyev, in which he introduced the idea of objects as partners, provided the necessary theatricality, and the scene wasn't without its success.

It was really through observing Filozov's work with Tom and Danny on Sebastian Barry's *Boss Grady's Boys* that I realised how the carving of the cabbage had been an activity rather than the pursuit of a physical action. The shift is actually very simple, but it's necessary: an *activity* may become a *physical action* through the pursuit of a psychological objective. The scene from *Boss Grady's Boys* involved two old shepherd boys, who live together in a hovel. In exploring the encounter, Tom and Danny sought strange pastimes to occupy the two chaps. When Tom suggested that he made tea as his concrete action, Filozov took the timbre of the piece (with its weird backwoods atmosphere) and suggested various eccentricities in what would otherwise be very normal naturalistic activities. These were very simple ideas, such as the ritualistic heaping of many teabags into the pot. Then on one occasion, when Tom brought herbal teabags on strings to the rehearsal, Filozov suggested that he attached a pencil to the string and used the teabag as a fishing-rod in his mug. As each action became increasingly odd, Tom's character sought to provoke, to entertain, to annoy, to distract Danny, who imperturbably read his paper, poured his tea, removed his socks and went to bed. Their ongoing 'score' of physical actions presented a dialogue which extended beyond the spoken words: all the time that Tom's absurd actions were attempting to elicit attention, Danny's actions illustrated his immeasurable calm and his tedious ritual, impervious to his room-mate's antic distractions.

The text, to which these physical actions formed an accompaniment, talked of sheepdogs and fires and the mundane occupations of the shepherds' lives. In fact the first time the boys improvised the text – before we'd really assimilated the concept of physical action – Tom had simply sat by the fire and recounted the tales to Danny. The scene was visually uninteresting and textually uninspiring – the performers seemed to be as bored by it as the spectators. But as soon as they found this curious montage of physical actions, the interaction between the characters revealed their history, their tedium, their intimacy and the inherent humour of the piece: yet the text was quite unchanged. Of course this is any director's job: to find a means of manifesting a play to make it visually interesting, to make sense of the words and to find multi-layers if appropriate. All that Filozov was doing was reminding the actors that a script needn't be taken at face value: by creating a juxtaposition between psycho-physical action and spoken word, the on-stage picture can become textured and unexpected. In this way, the performers can experience the real dynamic between text and partner, objective and action.

Uncle Vanya: contradictory life of the human spirit on stage

What really fascinated and delighted Filozov, as an actor and a tutor, was the unexpectedness of human behaviour. For him, the essence of physical actions lay in uncovering that unpredictability, whether the circumstances are everyday occurrences or something out-of-the-ordinary. One story in particular revealed his inspirational understanding of human behaviour: 'There was a friend of mine who, at the time of the Missile crisis, was in Cuba. One day they were lying in wait for the Americans to fly over. It was warm there, so my friend went to a puddle to wash his socks – he hadn't had clean socks for two days. Just at that moment, the American planes flew over and started to bomb. Out of pure fear, my friend mechanically continued to wash his socks in the puddle . . . because it was absolutely pointless to run away, they would have shot him. So he just sat there and washed his socks. After that, the Commandant said to him, "Signor, you are such a brave person, our soldiers are ashamed! Please could you not do that any more!" But the way he behaved in that moment came from pure fear, not bravery. He should have run away, shouting, but he couldn't – he just sat there washing his socks.'

This was precisely the unexpectedness of physical action which Filozov sought when breathing the life of the human spirit into a character on the stage. So in some respect, the physical action can be seen as something which colours the text, which undercuts the text, which manifests the subtext and which provokes emotion through its simple execution. Filozov's dynamic montage of word and physical action became particularly clear for me when Danny and I worked on Act Two of *Uncle Vanya*. It was the scene in which Sonya and Doctor Astrov are talking late at night, and he recalls the death of one of his patients under chloroform. In the course of the scene, Sonya subtly tries to draw Astrov's attention to the fact that she's in love with him. Through Filozov's work on *Uncle Vanya*, I began to understand the subtle differences between the Method of Physical Actions and Active Analysis.

For Filozov, the essence of this scene was Astrov's dilemma: 'To drink more vodka or not to drink more vodka. A Russian tale of everyday life.' Although Astrov has a number of long philosophical speeches, Filozov was adamant that the scene was not about Astrov's pontifications on life. To prevent us from falling into this trap, he led Danny towards a simple, achievable physical action – to refill his glass or not to refill his glass? This action served as a counter-point to Astrov's preoccupation with himself; it's his self-obsession at this moment which prevents him seeing that next to him is a potentially wonderful life-partner. As Filozov put it, 'Astrov has decided that he's behaving ignorantly in his life like a parasite, and he needs to *do* something to get his energy back. So he's talking, talking, talking to try and find what it is that he needs to do. In fact this scene is a very important moment for the character of Astrov, but I've seen it played in the theatre where usually they drink a little and then they philosophise for half an hour and it's all very boring.' The concrete action of sinking a bottle of vodka provides the actor with a physical backdrop, a physical dilemma, which stops the scene plummeting into generalised philosophising.

Finding physical actions needn't just be a visual texturing of a philosophical passage. By locating the appropriate physical action, an actor can ally him or her self with a character using very little effort. As Stanislavsky put it, 'To achieve this kinship between the actor and the person he is portraying, add some concrete detail which will fill out the play, giving it point and absorbing action.'[132] I discussed in Chapter 1 the way in which an actor can catalogue these physical actions throughout a script, so that a psychological objective can be fulfilled 'with a whole series of small, almost exclusively *physical* objectives (getting out of the carriage, ringing the doorbell, running up the stairs).' This catalogue of minor and major objectives is what Stanislavsky called the *score of the role*.[133] Compiling a score of physical actions is simply a matter of identifying a character's psychological objective and then breaking it down into manageable physical tasks. This was how Filozov led me through the scene from *Uncle Vanya*. He began by asking, 'What does Sonya want in this scene?' to which I replied that she wants to detain Astrov in her company for as long as possible. He then asked, 'And how does she do that?' My reply was, 'By making the room as inviting and comfortable as possible.' 'And how does she do *that*?' pursued Filozov. 'By offering Astrov some food and maybe lighting a candle,' I replied. And so gradually we identified my objective and pieced together the logical and coherent order of concrete physical actions needed to attain that objective.

Before long, I realised that an organic score of physical actions, discovered through unraveling what you want from your on-stage partner, had the potential to lead an actor dynamically and smoothly along the through-line of a scene towards the objective. In turn, an imaginative through-line of actions could arouse truthful emotion on the stage. With each improvisation, you can test the appropriateness or otherwise of each action, and adjust it accordingly. Stanislavsky maintained that if you 'work out a full score of inner and outer actions . . . you can be certain real tears will come to you.'[134] But you work them out through doing the scene, through 'on-your-feet' questioning. It doesn't need to be a telephone directory.

From demonstration to personalisation

Through Filozov's implementation of the Method of Physical Actions, it soon became clear that the application of a score of physical actions was a very delicate process. With the *Uncle Vanya* scene, Filozov's intimate knowledge of Chekhov's play led to a vivid and rather idiosyncratic interpretation, and gradually he began to take more of a directorial role than a pedagogical one. In retrospect, this seemed to be deliberate, though at the time it was rather disconcerting, as he started to give a very specific structure to the scene in terms of the score of physical actions. Some of the external actions stemmed directly from the text, as Sonya 'hunts in the sideboard' for food and Astrov 'gets a bottle out of the sideboard' and 'Pours a glass.' These were the playwright's signposts as to how the characters might manifest their objectives: Sonya wants to take care of Astrov, ideally as his wife; Astrov wishes to dispel his self-doubt, temporarily by getting drunk.

Some of Filozov's images for this scene were so specific that his teaching technique often included *demonstration* of particular moments. This confused me, given all the emphasis to date on improvisation, and finding an organic *mise-en-scène* through attention to the partner, and pursuing objectives through actions. What I didn't really appreciate at the time was that we weren't required to *imitate* his interpretation; all Filozov was doing was indicating how an actor might *personalise* a role. *Personalisation* was the process he was hoping to activate within each of us. Michael Chekhov (also a director as well as an actor) advocated that it's perfectly acceptable for a director to show his actors what he wants them to do by acting it out for them. 'The actors, if they are trained according to the suggested method, will easily understand what the director shows them, and will grasp its essence. They will not need to copy their director outwardly, as might be the case with purely external actors.'[135] Certainly, Stanislavsky advises that actors should never accept directions in the form in which they're presented. He states quite categorically, 'Do not allow yourself simply to copy them. You must adapt them to your own needs, make them your own, truly part of you. To accomplish this is to undertake a large piece of work, involving a whole new set of given circumstances and stimuli'.[136] Those new given circumstances and stimuli are, of course, your own imaginative connection with the script and all those psycho-physical factors, which make you *you*, and not the director who's demonstrating.

Rather than being a contradiction of Filozov's previous work methods, this process could therefore be seen as a continuation. He assumed that the actors' developing psycho-physical awareness would prevent them falling back on imitating him and instead would enable them to personalise the actions that he'd demonstrated. There's a certain vitality needed when you're executing a score of physical actions, which Grotowski sums up by saying that 'Theatre is an encounter. The actor's score consists of the elements of human contact: 'give and take'. Take other people, confront them with oneself, one's own experiences and thoughts, and give a reply. In these somewhat intimate human encounters there is always this element of 'give and take'. The process is repeated, but always *hic et nunc* [here and now]: that is to say it is never quite the same.'[137] So you don't have to adhere absolutely to the score of physical action. In fact, you can't. If you're really living in the psycho-physical moment, your limitless attention to your partners means that you're constantly making spontaneous adaptations, because in every moment *they* adapt.

This was something that Danny, playing Astrov, was particularly skilled at doing. He took Filozov's score of physical actions, personalised it, and on each occasion adapted it to the *hic et nunc* – the 'transient now'.[138] I discovered this during one rehearsal of the *Vanya* scene, and it led me to realise just how cerebrally-bound I still was. Having mentally constructed my score of physical actions, I found it incredibly difficult to accommodate the nuances of my partner's performance. My psycho-physical technique wasn't sophisticated enough yet to appreciate the freedom of Danny's spontaneous changes.

Striving (as Sonya) to create an ambience in which Danny/Astrov would want to stay, I felt completely inadequate when, in this particular rehearsal, he resisted sitting at the table and striking up an intimacy with me. I didn't know where to put myself physically. In previous rehearsals, he'd complied with my unspoken invitation and had sat down to talk, but this time – no!

In some ways, we were *both* living in the 'transient now', as I certainly hadn't pre-determined my overwhelming sense of inadequacy. The trouble was that I thought that I felt inadequate as the *actress*, rather than as the *character*. The inner policeman was doing overtime again, telling me that my physical inactivity was surely visually dull. I'd never attain my objective if I stood there looking like a lemon, just because Danny/Astrov wasn't complying with our previously executed *mise-en-scène*.

What was *actually* happening was that the inner tension created by my sense of impotence was completely in accord with the character's experience. Sonya is desperately trying to have some kind of influence, attractive pull, persuasive affect on Astrov, and he just doesn't see it. What suddenly struck me like a bolt from the blue was that the whole point about psycho-physical technique is that it requires absolute trust of whatever emotion the actor spontaneously experiences in the life of the on-stage character. In his book, *The Technique of Inner Action*, Bill Bruehl writes that 'The truly spontaneous response is *always* appropriate, without qualification. And how do you know it was appropriate? What is the test? Exhilaration. If the actors feel exhilarated by the interaction rather than bored or self-conscious, the response is spontaneous.'[139] Although I wouldn't have registered my sense of frustration on that day as a kind of exhilaration, I did suddenly realise that there was something happening, *hic et nunc*. These were *true feelings*: they came from the human raw material of the actor and, by turning the crystal and seeing them from a different perspective, they could be transmuted into the appropriate experience for the character. That realisation *was* exhilarating, and it was another moment of *Eureka!* Psycho-physical technique validates the present tense:

whatever is happening here and now is the material with which you work. You've already done all the homework, which supplies the structure for the present-tense encounter. But you don't have to *play* that homework – in fact, as I've said before, you can't play that homework. Finding the sense of fun and playing those present-tense actions on your partner is the source of real creative exhilaration. That's when you sense that there's a spontaneous chemical reaction taking place between you and your partner. And it all occurs within the given circumstances of the script and the *mise-en-scène* of the production.

Filozov's implementation of the Method of Physical Actions through our Self-Works led to some exciting discoveries. Because we were exploring texts that we didn't necessarily know very well, it wasn't difficult to find a spirit of unexpectedness and spontaneity – a constant state of inner improvisation. When we came to perform the extracts, some of them had hardly been rehearsed. This was because, in our rehearsals, Filozov was looking to see whether the actors understood the heart of the scene. If they did – in other words, if the improvisations had unlocked the essence of the encounter – Filozov would simply say, 'Yes, you know that scene; now all you need to do is go away and learn the lines'. Provided that there were certain lynch-pins throughout the scene from which the structure could depend, the actors were invited to improvise the *mise-en-scène* during the performance. It required limitless attention to the partner, not only to understand what action was being played by one actor on the other, but also to keep an eye on the stage-picture being created. Again dual consciousness was necessary, in terms of the on-going dialogue between the Actor (Technician) and the Character (as discussed in Chapter 2): the improvised *mise-en-scène* had to be aesthetically pleasing when viewed from the auditorium, as well as psychologically true on the stage.

Tom and I found ourselves in this very situation with our extract from Pinter's *The Lover*. After a few rehearsals, in which we psycho-physically charted the score of physical actions, we went away and learnt the lines by reading the text innumerable times. During the performance, we simply attended to each other's games and allowed the games to lead us through the action. This added a particular frisson to the scene, in which a sense of danger and unpredictability is supposed to permeate the interaction between Sarah and her lover/husband. The air of uncertainty between me and Tom as performers created an almost tangible sense of excitement, which corresponded directly to the emotions experienced by the characters of Sarah and Richard/Max. And so, the playwright's games and our chosen physical action happily united text and performers, as a result of which we found (rather pleasurably) that appropriate sexy feelings were aroused.

In the first three projects – *The Tempest*, *The Great Divorce* and the selected Self-Works – Filozov wanted the actors to identify their own spirit and bring it to the text through (1) games, (2) affective memories and concrete situations and (3) physical actions. We'd been equipped with certain components of psychophysical technique including Active Analysis, 'limitless attention to the partner', the Method of Physical Actions, and a constant state of inner improvisation. Inevitably some degree of 'character' emerged from time to time in our experiments, but it wasn't until the final project that Filozov consciously guided us away from the work on *our selves* towards the creative individuality of the *character*.

Summary of the Key Components in Finding the Fun and the Physical Actions

- Through working on self-selected extracts, you can harness elements of Stanislavsky's 'system' without 'invading' your spiritual state and logical understanding of a role.

- Physical activity becomes physical *action* by the introduction of a psychological/dramatic effect, which the executor of the action (activity) wishes to have on his or her partner.

- Physical actions can create a dramatic montage with the play-text, revealing subtext and (if appropriate) humour or dramatic irony in textured and unexpected ways.

- Cleverly chosen physical actions can often reveal the true contradictions in natural behaviour, thus creating a dramatically interesting and psychologically reverberant *mise-en-scène*.

- A score of physical actions is discovered through improvisations; it is noted, repeated and tested for usefulness or truth, and retained or rejected accordingly.

- In the Method of Physical Actions and Active Analysis, what you feel here and now is legitimate material with which you can work. The challenge then is to find the appropriate physical actions to marry your own inner sensations with the dramatic action of the character. Games are often the means for achieving this.

Stage Four:
Releasing the character through *Crime and Punishment*

The final project was due to be presented as the culmination of the ten-month training programme. So Filozov encouraged each actor to take a tentative but necessary step beyond his or her everyday personality to experience the rhythms and energies of the created character. To this end, he chose the dark and dynamically psychological material of Dostoyevsky's *Crime and Punishment*. The development of Russian acting has always been intricately interwoven with social, historical and cultural events, so it was very important to the tutors that we explored their native material. The relevance of this was stressed by VGIK's Pro-Rector, Tatiana Storchak, who described how 'Russian literature is one of the parents of the Russian acting school, including the images of Dostoyevsky, Chekhov and Tolstoy, with the heavy emotional colouring of a character. And if you take this long journey into the inner state of the character, eventually you find something new about *yourself* in the role. Foreign students have to work on Russian material as we believe it's one of the principles of creating a new side to acting; therefore, it's very important for our actor-training.'

Filozov was specific in his choice of Dostoyevsky as being appropriate material for the culmination of our psycho-physical acting programme. He believed that Dostoyevsky is so psychologically rich as a writer, that 'you can't just show emotions – you'll find you actually feel them. When you start to feel it, that's when you stop showing, and that's when you find the "life of the human spirit", as Stanislavsky says.' It was this 'life of the human spirit' which Filozov now wished us all to find through the 'creative individuality' of our characters.

As I mentioned in Chapter 3, our group had gradually diminished over the course of the ten months, so that a hard-core of four now remained in the ensemble. Vivien took the role of Katerina Marmeladova, the eccentric and fastidious widow with not a kopeck in the world and a house full of children; Danny was the student Rodion Raskolnikov, the Nietzschian anti-hero, who murders an old money-lender and her sister, Lizaveta, because they are 'lice'. Tom played Porfiry Petrovich, the cheerfully sly detective in the Criminal Investigation section dealing with the murders; and I was Sonya Marmeladova, the religious prostitute, to whom Raskolnikov confesses his murders. Katya Kamotskaya joined the ensemble to play Raskolnikov's sister, Dunyasha, along with a wonderful Serbian actor, Serge, taking the role of Arkady Svidrigaylov, who shadows Raskolnikov, and attempts rape on Dunyasha before committing suicide. The emphasis of the adaptation shifted from a direct presentation of Dostoyevsky's narrative to an exposé of the relationships and power struggles inherent in the novel. Kamotskaya and Serge performed in Russian, the English-speaking actors performed in English, and Filozov directed in Russian as usual.

The first steps

Throughout the course, there had always been a very close connection between Kamotskaya's Actor-Training sessions and Filozov's approach to physical action. The staging of *Crime and Punishment* developed from that connection, and in fact Kamotskaya took responsibility for the early rehearsals. The preliminary session involved round-the-table discussion, which enabled us to pinpoint the essential scenes for the adaptation. For the second rehearsal, Kamotskaya asked each actor to bring one or two objects, which might provide powerful springboards into characterisation. Continuing Ananyev's idea of Dialogues with an Object, we were to choose items which we felt might provoke the inner life of the *character*, and (in return) could be endowed with imaginative meaning for us as *actors*. So there was a two-way street: we were beginning for once with character, and allowing choices we made on the character's behalf to provoke our own sensations and imaginations. For Sonya, I chose a Bible and a candle.

The second rehearsal began with an Actor-Training exercise, which involved us focusing our imaginations on our chosen objects, and observing which images arose, which sensations and associations were created, which affective memories were ignited. It was a chance to test whether these objects were as powerful in practice, as they seemed in theory. This exercise lasted for quite some time, and then we began to rehearse. Danny and I read the first encounter between Raskolnikov and Sonya; we then briefly discussed with Kamotskaya the dynamics between the characters, what their given circumstances were and what their objectives might be (i.e. what they wanted from each other). Then we got up and improvised it according to the first stage in Active Analysis.

In this first improvisation, Danny and I used our own words. Sometimes we stuck quite closely to the narrative of the scene, if that's where our encounter took us. Other times, we explored whatever imaginative directions the improvisation naturally led to. To be honest, I felt horribly ill-equipped to do this. When Kamotskaya said after the preliminary discussion, 'Now get up and do it,' I thought, 'Crikey, I haven't got enough textual information to start this kind of improvisation.' But Kamotskaya was reassuring: 'You'll know what you need to know.' At this stage, intuition could be far more revealing than cerebral knowledge. Michael Chekhov strongly encouraged an initially intuitive approach, in the belief that when we first encounter a role, we musn't allow our intellect to take part. 'We just have to fight it mercilessly,' he wrote; 'we must become in this first part of the work somehow foolish. Really there is a fool within us which creates . . . If you really trust yourselves, in an hour you can create a part.'[140] The significance of intuition is perhaps where Active Analysis differs from the Method of Physical Actions, where cerebral analysis is still dominant in fixing the score of physical actions. The Method of Physical Actions can almost be seen as a transitional phase in Stanislavsky's development between Round-the-Table analysis and the highly holistic approach of Active Analysis, where *experience* of a scene predominates.

This is where the power of Dostoyevsky's writing really did seem to bear fruits. Because we appealed to the psycho–physical experience of *doing* the scene as opposed to cerebral analysis, we found an immediate and profound engagement with each other and with our characters. Although beforehand I'd thought I didn't know the text well enough to improvise anything, the psychological truth of Dostoyevsky's characterisations was so well-defined that we effortlessly retained much of the original text even during this first improvisation. It may be that our understanding of the psycho–physical approach had developed now, to the extent that we trusted the process, we trusted each other and we trusted our own intuition. Certainly, after the improvisation had finished, I was suddenly aware of how empty my head was – my inner policeman had gone on leave.

From actor-training to rehearsal

After the first week, Filozov took over rehearsals, although Kamotskaya began every session with some kind of Actor-Training. For this training, each actor created his or her own area in the studio with the particular props and essential furniture appropriate to each character. They didn't have to be the same objects that we'd chosen for the initial exercises; we were working on Ananyev's principle that when an actor is psychophysically open, everything can become a partner – props, set, music, lighting, and, of course, other actors. Tom chose a mahogany desk and a musical box for Porfiry Petrovich in his formal police office. Danny selected a broken bench and a grubby old blanket for Raskolnikov in his pokey attic room. Vivien found a wooden sewing box and an old table for Katerina Marmeladova in her cluttered kitchen, and I chose a box of tin soldiers and a stained mattress for Sonya in her squalid quarters. Once the small 'living areas' were established, each actor then engaged in the Circles of Attention exercise: listening to their own thoughts, listening to the sounds in the room, the building, the street, etc. During this exercise, I discovered that Sonya's attention was most alert to sounds outside the room, responding, startled, like a frightened animal. As and when we were ready to – each at his or her own pace – we began to expand our personal circles of attention and connect with the others in the studio. This allowed simple connections between two or more characters gradually to lead on to improvisations of the scenes. Since each actor/character had established his or her own living area, it was a question of 'visiting' each other's spaces and using dialogue from respective scenes. Sometimes Danny would come to my 'hovel', and we might begin the encounter between Raskolnikov and Sonya, in which he asks her to read from the Bible. Or we might simply sit in silence sensing each other's presence.

Sonya and Raskolnikov: reading the Bible

Filozov was adamant that these scenes from *Crime and Punishment* were not just dialogues of text, they were dialogues of human energies, so it was very important that the actors didn't play what he called 'psychological literature'. To avoid this, he encouraged us to find the elements of game, which had been explored in *The Tempest*. Because the character of Sonya seemed to be so psychologically dark, it was difficult at first for me to find this quality of playfulness. However, it wasn't long before Danny's openness as an actor, as well as his interpretation of Raskolnikov's challenging directness with Sonya, provoked the necessary adaptability in me.

Two encounters between Sonya and Raskolnikov were included in the adaptation: the first scene was the one in which he asks her to read the story of Lazarus from the Bible, and the second scene was his confession of the double murder. In the early, improvisation-based rehearsals, we soon discovered that, if we paid limitless attention to one another, it was possible to accommodate each other's spontaneity, at the same time as being close enough to the text to allow both of us to explore our respective characters. There had to be a strong sense of complicity – free improvisation, but with enough structure to enable us to go deep into what the author had provided. In many respects, it was Danny's natural ability to be in a constant state of inner improvisation which enhanced my own freedom on the stage. There was always a kind of game between us; as Stanislavsky put it, 'as long as we are on the stage, we are in an unending contact with one another, therefore our adjustments to each other must be constant.'[141] Although we remained within the given circumstances of the characters, there was a simultaneous unseen game going on between us as performers. It made the on-stage interaction vital and exciting.

This contact struck me full in the face on two occasions when we were rehearsing the scene about the Bible reading. The encounter begins by Raskolnikov arriving unexpectedly at Sonya's quarters, much to her shame and anguish. After disparaging her accommodation, Raskolnikov asks her if her mother, Katerina, used to beat her. This distresses Sonya beyond words as her life is devoted to her mother and siblings, just as it was to her father before he was killed recently in a road accident, and Sonya describes how he used to ask her to read to him. Raskolnikov taunts Sonya by telling her that it won't be long before her mother dies, too; both she and Sonya's sister, Polechka, have consumption, and – in spite of all the money that Sonya tries to earn by walking the streets – mother and child will soon die. In this way, Raskolnikov keeps twisting Sonya's heart. At the same time, he notes that there are only three options for her: 'to fling herself into the canal, to end up in a madhouse or to abandon herself to debauchery that will numb her mind and turn her heart to stone'. Suddenly he asks her if she prays to God; at the mention of God, Sonya becomes extremely agitated, silencing him with the accusation that he is unworthy to speak of God. But still he can't keep silent. Almost as if he's pulling the legs off a spider, Raskolnikov pursues his taunting, asking Sonya what God can possibly do for her, wretched as she is. Picking up an old leatherbound Bible (given to her, ironically, by Lizaveta, the murdered sister of the money-lender), he asks her to read the story of Lazarus. After two failed attempts, Sonya at last begins to read, her voice breaking 'like an overstrained violin string'.

The inner and outer action in the scene is full of contradictions and conflicts, rendering it deliciously dramatic material and easily accessing big emotional responses within both of the characters. The first two times that we improvised the scene, Danny/Raskolnikov presented me with an algebra book for a Bible, demanding that I/Sonya read the story of Lazarus from it. The first time he did it, I wanted to laugh and ask how he thought I could possibly do it. The second time, it was deeply distressing. I was suddenly struck by how cruel he was being. More than that – it felt *sadistic* that he was trying to make me do something which I couldn't possibly do: read a Bible story from an algebra book. Each of these occasions unconsciously demanded inner adjustments, the result of which was a different and spontaneous emotional sensation. There must have been something different about each interaction, some exchange of energies between us which meant that the first time amused me and the second time confused me. As Stanislavsky proposes, it's when we are concerned with a constant interchange of thoughts, feelings and adjustments that the subconscious comes into the picture.[142]

Porfiry Petrovich and Raskolnikov: 'Don't put your money in a different bank'

As I've already suggested, this 'constant interchange of thoughts and feelings' requires the performers' complicity in the free improvisations, so that there's a delicate balance between the needs of the actors and the given circumstances of the characters. If this balance between character and actor isn't finely tuned, it becomes very difficult to find the characters' creative individuality. This is what happened with Danny as Raskolnikov and Tom as Porfiry Petrovich; they were working on the scene in which Raskolnikov visits the police station and Porfiry attempts to elicit a confession of murder from him.

Throughout the ten-month programme, Filozov had encouraged the actors to find games and constant improvisation. But with any directive, there has to be a sense of balance. Tom had found a fantastic sense of play and eccentricity in *Boss Grady's Boys*, but what had worked with that somewhat absurdist text wasn't necessarily appropriate for Porfiry Petrovich. There were, however, some moments in this scene from *Crime and Punishment* when his eccentric mischief was wonderful and fascinating. Every time that Danny/Raskolnikov began to speak during one improvisation, Tom/Porfiry opened his music box and began to eulogise over the beauty of the tinny music. The ensuing tension was powerful and exciting, particularly as it was ambiguous as to whether it was the actors' tension or that of the characters. Sometimes, though, Tom's interpretation of Filozov's directive to find a game grew rather too quirky to apply to all encounters. It became almost the actor's trademark, making it harder and harder to step beyond personality to find the character's individuality.

An interesting dynamic began to develop between the two actors. Whilst Tom's Porfiry became increasingly eccentric, Danny's Raskolnikov became increasingly taciturn. In our early improvisations of the Raskolnikov/Sonya scenes, Danny and I had found that we followed the text fairly closely, as the writer's words just seemed to lead us effortlessly to the heart of the encounters. Here, however, Tom and Danny seemed to take a different inroad into their scene. Their references to the text became fewer and fewer as their improvisations led them to explore atmosphere and emotion in a more general, tangential way. Initially this led to some interesting discoveries, but the balance between improvisational freedom and textual structure was overturned. With each improvisation, they seemed to travel further and further away from Dostoyevsky's intention. The aim of Active Analysis is that the improvisations bring you closer and closer to the playwright's words, to the point where the most succinct way of expressing the characters' physical actions and psychological objectives is, of course, the script itself.

Little by little, the actors seemed to lose sight of what the point of the improvisations was, until, at the end of one particular session, each actor admitted that they hadn't received from the other what they needed for the scene to move logically forward. They'd reached an impasse. Danny's response to Tom's overtly sinister Porfiry was to remain silent, knowing that he, as Danny the actor, was powerful in his silence. This dynamic wasn't really appropriate to Raskolnikov, and Filozov accused him of 'putting his money in another bank'. He was referring to the improvisation set up by Stanislavsky's semi-fictional 'Tortsov', in *An Actor Prepares*, in which he tells the students that the bank has burnt down. Everyone begins running all over the stage in a state of dire distress. Except one student, who sits quite calmly. When asked why he remained so calm, the student replied that it didn't worry him that the building had burnt down – he'd put his money in another bank. This was in fact cheating, as Tortsov declared that it didn't accommodate the necessary given circumstances of the improvisation. And that's what was happening here with Tom (Porfiry) and Danny (Raskolnikov).

What Filozov was doing at this point in the programme was taking the next step in psycho-physical development; he was now talking overtly about 'playing the character'. Danny and Tom were certainly paying attention to each other and experiencing true emotional responses. But they weren't embracing the needs of the characters and the given circumstances of the text. Without assimilating crucial facets of the characters, it was impossible for them to find the through-line of the scene. They were both 'putting their money in another bank.' Since neither of the actors seemed to be prepared to take the first step towards 'the character', they remained locked in a battle of personalities.

From personality to creative individuality

An actor's personality is, of course, a crucial weapon in his creative armoury. However, Michael Chekhov's vision of *creative individuality* begins with the subconscious or 'higher self' moulding and reassessing the actor's raw material, (i.e. his or her personality, voice and imagination). It's this reassessment – or even 're-assembly' – of the actor's instrument, which can prompt inner activity. Chekhov believed that *creative individuality* 'grants you genuine feelings, makes you original and inventive, awakens and maintains your ability to improvise. In short, it puts you in a creative *state*. You begin to act under its inspiration. Everything you do now surprises you as well as your audience; all seems new and unexpected. Your impression now is that it is happening spontaneously and that you do nothing but serve its medium of expression.'[143] That kind of spontaneous activity sounds marvellous, but isn't it just too idealistic and far-fetched? I'd like to suggest that it isn't. Both Ananyev in his Scenic Movement discipline and Filozov through *Crime and Punishment* were providing us with the means to release the inspiration of our creative individuality.

However . . .

It took me some time in rehearsal to understand what Filozov meant when he said he didn't want 'psychological literature', as I didn't really know what was intended by concepts of *non-psychological playing* and *character*. My instinctive empathy for Sonya was drawn towards the darker side of her psychology, so that it was some time before I could find the lightness and openness that Filozov was advocating. He could see that I was struggling, that I was making everything rather significant and heavy, so he suggested that the key to Sonya's character lay in finding her inner 'child'. The thing about Sonya is that she doesn't probe Raskolnikov's motives; she doesn't question anything before speaking – everything just emerges immediately, unfiltered, like a child. Filozov firmly believed that if I could find this child-element, I would ignite Sonya's character, while still being totally true to my own feelings and to the sentiments of the novel. To some extent this corresponded to the quality of 'Child' that Ananyev had talked about in Scenic Movement, with relation to Eric Berne's three ego-states of Adult, Parent and Child (see Chapter 2). But, of course, you can't play an ego-state. Freedom from 'psychological playing' lay in the pursuit of the appropriate physical actions. While Filozov was aware of the pitiable state of Sonya's life, he was ardent in his belief that any pain surrounding her lay in the audience's perception of Raskolnikov's cruelty and in Sonya's total embrace of him despite that cruelty. In other words, if the actress can find the appropriate actions for the child, the audience will provide the psychology and emotion. Again, I could intellectually understand what Filozov was saying, but I couldn't quite figure out how to put it into practice.

To help me with the complex transition from personality to creative individuality, Filozov asked me to make a very technical transformation: he directed me to lighten my vocal timbre. At first, his advice seemed completely phoney to me: after all this organic work we'd been doing, he suddenly wanted me to put on a funny voice? Something in my brain did not compute. But he was adamant: first of all the actor has to locate him or her self in a role (which I felt I had) and find the trigger which activates his or her connection with it (which I felt I had). If that psychological work has been done, it shouldn't be intrusive making *technical* adjustments to shift the perspective from the actor's personality to the character's individuality. If the actor's psycho-physical motor is fully functional, these adaptations can be made in such a way that they are intrinsic to the character and in no way superimposed.

In addition to changing Sonya's voice, Filozov gave me another important piece of advice: I didn't need to be emotional with the part. Although Dostoyevsky describes Sonya as 'almost wailing . . . despairingly wringing her hands in excitement and distress',[144] Filozov pointed out that those descriptions are *literature* and the actor cannot play literature on the stage. He was wise in giving me this advice. Since the work on *The Great Divorce*, I'd discovered that my emotional reservoirs had been released and that that particular part of my psycho-physical mechanism was fairly active. The danger then was that, at any available opportunity, I'd start weeping on stage. Filozov insisted that if I was really going to make the transition from the limits of my own personality to the character of Sonya, this emotion had to be contained. On those occasions in rehearsals when I'd found myself crying, Filozov conjectured that it was *my reaction* to Sonya, and not *Sonya's experience* of a situation. They were my tears for Sonya, not Sonya's tears: she doesn't focus on her own suffering and hopelessness, she doesn't cry out of self-pity. Sure enough, the combination of Filozov's directives (1) to find the child by changing the vocal timbre and (2) to detach from the emotions of psychological literature, set in motion a curious transition into a creative individuality. Although the process of emotional detachment was disconcerting at first, I soon realised just how appropriate it was for Sonya. All I had to do was to locate the inner and outer actions of the scene and execute them openly. I didn't have to worry about emotion.

Sometimes an action was as simple as 'to watch Raskolnikov' – in disbelief, with incredulity, in shame or with horror. What I *then* discovered was that when Raskolnikov directed this kind of intense observation back on Sonya, her sense of self completely disintegrated. The experiential process of Active Analysis had unlocked something very useful. I realised that Sonya can only exist by channelling her energies into other people. The consequence of that outward-flowing attention is that the real moment of penetrating pain occurs when Raskolnikov shines the spotlight back on her. Perhaps the most painful words in the novel are when he tells her that all her efforts are futile: 'That you are a great sinner is true, but your greatest sin is that you have abandoned and destroyed yourself *in vain*. Is that not a horror? Is it not a horror that you live in this filth which is so loathsome to you, whilst at the same time, you know that you are helping nobody by it, and not saving anybody or anything?'[145] As Danny/Raskolnikov drove home these painful truths, I understood that Sonya simply cannot bear to focus on her own pathetic existence. At that point, both action and psychology were fused.

The 'Method of Physicalisation'

It was from the realisation that Sonya can't bear the spotlight being turned on her life that I found her physicality began to develop. It was a subconscious development, largely due to my own physical receptivity being awakened in Ananyev's parallel Scenic Movement work. As my vocal timbre altered and as the psychological responses began to change, my body gradually adopted another form. I wasn't deliberately imposing this: the physical transformation arose purely from improvising the scene. It was strongly connected to Ananyev's work on wave movements from central to peripheral, and the correspondence between wave movements and the information we give and receive from the world at large. Sonya's connection with the world is very precarious. What happened during these rehearsals was that I kept wanting to occupy less space – I'd find that I was sitting very small, either curled up, scrunched up or with my hands tucked tightly in my lap. I rarely kept eye-contact with anyone, succeeding only when I knew the other person wasn't looking at me. Through Active Analysis, I discovered that my Sonya carried a lot of tension in the muscles of her shoulders, which I knew from Ananyev's classes were emotion-centres. It was as if she was trying to hide inside a shell, to contract her head into her body. Her centre of gravity constantly shifted between her two feet, as if she couldn't quite possess her own space, and she continually looked about her, alert, watching, questioning, like a frightened animal. Although on the page, it sounds as though I turned Sonya into a hunch-backed, quaking grotesque, in reality of course (I hope . . .) it was all much subtler.

While most of this physical work evolved of its own accord, it was necessary to boost it *consciously* from time to time in order to unleash the appropriate rhythm. I was aware that Sonya's character wasn't yet 'breathing for itself'; I knew I still hadn't found the right inner tempo-rhythm. Like Stanislavsky, Filozov believed that physical actions and tempo-rhythm were mutually dependent. So I decided to use some of the exercises in Ananyev's parallel Scenic Movement classes as a mini-laboratory in which to investigate Sonya's possible tempo-rhythm. During one of Ananyev's free improvisations, I discovered that the interactions between thought, feeling and action were very swift when I explored them with the quality of a child. Sonya seemed to be a mixture of contradictions, summed up by Dostoyevsky's description that, when Raskolnikov arrives at her apartment, 'She felt at once sick and ashamed and glad.'[146] Her absolute love for the murderer sends her from peaks of joy to depths of despair within moments. In other words, her inner tempo-rhythm was quick and extreme in its dynamics.

One of the scenes in our adaptation was the confession between Raskolnikov and Sonya. Filozov's understanding of tempo-rhythm led him to include various actions specified in the novel at certain moments during the dramatisation. He believed that if the actors executed those particular actions at those particular points, the appropriate emotion would be released. One of these instances was Sonya's realisation that Raskolnikov is

Lizaveta's murderer. At this point, Filozov insisted that we incorporated Dostoyevsky's 'stage direction': 'Suddenly, as if she had been stabbed, Sonya started, cried out, and flung herself, without knowing why, on her knees in front of him. "What have you done, what have you done to yourself?" she said despairingly, and, starting up, threw herself on his neck, embraced him, and held him tight.'[147] The repetition of the verb 'started' provided a clue to Sonya's tempo-rhythm. We did actually find this moment of prostration through improvisation, and I discovered that the physical impulse of Sonya flinging her arms around Raskolnikov really did release the appropriate, truly-felt emotion, without any recourse to affective memory or other psychological tools. It was an impulse from centre to periphery – a true declaration of Sonya's 'self'. The connection between body, mind and emotions was made by simply executing the specified action at a particular tempo-rhythm in the determined given circumstances of the scene. This was all facilitated by my having completed the necessary psycho-physical preparation.

Dual consciousness

Filozov suggested another technical 'trick' to stimulate inner action: I should try *smiling* at the top of the first encounter with Raskolnikov. Again, this sounded rather strange at first, as smiling certainly hadn't been my instinctive response as Sonya to seeing Raskolnikov here in my shameful rooms. In practice, however, I found that the simple concrete action of smiling juxtaposed the sense of shame. This, in turn, accessed the childlike openness which Filozov had been looking for and which contradicted my previous dark psychological reaction. Out of this childlike openness arose a vulnerability, as well as a kind of naïve hopefulness, both of which were wonderfully resonant for the character of Sonya.

Filozov certainly wasn't advocating a saccharine interpretation. In fact, quite the opposite; through her childlike openness, Sonya could have a cruel honesty. This provided me with another useful, potent springboard into the characterisation. I found that a kind of dual consciousness began to develop in rehearsal, as I became increasingly aware of moments when the *character's* energy was leading the scene and when my *own* personality was jutting out of the action like a broken sofa spring. From time to time, I would hear in my voice a sort of school-ma'am-ish disciplinarianism permeating the cruelty, a kind of intonation that didn't ring at all true for Sonya. Her cruelty and morality come from childish simplicity, not intellectual judgement; it may be true for *me* sometimes, but it just wasn't Sonya. What was happening was that, through the process of Active Analysis, I sensed the inappropriateness of a particular hand gesture or the harshness of a vocal expression within a split second of delivery. This then jolted my consciousness from character to technician. It was just as Stanislavsky described it: 'Every external movement which may be natural to an actor off-stage separates him from the character he is playing and keeps reminding him of himself.'[148] This isn't a *bad* thing: it's all part of the process of releasing the character's creative individuality. Shomit Mitter describes it as the moment when 'the actor "recognises" the character and thereby confirms his/her sense of its rightness – as though it conformed to some previously imagined plan.'[149] That was exactly how I felt: I was beginning to 'recognise' Sonya. The process of Active Analysis allows the sense of dislocation between character and self to become less and less. Each time you improvise the scene, the more you eliminate these moments of dislocation, coming closer to the character's creative individuality.

Crossing the threshold

In his book about Stanislavsky's 'protégé', Reuben Simonov quotes Evgeny Vakhtangov as saying that 'When an actor frees himself from his own personality, when his "I" becomes different, then his boldness, his freedom of scenic resourcefulness, is inexhaustible. The character's temperament prompts in the actor the most unexpected reactions and adjustments. The outer character moulds the feeling with lightning speed, no matter how unexpected it is, and directs it into the correct channel. It takes so much more courage for an actor to live in a strikingly characteristic image than to play the role *from himself*.'[150] Filozov's work had been a process of inspiring the actor to develop this 'courage'. He'd created the grounds in which true psycho-physical activity might flourish by inviting his actors to consider physical actions, tempo-rhythm and attention to the on-stage partner.

After six weeks of work on *Crime and Punishment*, I sensed the character's inner momentum developing a natural flow. I don't know what exactly prompted it, but during one rehearsal, I suddenly experienced a very powerful sensation of transformation, one which I had in no way consciously pre-determined. My voice sounded completely different, and I found myself speaking with a timbre that felt quite new. It really was as if somehow Sonya had 'found herself', to the extent that when Raskolnikov told her what a waste of a life her existence had been, that she had abandoned herself in vain, 'Sonya' began to weep. It was my body, my emotions, but absolutely Sonya's reasons. At that point, I understood Filozov's previous differentiation between *my reaction* to Sonya's predicament and *Sonya's experience* of her own situation. I also understood the true meaning of dual consciousness: all the time that I was involved in the scene, part of me was watching, enjoying wholeheartedly the satisfying feeling of 'transformation'.

It seemed as if Filozov's psycho-physical technique was at last beginning to reside within me: I'd found the faith to trust 'Sonya's' expressiveness, and the unexpectedness of the on-stage actions was liberating and exciting. I felt I could run with the wind. It corresponded to what Michael Chekhov calls the 'boundless sea of emotion'[151] that can open up within an actor when he or she is working with creative individuality. Russian actor-director, Alexei Popov, described this sensation as a 'reincarnation'. 'Reincarnation into the character,' he wrote, 'implies the mutual penetration of character and actor, i.e. the character created by the dramatist and the psycho-physical material of the actor.' He goes on to say that the result of this fusion is a new being, but one who lives completely 'within the framework of the theatre'.[152] This idea of living 'within the framework of the theatre' is very important. The reincarnation is simply a natural outcome of creating and working with the raw materials which are your own body, imagination and emotions. There's nothing psychotic or schizophrenic about it: all the time that the character is 'existing', the actor remains technically in control in just the way I discussed in Chapter 2 when talking about dual consciousness. The actor's technique (Actor-Parent) works collaboratively with the actor's own sense of self (Person-Adult) to liberate the life of the Character-Child.

This fusion of actor and character (or 'reincarnation') described the sensation I had of experiencing Sonya's momentum within my own psycho-physical apparatus. It was organic in its formation and exhilarating in my experience of it. In a practice reminiscent of Filozov's and born directly from Stanislavsky's own research, the Russian director, Georgi Tovstonogov, describes this very experience: 'The actor submits to the first law of reincarnation and begins work as himself; if he truly exists in the given circumstances, if for a long time he performs actions which are peculiar not to him but to the character, making them his own, then, at a certain stage in the assimilation of the role, a leap in quality occurs and something new appears, something which is essential to the role: the actor stops being himself and merges with the character. *The transformation occurs in his way of thinking, in his relationship to the surrounding work, in the rhythm of his life.*'[153] This is what I understood to be the Russian idea of working with 'the spirit'. And it was wildly exciting.

But for Filozov, the work didn't stop there. On sensing that my psycho-physical process was beginning to be activated, the final change that Filozov made to my interpretation of Sonya involved the Bible reading. He wanted me to bring a new subtlety to my reading of the Lazarus story. In our very first rehearsal of the scene, I'd found to my surprise that when I read the story (investing it imaginatively with the dreams of a child-prostitute) its effect was very potent. Suddenly I'd seen religion from Sonya's childlike perspective: the thought of Jesus being put to the test, afraid that God wouldn't answer him, the thought of the injustice of going through that humiliation and, until the last moment, believing God had forsaken him. These thoughts unleashed emotions that were more pertinent to Sonya than to me. And yet they were *absolutely me* in the sense that they were real human feelings, expressed by my body, and therefore part of my raw materials.

After that particular rehearsal, Filozov could see that I'd found some sort of trigger into the story, so the first phase of identification was complete. But now he sought a delicacy, a feeling of ease, *a secret*. Earlier in this chapter, I suggested that much of Filozov's skill as an actor lay in the textures that he brought to a character through his notion of 'secret'. Now he described to me how 'the Bible-story is Sonya's secret, her beautiful secret that fills her with joy and light when she reads it. *She* mustn't be dramatic – the emotional drama takes place within *Raskolnikov* and within *the audience*.' The implication was that the character's secret could lure the spectators into the workings of the character's mind, drawing them into both the play's dramatic narrative and the actor's inner action. At the same time, Filozov's idea for the reading was absolutely in keeping with the timbre of Dostoyevsky's original description: 'She was approaching the moment of the greatest, the unheard-of miracle, and was filled with immense triumph. Her voice rang like a bell with the power of triumph and joy.'[154] The sense of secret, combined with the visual juxtaposition of the Bible-reading child-whore and the delirious murderer, was in itself the theatricality of the piece. It needed no psychological emotion in my interpretation of Sonya. That was her creative individuality.

Summary of Key Components
in Releasing the Character

- Actor-Training sessions were incorporated into the early stages *Crime and Punishment*. Each actor found objects to create a living space for his or her character. Following Circles of Attention or the Five-Minute Recollection, a free improvisation unfolded, during which characters visited each other's spaces. Encounters ensued, using improvised text or words from the play if they arose.

- *'Don't put your money in a different bank'*: It is important with a rehearsal process incorporating Active Analysis that there is a complicity between the actors, in terms of the games played and the gradual progression from free improvisation to a structured improvisation of the playwright's text. A time must come when free research into the way in which the characters interact is replaced with an investigation into the structure and *mise-en-scène* of the text as it will ultimately be performed. If this development doesn't happen naturally, the actors need the guidance of the director or workshop leader.

- *Developing Creative Individuality*: Through technical adjustments, perhaps proposed by the director in terms of physical or vocal characterisations, or arising from the improvisations of Active Analysis, actors may take the step from personality into creative individuality.

- An emerging *physicalisation* can inform or illuminate a character's motivations, objectives and psychology.

- *Tempo-rhythm* (the speed of inner/outer action and its intensity) of language can also unlock creative individuality.

- Find *contradictions* – smiling in fear, pitying in scorn, etc. Such contradictions can unlock surprising discoveries and facilitate the step into 'creative individuality'

- Allow a transformation/incarnation to take place creatively, finding pleasure in the discoveries and always allowing your inner Parent-Technician to work in harmony with your spontaneous, creative 'Child'.

- Celebrate the unexpected. It illustrates that you are developing a sense of a constant state of improvisation.

The end

The work on *Crime and Punishment* illustrated how inspirational Active Analysis could be. All decisions regarding character, interpretation, staging, and to some extent set and lighting had come through the actors and director actively analysing the text on their feet in the rehearsal space. It hadn't always been easy and, given the workshop nature of the project, the right choices hadn't always been made. What was exciting, though, was the way in which each of the inner motive forces – the thought-centre (both intellect and imagination), the emotion-centre and the action-centre (or body) had been collaboratively and often unexpectedly harnessed in the process of active character research.

Looking back over the year – which, as I've said all along, was very experimental for tutors and participants alike – it was clear to see (through our failures as much as our successes) the extent to which our psycho-physicality had developed. When Filozov had tried to structure our work with *The Tempest*, we'd come a cropper, as we couldn't yet integrate the freedom of improvisation with the structure of directorial decisions. By the time we came to work on *Crime and Punishment*, that particular issue had become less significant. Active Analysis illustrated how each actor needs to take responsibility for finding his or her own connection with a character, but the crucial element is constant referral back to the script. Only by mining the text can an actor glean all the details which will take the character beyond an actor's own personality, beyond an author's own creation, into that union of both artists which is *the creative individuality of the character.*

Throughout his ten-month programme, Filozov aimed to connect each actor's personality with a dramatic text through games, affective memory, concrete situations and physical actions. By using these components, the raw material of true emotions could be aroused and invested into the life of the human spirit on the stage. Once the actor's psycho-physical mechanism was sensitive, the director could then make technical decisions to adapt the actor's raw materials to those of the playwright's character. The emphasis of all this work was on process, not result; on spirit, not material; on collaborative ensemble, not solitary success; and on creative individuality, not personality. Psychophysical work is delicate and precise, and different practitioners meet with varying degrees of success and proficiency. Ten months was really far too short a time to eliminate all the habits accumulated by each actor. And the fact that the group diminished from ten participants to four indicated the extent and rigour of the personal challenges. It was with a huge amount of trepidation that I returned to England. Would I remember everything that Ananyev, Kamotskaya and Filozov had taught me? Would I even be able to find work? If so, would I be able to incorporate the possibilities of Active Analysis into my work as an actor in the British theatre? It all remained to be seen . . .

ACT 5
Working in the Theatre

The sea, not an island

There are two given circumstances which have to be considered above anything else in rehearsal: what is the medium and who is the director? The medium dictates the way in which you make choices (usually dependent on the amount of rehearsal time you'll get) and the director's work-method is the ultimate guiding factor in how those choices may be made. At one extreme, some directors arrive at the read-through with the *mise-en-scène* planned out in great detail. At the other extreme, some directors enjoy the collaborative work of the creative team, to the extent that they may know little more at the start of rehearsal beyond what the chosen text is. Some directors encourage detailed detective work on the script through analysis of actions and objectives; others introduce a variety of improvisations or devised scenarios to access the text or to create the script from scratch. The pleasure of psycho-physical preparation is that, as an actor, you're physically, emotionally and imaginatively open to whatever circumstances you find yourself in, through media or directorial choice.

That's the ideal state, of course . . .

In practice, it isn't always so easy. Nonetheless, the joy of psycho-physical acting is that it begins from the premise that 'what I feel here and now is a valid and valuable starting point'. In other words, you're not left thinking, 'I work with oil paints, but this situation demands I use pastels', but rather, 'How can I use my oil paints to create the effects of pastels?' In this final chapter, I want to look at the use of psycho-physical techniques from the perspective of an actor in Britain. I've chosen two particular experiences immediately following my return from Moscow, both of which shared successes and failures. To some extent, they illustrate the fact that the difficulty with acting is that you're using your own self as your basic raw materials, and those raw materials are in a constant state of daily flux and development. Therefore, there can be no hard-and-fast implementation of exercises or ideas: what works on one occasion may not work on another. Underlying everything, however, there should be *a constant state of inner improvisation*: nothing need obstruct the actor, everything can be accommodated. Although I was isolated sometimes in terms of trying to implement a specific approach, that wasn't necessarily a problem. 'Don't be an island, be the sea that connects the other islands.'

From brain to body

I returned from Moscow as a 'born-again actress', driven by wild visions of how I could revolutionise my acting practice and seek converts. It wasn't long before I was cast in a season at the Swan Theatre in Worcester, a small but determined repertory theatre, with an interesting choice of plays and two lively, impassioned directors – Jenny Stephens and Mark Babych. Both directors incorporated aspects of Stanislavsky's system into their rehearsals in slightly different ways, and two of the roles in which I was cast (Masha in *The Seagull* directed by Jenny Stephens, and Josie in *Steaming* directed by Mark Babych) threw light on the strengths and difficulties of psycho-physical processes.

The Seagull was one of the first challenges which rose up in front of me shortly after my return. Like myself, Jenny Stephens was a graduate of Birmingham University, so we shared several points of contact in terms of our acting vocabulary. Rehearsals began with Stephens breaking the text down into sections, pragmatically determined by which characters were on stage during any one scene. Within these sections, actors were then invited to identify bits or, as she called them, 'units' – that is, where a character's objective is achieved or thwarted and consequently an intention changes. This is a fairly straight forward and quite common use of Stanislavsky system. Once the units had been determined, they were then given a label such as 'to shine a spotlight on Konstantin' or 'to invite intimacy'. Each actor named the unit according to his or her own objective, so that two or more actors could label the same unit using completely contradictory verbs. So, in the opening scene, my label (for a unit spanning from the top of the play until Sorin and Konstantin enter) was 'to repel Medvedenko', while the actor playing Medvedenko, Simon Wright, chose the label 'to embrace Masha'. Instantly, we'd unwittingly highlighted the contradictory inner dynamic of attraction and repulsion between these two characters.

Having defined these labels, the actors and director collaboratively identified moments of change within each unit, to pinpoint the specific tactics or *actions* used by the characters in achieving their objectives. These sub-divisions might cover as little as one line of dialogue or as much as half a page; so the first exchange between Masha and Medvedenko held five moments of shifting actions. Only at points in the play where particular difficulties arose were the actors asked to label individual actions specific to each line.

However . . .

I found Masha incredibly troublesome. I just didn't know who she was or what she wanted. Despite my awareness that the body can give the actor as many clues to a character as the brain can, I decided to notate my script with actions appropriate to almost every line. So, in reply to Medvedenko's 'Why do you always wear black?', I determined that the action for 'I'm in mourning for my life' was *to dismiss*. I thought that my next line ('It's not a question of money. Even a beggar can be happy.') needed two actions: *to dislocate* for the first sentence and *to humiliate* for the second. I actually enjoy this sort of analysis, and it can provide a necessary complement to a more intuitive physical approach. But for some strange reason with Masha, it wasn't really helping. Part of the problem was that I was doing it independently (therefore rather cerebrally) instead of psycho-physically on the rehearsal floor with the other actors and the director.

Another aspect of the problem was that I wasn't really 'psycho-physically warmed-up' before rehearsals. After the intensive training in Moscow, I found myself floundering about without daily, collective actor-training, during which each actor could prepare his or her 'instrument' for really organic creativity. The financial limits imposed on small theatres means that rehearsal periods are often only three and a half weeks long, and the main thrust of the schedule has to be to get the play on its feet in the most time-effective way. It was usual for actors to start from 'cold' each day. Because we were usually only called to rehearsals for those scenes we were in, it wasn't uncommon for an actor to join a group who'd already been working for a few hours, so that it was impossible to maintain a common level of preparation. Of course it would be silly to compare too closely a repertory set-up like the Swan Theatre with a training environment like VGIK. Nonetheless, the atmosphere of any working environment is fundamental to the work produced within it, regarding the actors' own psycho-physical preparation (relaxation, concentration and imagination) and regarding the ensemble as a whole. Much of the ease with which Albert Filozov had been able to develop characterisations and *mises-en-scène* was because we'd spent time beforehand preparing our 'instruments' through the work of Ananyev and Kamotskaya. He also knew the individuality of each member of the group, and we were familiar with his work-methods, which were steeped in Active Analysis, integrating improvisation with text-based work. While Jenny Stephens was theoretically in favour of pre-rehearsal preparations, neither myself nor any of the other actors made an attempt to unite in a collaborative warm-up. And so it was up to each actor to prepare him or her self for creative work. But this wasn't really the main problem. It was the scripts . . .

It's perfectly usual in most rehearsal situations for the actors to start with their scripts in their hands. This is certainly the case for the first few days while the play is being 'blocked', and probably until mid-way through the second of the three weeks' rehearsal period. (Where rehearsal periods are longer, the assimilation time is obviously much richer.) After that, actors and directors hope that play-scripts can be abandoned, and the task of exploring and polishing the play can proceed. Although (I repeat) the first given circumstance *must be* the director's work method, this process of rehearsal (in the light of psycho-physical acting) suddenly seems rather odd. First of all, it places the actor's exploratory work quite clearly in the thought-centre, as the printed word is more important at the start of the rehearsal than organic physical activity. You might argue, 'Well, of course the printed word is the most important thing: you've got to honour the playwright's text.' To which I'd reply that it must be both the starting point and the finishing point for a production, but the journey from start to finish has to harness body and imagination, as well as intellect.

The second point about script-based rehearsals is that they actually render the concept of psycho-physical activity a non-sense. The point about psycho-physical activity is that every movement or gesture made by the body has an impact on our psychology and emotions, and vice versa. Every emotion vibrates to a greater or lesser extent around the human being's musculature. Picture ten actors walking around the room with a script in their left hand, at which they glance from time to time. In such a situation, an actor has to completely *silence* any dialogue between bodily gesture and inner sensation, otherwise all characters would be developed with a raised left hand and an occasional downward glance. Actually, that might be very useful for a character like Trigorin, who endlessly scribbles things down in a notebook, or even at a push maybe Hamlet. But when it comes to incarnating most characters, the first few days of rehearsal are really only helpful for the brain's understanding of a general picture of the play. And even then, I'm sure many of us have found that the 'blocking' that arises out of the first few days of script-bound rehearsals is quickly abandoned – or at least, dramatically altered – once the actors are free from the text and can start really looking at each other in the eye and handling the props with both hands. Which leads to another problem that arises once the scripts are put down: often actors just don't know what to do with their hands. They've been so used to walking around with the security blanket of the script, that once they put it down, they suddenly become conscious of their empty hands. They then start making meaningless gestures. I'm no great fan of repeated pointing (do we really point as often in life as actors do on the stage?). Or what I call 'plate-of-meat' acting, where the actors thrust the palms of their hands at you, as if they were waving slices of cold ham under your nose as they speak. All to fill the physical void left by the absent script. (To be honest, I don't even like the word, 'blocking'. That's often exactly what the process does – it blocks the emotions, the imagination and real psycho-physical interaction between actors.)

Finally, true contact with an on-stage partner is at one remove, as there's a physical obstacle stuck between the actors – the paper-and-glue play-text. A strength of Active Analysis is that limitless attention to the partner can take place from the very first moment you enter the rehearsal space, and a truly interactive ensemble can start to be created. Since non-script-bound exploratory work is often (by necessity) fairly limited in the British system, the alternative option is to learn your lines as quickly as possible. The negative side to this is that once again the word becomes the focal point of attention; the minute you put your script down, you're more concerned with memory-test than true connection with your on-stage partner. It's very easy for intonations and interpretations to become fixed, before you've really had the opportunity to assimilate fully what your partner is saying and what your true response to that might be.

All this may sound like a poor craftsman blaming his tools, because the long-and-the-short of it was that I wasn't very good as Masha. Much of it was to do with the fact that ten months in Russia hadn't really been long enough to unlearn my bad habits. It's probably become more than obvious by now that I'd always been rather a cerebral actress. A return to a script-based rehearsal forum had partially obscured much of the work I'd uncovered in Moscow. Masha was eluding me, because I was trying to tie her down with bad, old cerebral techniques and it wasn't working. But I hadn't really found the way of independently exploring her psycho-physicality. That was until we got to the technical rehearsal, when suddenly Masha underwent a substantial development. As I've repeated endlessly throughout this book, psycho-physical acting allows every part of the stage experience to become a partner with which you can work – lighting, atmosphere, space, music, other actors, the audience and the set itself.

The all-wooden set, designed by James Merifield in close collaboration with Jenny Stephens, was fantastic. During the technical rehearsal, I underwent a peculiar metamorphosis: I discovered that the actual construction of the set unlocked the gate to Masha's physicality and psychology. Ananyev had always said that the floor is your best friend – it's the one thing that will never let you down. And it certainly proved very supportive in this instance. We'd been rehearsing in a room with a linoleum-covered concrete floor; the transition to the set's raised wooden platform provoked an entirely new sensation. The springiness, the insecurity, the thinness of the contact. It made me feel rather anxious, as its hollowness made everything reverberate. This was an exciting discovery to make in a technical rehearsal, and over the course of the four weeks of performances the sensations increased. Because walking on the wooden floorboards could be very noisy, I began to find that a slightly lopsided walk was developing, as I struggled to avoid putting my heels down first and making my footsteps loud. The result of this weird sensation was two-fold. On a physical level, I felt as if I was slightly drunk and straddling my centre of balance: this was a great sensation for the vodka-swigging, snuff-pinching Masha. On a psychological level, I was aware of being very peripheral, like someone who never wants to draw attention to herself, but lurks in the black shadows, watching and absorbing. Curiously, this sense of

Masha's psycho-physicality was arising through the continuity of performance, rather than the fractured process of rehearsal. After each act, I'd walk off into the wings and feel my shoulders completely relaxing. It was almost as if, when I was on stage, there was something other than myself sending all Masha's tension into her upper back. This made perfect sense in terms of Ananyev's work on the centres: Masha is a very emotional person in a very restrictive environment. She rarely voices how she actually feels; instead it's all carried in one of her emotion-centres: her shoulders. It was very strange, as I hadn't consciously *decided* to do that, but I'd find myself coming off stage and thinking, 'Phew! Let's drop that away now!' Somewhere along the way – more in performance than in rehearsal – Masha had 'come alive', to the extent that I found I didn't even walk in a straight line on stage, and that definitely wasn't something I'd cerebrally conjured up!

Despite these subconscious psycho-physical developments, I was still aware of a dislocation between myself as an actor and the playwright's character. In our work on *Crime and Punishment*, Filozov had incited actors to step beyond themselves into the author's creation, and I was now feeling conscious that I hadn't found the resonances of Masha's creative individuality. I felt very unsatisfied, not understanding what made Masha tick, stranded somewhere between myself and the character. However, Filozov had also said – in terms of Active Analysis – that if the actor is going to live on the stage truly in the moment, then he or she can only use those sensations which are aroused by the present-tense circumstances. Here and now I was feeling dislocated, so there was nothing to do but to feed that inner dislocation back into the character. And it wasn't as difficult as I imagined. Masha *doesn't* quite know which identity she fits: she fluctuates between normality and a brittle fragility, and this is what I needed to work with.

It was only during the performance run that I discovered, for me, Masha *was* elusive: like a strange butterfly, the more I tried to pin her down, the quicker she flew away. The pressure of time had meant that the rehearsal approach had to be more cerebral than psycho-physical, and in an attempt to unlock Masha, I'd employed analytical tactics, such as determining through-lines and objectives. With this particular character, it hadn't been a helpful tool. Having struggled in my homework to find her through-line (and, in the process, made some fairly contrived decisions), I discovered in performance that, within each act, Masha was a different person. In other words, she didn't have a clear-cut through-line. Like a crystal turning in the light, each scene presents the spectator with another facet of her complexity. Her development, then, is almost static. Once I'd freed myself from trying to find the logic of her story and the through-line of her character, and instead simply played the action of each scene, she gradually began to fascinate and not to frighten me. Once I'd relaxed the intellectual preparatory work and allowed the psycho-physicality of performance to lead me, I gradually 'found' Masha.

What also happened was that I started to have fun with her. I suddenly understood Michael Chekhov's quality of ease and how you have to love everything you do on stage and *play the game*. I discovered that there was great fun to be had at the top of Act Three when Masha and Trigorin are sharing a drink. There were little games that could be introduced, which were simple and unobtrusive, but which gave a real sense of vitality and risk to the scene. Who dared to fill their tiny vodka glass the highest without spilling it? Could I eat the grape off Trigorin's plate without him noticing? The games were so simple and yet they required both myself and Glenn Cunningham as Trigorin to pay limitless attention to each other and to the props. These games were never consciously discussed or agreed upon; they just arose from our mutual playing of each moment, and they textured and sharpened our interaction, provoking a warmth and openness between us as actors and as characters. That in itself gave credence to Masha's line to Trigorin, 'I'll be sorry to see you go.' These adaptations to each other were small, and generally they involved nuances to an established structure, rather than major changes of *mise-en-scène*. Since they arose out of a mutual but unspoken consent between the actors, in no way did the adaptations disturb the stage action, as long as we remained attentive both to each other and to the script.

The willingness of individual actors to engage in this kind of dynamic interaction varies, and indeed there were some cast members of *The Seagull* who, having carved out in rehearsal their intended interpretation, clung onto it in every performance, regardless of others' spontaneous timings, inflections, movements, etc. Negotiating this kind of 'fixed' acting is in itself a component of psycho-physical adaptability; you have to remain open to those actors who prefer to remain closed, in order that you may complement and work with their performance without jeopardising or threatening their particular working method. There are other actors, however, for whom the intrinsic nature of *play* in performance is not only an enjoyable, but an essential part of on-stage interaction. I encountered one such actor, during a production of *Hard Times* included in the following season at the Swan Theatre, Worcester; the actor in question, Alexander Delamere, played Harthouse opposite my Louisa Gradgrind. Harthouse is manipulative, almost cad-ish, and each night Delamere introduced tiny, but vital changes to his performance, rendering it a joyful and excitingly electric experience to play a scene with him. I was never entirely sure – just as in real-life interactions – what might happen next, whilst at the same time, neither of us disrupted the director's staging or the playwright's text. Such actors are a real find if you're interested in Active Analysis and psycho-physicality.

But returning to *The Seagull*, I realised by the end of the four-week run that, each night, my task as an actress was simply to turn the crystal, and the audience would amalgamate the character from the montage of impressions they received. It was in this way that I glimpsed the colours and humour within Masha's apparent blackness and sorrow. It follows Stanislavsky's premise of 'heroic tension', of finding good in evil, black in white, desire in repulsion, temperance in excess. By giving limitless attention to the partner and simply playing the action of each scene, Masha's warmth and wisdom developed, and the part became a joy to play.

Jenny Stephens had done a fantastic job on the production as a whole: *The Seagull* was a great success and received some generous crits. For my part, I'd learnt some major lessons, although the whole experience of incarnating a role had left me curiously nervous. It had reminded me of my propensity to be cerebral, not intuitive, to be rational, not contradictory. It had illustrated the fact that ten months wasn't long enough for real psycho-physical activity to permeate my bones. It was with this degree of trepidation that I entered the next project, *Steaming* – which in some ways couldn't have been further from the subtleties of Chekhov's dialogue.

From body to brain: *Steaming*

Steaming is set in the East End of London in the steam-room of a decrepit Public Baths, which, as we discover, is under serious threat of closure. The play tells the story of five women who frequent the steam-room. As the action unfolds, we are let into the lives of Mrs Meadow, the elderly mother of the mentally-impaired Dawn, the Bohemian Jane (who gave up the rat-race and travelled the world with toddler in tow), the middle-class Nancy (a modest, steam-room 'virgin', who stays with her husband due to pure financial dependence) and the working-class Josie (beaten-up-by-boyfriend and a part-time prostitute). When the play first opened in 1981 at the Theatre Royal, Stratford East, it caused something of a stir. It is clearly a 'feminist' piece, with significant chunks of pseudo-political diatribe, and it's also a celebration of the female form. One by one, Josie, Jane and Nancy take all their clothes off to relax in the steam-room, and – in a flourish of liberation – Dawn (usually encased in semi-transparent pink plastic) strips her top off and paints her nipples red. Considering the flurry of stage-nudity in the 1960s and '70s, it could be thought that there's no great shakes about an actor *sans* clothes these days. However, the London re-run of *Steaming* in 1996, as well as the commotion caused by Hollywood greats baring all on the West End stage in the early 21st century suggest that the combination of live theatre and the female form still creates excitement, an issue which Dunn is undoubtedly exploring in *Steaming*.

The director of the Swan Theatre's production was Mark Babych, whose provocative production of Chris O'Connell's *Car* took the Edinburgh Fringe Festival by storm in 1999. He subsequently took the helm at the Octagon Theatre, Bolton, where he received three of the six 'Best Production' nominations in the Manchester Evening News Awards 2000, and did indeed win, evidence of his skill and innovation as a theatre practitioner. Babych's approach to directing is eclectic: his own Eastern European roots have instilled in him a taste for the esoteric and the experimental. And his appetite for innovation leads him to challenge and question his own understanding of theatre directing, as well as inspiring his actors to take personal and creative risks. At the time of *Steaming*, he had just read Max Stafford-Clark's *Letters to George*, and was stimulated by the notion that 'analysis is a more formidable tool for cracking a scene than instinct.'[155] To this end, Babych decided to begin the rehearsal period with intense round-the-table analysis, in which the whole company was involved in collaboratively determining the actions and objectives for each scene.

The immediate obstacle was time, in that while Max Stafford-Clark spends a matter of weeks on this phase of rehearsal, Babych was reduced to a couple of days. Nonetheless, and despite the fact that he'd never worked like this before, he was convinced by Stafford-Clark's reasoning behind this approach: first of all the general shape of the play and the specific shape of each scene is rapidly exposed, giving the company a basic working structure. Secondly, the company is united in its interpretation, as 'each actor knows and subscribes to a particular shape to a scene'[156], a shape which has come out of collaborative discussion, not directorial imposition. This also allows for cast and director to form a common language in terms of what the play's about and in terms of how to manifest that play through actions and objectives. All this takes place almost immediately so that, as Stafford-Clark points out, 'the first stage of rehearsals is both intimate and intense'[157], allowing for the working atmosphere to embrace all the actors, however great or small their roles. Perhaps the most significant benefit of this way of working is its precision; it makes actors think about what they're doing, so that those moments when it's unclear what's really going on between the characters can be put under the microscope and the subtext can be penetrated. This is useful for any kind of text, from *Coronation Street* to *Coriolanus*, especially with the classics, when 'the choices that those great writers give you are so many that you actually do need to define yourself.'[158]

It's important to remember with this degree of analysis that decisions aren't set in stone: Stafford-Clark describes it as the first-stage rocket designed to fall away once the scene has been launched into orbit. It allows the brain to get the juices flowing before the actor walks into what David Mamet describes as the 'terrifying unforeseen'[159] of the rehearsal space. And Stanislavsky was only too ready to admit that an actor can't always create subconsciously and with inspiration: no such genius in the world exists. If you start by creating consciously and precisely, you can 'best prepare the way for the blossoming of the subconscious, which is inspiration. The more you have of conscious creative moments in your role, the more chance you will have of the flow of inspiration.'[160]

And so this was the starting point for Babych's work on *Steaming*, inviting the actors to ask questions and look for the details that would put life into their parts. It also allowed them to take responsibility for their own creativity, by responding to the director's questions, 'What's your intention? What do you want?' The trouble was that I had a problem with this. Given the recent experience with Masha and my need to integrate psycho-physical training with the demands of short rehearsal periods, I could feel myself resisting. I didn't allow myself to acknowledge that the truly psycho-physical actor can take any circumstance presented by the director and translate it into pastels, oils, charcoals, watercolours, or whatever medium is required. And this was really all that Babych was demanding. He believed that 'if I cast the right people then it's about *openness* and *freedom* and *impulse* and translating *intelligence into play*. In fact, that's what I hope my work is about: play.'

Play was an important part of the Russian training, and in many ways, *Steaming* offered me several opportunities to incorporate tools acquired in Moscow. This was partly due to the fact that the role of Josie revealed a very clear through-line, as well as having a wonderfully active psychology. The threatened closure of the steam-room 'haven' in the course of the play motivates the women into action, facilitating Josie's transformation from a foul-mouthed sex-fiend into an articulate public speaker. As she begins to realise that her talents don't just lie in the bedroom, she understands that she has the power to change her life and get herself educated. In terms of a dramatic through-line, her development is clear and extreme. That aside, one of the main reasons that the Russian approach was so applicable was that Josie was by nature a *physical*, action-based character. Therefore, it invited a psycho-physical perspective along the lines of the work done with Ananyev and Kamotskaya to get inside her. This was why I found myself resistant at first to the idea of 'actioning' the text. I was afraid of being too cerebral with Josie, because *she* wasn't very academic. Trying to be too mentally logical with some of the non-sequiturs in the writing might deny a more unfathomable, visceral logic, stemming from Josie's experience of life rather than from any intellectual knowledge.

Some of this resistance to cerebral analysis came from my need to 'get inside Josie' as quickly as possible. The Russian premise of locating your own personality in a script before working towards the unknown territory of the character was particularly difficult on this occasion, as (if the truth be known) I was *intimidated* by Josie. She was alien to me in so many respects that I didn't know where to find her. I knew this was a bad beginning: you can't start by thinking that the character is on one side of the room, and you're on the other, and somehow you're going to make the journey over there to find it. You can only start with You, Here, Now. And that was what was scary. One of the biggest differences between me and Josie was the pride she took in her body: this was a major aspect of her psychology and her inner motor. Given the nudity in the play, it was absolutely imperative that I somehow developed a comparable relation to my own body if I was going to portray Josie's essence with any degree of conviction. That kind of pride was entirely foreign to me, which was why I was so eager to find a trigger into her character as early in the rehearsal process as possible. And that was why I was afraid that examining her cerebrally through round-the-table analysis would dislocate me from her at the very first hurdle.

Because Josie was dominated by her action-centre, not her thought-centre, I was reluctant to take my preparatory work into my own thought-centre, for fear that it would actually push her further away from me, rather than let me in. Josie's psychological journey through the play moves very clearly through her inner motive forces. She starts in her action/sexual centre (getting through life as a semi-prostitute), moving to her emotion-centre (realising she's got to be more than her boyfriend's punch-bag) finishing in her thought-centre, when at the end of the play she decides she's going to 'get meself . . . an education.' That was her journey – but how was I to take her there?

The only real problem with the round-the-table analysis was the time element: with only a few days to work like this, we were in danger of making decisions which were actually blocking the impulse rather than freeing it up. When Stanislavsky used this approach, the company would literally spend months on it, and Max Stafford-Clark's actioning practice lasts several weeks, not days. During those weeks, lines are read and re-read to test the pertinence of the actions chosen; it's not assumed that the first choice will always be the right choice. Despite my reservations and as far as Babych's use of the work was concerned, a collaborative atmosphere emerged almost instantaneously, which meant that once we began putting the play on its feet, the degree of ensemble interaction between us was enjoyably well-advanced. This in itself was an exciting and important contribution to psycho-physical activity: as we've seen in Chapter 3, it requires faith in the on-stage partners to develop the risky state of constant improvisation inherent in vibrant acting.

I was aware that all avenues have to be pursued for an actor to unlock the creative individuality of a character. To this end, I embarked on the necessary independent detective work on the script. I began to piece together the facts of Josie's life to compile her biography and attempt to take the first tentative steps towards (what Michael Chekhov calls) 'transformation'. Chekhov describes it as 'a crime to chain and imprison an actor within the limits of his so-called "personality", thus making him an enslaved labourer rather than an artist.'[161] In this instance, my need to develop a creative individuality was nothing to do with expanding my artistry, but more to do with the fact that I knew my own personality would limit and even distort the character as written by the playwright. (If I'd have had my way, Josie would've wandered around in her thermals.) Yet I also knew that I had to begin with the tools I possessed, if I was going to get anywhere at all.

I decided that one tactic I'd adopt would be to tackle the transformation from a physical angle. Daily trips to the gym ensued, followed by dyeing my hair blonde, having a set of false nails glued on, and generally entering the female domain of the beauty salon. This in itself was incredible! My eyes were opened: I didn't realise that so many ordinary women spent their hard-earned cash and well-earned time beautifying and glorifying their bodies. It proved to be surprisingly relevant research for Josie, who primps and preens her body, since it's the only thing she feels she's got of any worth in the world. But while all this helped enormously (I even began to feel quite vain), I still hadn't found the trigger.

Rooting a character in your own personality can involve a variety of manifestations: the identification may come from finding a subjective affective memory or through objective observation of other people. Once this key into the character – this *trigger moment* – has been found, the riddle of the character's inner life can suddenly be solved. Stanislavsky describes the trigger moment he experienced during his preparation for Sotanville in *Georges Dandin*, when one feature in his make-up gave a living, comic expression to his face and suddenly something turned inside him. 'All that was dim became clear, all that was groundless suddenly had ground under its feet, all that I did not believe suddenly found my trust. Who can explain this unexplainable, sudden and magical creative motion!'[162] This was exactly what happened with Josie at the end of the first week of rehearsals. I'd been fretting over the cerebral bit, and wondering whether the trips to the gym would really start making me feel excited about taking my clothes off in front of five hundred people. I was generally doubting whether Mark Babych's decision to cast me so far against type was really going to pay off. With all this confusion throbbing through my head, I turned on to watch late-night Friday telly, to find a magazine programme all about the new phenomenon of the late twentieth century – women with the vigorous sexual appetites and predatory social behaviour traditionally associated with men. During the lively debate, I watched these immaculately dressed women, in feathers and furs, with blood-red talons and coiffures to die for, with the physical gestures and deportment of *men*. Their hand gestures were aggressive, their expressions were almost pugilisitic, their energy was action-based, and they were out for sex. They were 'laddettes'. This gave me the trigger into Josie's inner contradiction: bravura versus vulnerability. I started strutting round the living room, trying to find the right contact with the floor. And suddenly a swagger came into my gait and a confidence came into my posture. It began to grow, it began to live! I started to feel like some sort of slicked-back dude from the 1950s, with arm movements that roll from the shoulders, and leg movements that open from the pelvis. Like Elvis! No, maybe it was more like the Fonz! It was bizarre, but it was great! I really felt the *Eureka!* of the 'unexplainable, sudden and magical creative motion' that Stanislavsky had promised. My body was giving me the psychology of the character, and the more confident my body felt, the more paradoxically fragile I felt inside: *that* was Josie.

The next day at rehearsals, we worked with the actions we'd already discussed, but now allowing *the body* to manifest those actions and possess them. I began to feel the interdependence of Ananyev's psycho-physical movement work and Filozov's pursuit of physical actions within the context of Babych's rehearsal format. This interdependence became particularly evident with Josie's first entrance, when within moments of arriving at the steam-house, the stage-directions tell us that we see her 'beginning to undress.' There's nothing sexy in this. What she's doing here is unloading her emotional baggage on the steam-house manager, Violet, and her physical undressing is a visual symbol of the psychological unburdening of her life. The steam-room is the one place in the world that she can unload all that garbage and 'find herself' again; where a state of undress isn't sexual or provocative, it's matter-of-fact, it's liberating and it's innocent. Although Babych didn't want us to get too hung up in rehearsals about the intricacies of getting undressed, it soon became apparent with all of the characters, that the points at which they took their clothes off, the reasons why and the manner in which they did it, gave a direct in-road into their psychologies. Their physical actions had psychological reverberations, and executing those physical actions would effortlessly provide us with the appropriate text. Before long, the element of the production from which we'd all initially shied away (stripping) became an aspect of the play that we were keen to put into *action*. Even if (in rehearsals) the final layer was a leotard, not bare skin!

The manner in which the characters got undressed, as well as other activities, of course, be it making a cup of tea or tucking into an Indian take-away, was an immensely important part of the transition from textual analysis to psycho-physical activity.

Babych was especially interested in Stanislavsky's understanding of tempo-rhythm, in terms of individual character and in terms of the action of the play as a whole. A lot happens to Josie between scenes. So the very speed at which she enters the steam-room, and her moments of orientation, betray something of the psychological changes that have taken place within her since her last appearance. This was tricky, especially because I also had a series of very quick costume changes, which technically didn't allow me any imaginative transition time between scenes. I needed to find some sort of short-hand for assimilating all the necessary information before coming on stage. Babych was very intrigued by 'the Russian experience', with regard to the practitioners I'd encountered and the ideas of Chekhov and Stanislavsky. So the short-hand we devised was based on Michael Chekhov's *centres* and *qualities*, and rooted in the psycho-physical work I'd undertaken with Ananyev. Before coming on to the stage each time, I focused my attention on an imaginary point of energy (an 'energy centre') somewhere in my body, and allowed the image of the centre along with an accompanying 'sensation quality' to affect my physicality. That in turn affected my tempo-rhythm.

What does all that mean, then? Well, my point of focus for Act One, Scene One, in which Josie is bored with her life and her lover, was a small, gristly centre between my eyes, endowed with a quality of burden. The focus for Scene Two was a large en-gorged centre on my top lip endowed with a quality of confusion, as Jerry (Josie's German lover) has just moved out of her flat after punching her in the face because she tried to get herself a job. In the third scene, the focus was a sparkly silver centre in my groin, endowed with the quality of a cockerel, as Josie has just succeeded in securing herself a job, albeit in a topless club. The focus for the fourth scene of Act One was a swollen purple centre at the back of my head, filled with a quality of 'flu, as Josie has been beaten up by Jerry and abandoned for good this time. Coming into each scene with these imaginative stimuli made it possible for me to take a preparatory short-cut into the character's psyche. Because each image inevitably changed the speed at which I moved and the rhythm of my inner life, it was comparatively easy to motivate Josie's psychological journey through the action of the play.

The accumulation of information acquired by actioning the script, determining centres, connecting with physical activities, awakening tempo-rhythms, detecting the character's biography and in a small way transforming my own body into that of the character meant that by the end of the rehearsal period, I felt that the work had 'outgrown' the rehearsal space. Josie was a 'big' energy: to take the final step into her creative individuality, it was time to get out into the performance space. As soon as we reached the technical rehearsal, where we could develop our interaction with the space and the atmosphere as much as with each other and the text, all the characters seemed to have developed a life of their own. None of us were afraid of the exposure – of skin and of heart. We had room to breathe, we knew who we were.

Journey to the centre of your self

While the combination of Mark Babych's rehearsal technique and my independent research evoked the energy and rhythm of Josie, the basis of the character was of course founded in my own personality. Many times I've said in this book that, as actors, we only have our own bodies, emotions, and voices. When Filozov spoke of developing beyond our own personalities into the creative individuality of the characters, he was really inviting the blossoming of our own personalities into new experiences. I'd begun the rehearsal process with the sensation that the character was at one end of the spectrum with my self at the other and somehow, *through* the rehearsal process, I had to find a union of the two. In reality, Josie turned out to be far closer to my own personality than I'd anticipated. Putting on her mask in fact revealed me to myself. As Peter Brook suggests, the mask of a character allows the actor unwittingly to penetrate his or her own

psyche in the confidence that the self is disguised. The fact that
the mask gives you something to hide behind, he writes, 'makes
it *unnecessary* for you to hide. This is the fundamental paradox
that exists in all acting: that because you are in safety you can go
into danger . . . because here is *not* you, and therefore everything
about you is hidden, you can let yourself appear.'[163] The mask
allows you a kind of 'otherness', and really that 'otherness' is
Creative Individuality. The journey to the core of Josie had
required analysis of her biography, her actions, her motivations,
and her physicality, including some changes to my own body and
more importantly to my own *relation* to my own body. This had
in fact taken me full circle back to myself, or rather to a deeper
understanding of myself. This journey had called upon psycho-
physical exploration, trust and interaction with a potent and
generous director and ensemble. The roots of Josie's creative
individuality were located in true emotions, inner tempo-
rhythm, a sense of play and a delight in taking risks. I actually
relished the thrill of leaping into the 'terrifying unforeseen'.

Through Mark Babych's production of *Steaming*, I realised
that the implementation of the Russian training (with its emphasis on psycho-physical activity and the marriage of personality and character) in an essentially (and necessarily) text-based
environment was not only possible, but rewarding and challenging. When rehearsal schedules are so brief, the ideal situation
would be the formation of an ensemble of actors with a common
vocabulary and a shared interest in the potential of an actor's life-
long learning. Practitioners have been striving for such a thing
from the Moscow Art Theatre to the Teatr Laboratorium to the
Open Theatre to Peter Brook's ensemble to Mike Alfreds'
Method&Madness to name but a few. Until such an ensemble
exists in the West, a truly satisfactory implementation of Active
Analysis will be hard to come by. (Maybe there's one out there
already, I just don't know.) In the meantime, the realisation that
Here and Now is valid and valuable, and that you can open
yourself up to any method, director and ensemble, is the heart of
Active Analysis which can liberate and inspire.

Summary of Key Components in working in the theatre

• *Be the sea, not the island*: You can't *make* others work in the way that you do, and why should they? But there's no need to be isolated. Psycho-physical adaptability allows you to work in any medium with actors and directors from any culture or training background. By paying limitless attention to your fellow artists, you will find the points of contact or compromise without losing your sense of improvisation or disturbing another practitioner's working method.

• Aside from the conditions imposed by medium (theatre, radio, television, film or video), one of the first given circumstances the actor negotiates is the director's creative method. You must work within that, and find your own adaptability within it, if it isn't essentially psycho-physically orientated.

• *Brain and Body*: Understand the extent to which textual analysis can be complemented by psycho-physical exploration, even if it means doing your own preparation before rehearsal. Body and brain need to work together to fill form with content, and give content a rock-solid foundation and form.

• *Hic et nunc*: What's happening here and now is valid. If you feel insecure or nervous, understand how that informs your character and dialogue. Don't ignore the valuable information of the *hic et nunc*.

• Have fun: acting is play.

• Have integrity: acting is an art.

• Find your *trigger* – from any source, down any avenue: the text, the director, books, films, recordings. Dare to go beyond the small per cent of consciousness which comprises your daily personality. Liberate the components of your psycho-physical mechanism – body, intellect, imagination, emotions and spirit.

• You are only limited by your imagination.

• Step into the 'terrifying unforeseen', and take your fellow creators with you.

Active Analysis in production

Active Analysis needs time: to date, I've directed two complete productions using the technique – Lillian Hellman's *The Children's Hour* in three and a half weeks and Ostrovsky's *Innocent as Charged* in four and a half weeks. Both productions involved a cast of drama students at Birmingham University, and although the rehearsal schedules were far too short, both productions were encouragingly well-received. The students committed to the non-script-based approach with remarkable ease. On the one hand, their inexperience was a positive asset, in that they were comparatively open and willing to experiment, and, in general, they had no deep-rooted methods to which they might cling. On the other hand, a university course in no way purports to provide a complete drama training: most of the students with whom I was working had no more than three hours of practical classes each week. While their freshness and rawness enabled them to make some intuitive and exciting decisions, they were sometimes more inclined to do the work with their brains rather than with their bodies.

Another interesting discovery was that the more subtext a scene had, the easier it was to work using Active Analysis. The wittier the characters and the more the action happened through speech rather than communion, the harder it was for the students to have the confidence to trust their own connections with the text. But that doesn't matter. The final stage in Active Analysis is 'learn the lines'. As long as the essence of the scene has been engaged with truthfully, the actors can learn the lines as early as they wish. It's only when memory test replaces real listening that the process is short-circuited. And if the actors are really working in a state of constant inner improvisation, then one actor may be word-perfect while another actor is still improvising, and that's absolutely workable – as long as they are both listening to each other and internally alive.

Despite the occasional difficulties in my students' exposure to Active Analysis, the majority of the participants agreed that they'd found out details about their characters far sooner than they might've done in a more traditional text-based rehearsal. And I'd argue that some of their discoveries might never have been made at all if the actors hadn't been able to strike up direct contact with their on-stage partners from the very first moment they entered the rehearsal space. They also discovered the joy of props and set, and how the relationship with a chair or table can be just as informative (more so, in some cases) as their fellow-actors.

Once the actor's body and heart are truly awakened and alerted to the enormous amount of information around him or her – from set, music, objects, space, actors and audience – there need never be a dead moment on stage again. If every actor could re-member him or her self, the theatrical experience could once again become as vibrant, exciting and dangerous as it was for Shakespeare's audience or medieval man. If actors would enter bravely the 'terrifying unforeseen', we'd no longer turn on the television or video, where directors, editors and cameramen do so much of the actor's work. We'd take the time and pay the money to watch the truly happening interaction of real people, engaged in front of our very eyes in the Active Analysis of our human existence.

Epilogue

At the very beginning of this book, I warned the reader that it was a personal journey into a particular approach to actor-training in Russia. In no way have I wished to imply that the standard of British acting is any less than its international reputation warrants. It's just that the present-day acting climate in Britain often puts actors in an untenable position. We want to care about our craft, but we also have to pay the mortgage. If that means doing the commercial where we have to be a goldfish, or forking out on Spotlight photos rather than investing in some voice classes, so be it. But it needn't stop our intentions being golden.

When I left drama school, I remember being very snooty about one of my peers who had started going to the Actors Centre for extra coaching. I thought, 'But, darling, we've just finished drama school; we've done our training. Are you really so bad that you need to continue your classes?' Much as I blush at that bias now, I know that it isn't unique. Doreen Cannon (appointed Head of Acting at RADA in 1985) believed that a 'traditional attitude still prevails that once you've trained and are a professional, you needn't train again'.[164] It's a foolhardy attitude given that even the most celebrated of actors experience bouts of unemployment, during which their creative muscles can atrophy. Not forgetting the fact that the raw materials of our craft – body, emotions and voice – are constantly changing throughout our lives, and even from dawn to noon to night.

The trouble is that we don't always know where to go for the kind of re-training we need. And we don't necessarily trust the range of practitioners offering their services. And we don't always feel like getting things wrong in a classroom or showing ourselves up in a workshop. When it comes to appropriate teachers, of course, I'm a Stanislavsky-ophile. Yet, despite the fact that Stanislavsky has had an indescribable effect on international acting, he's still misunderstood and marginal in contemporary British practice. Of course there are directors who actively use elements of the 'system' in rehearsal. And *most* British practitioners have come across *An Actor Prepares* by title, if not by content. That said, there's a wonderful quotation from Michael Redgrave, which is as applicable now as it was when he wrote it back in the 1950s. He knew quite a few actors had read *An Actor Prepares* and 'found it immensely interesting. Other actors have read it and find it fairly frustrating. Some others again say they have read it when what they mean is that they always meant to read it. Some have read it and will, frankly, have none of it. Some would sooner be seen dead than reading it. For all I know some may even have died reading it. Very few have read it again.'[165] There's no denying that the style of the semi-fictional Tortsov trilogy can be very annoying at times. Despite that, there are countless pearls of wisdom tucked in every book, on almost every page – something somewhere to tackle the nagging neurosis or insidious insecurity that you might be feeling after that crazy casting or apocalyptic First Night.

It's always struck me as odd that dancers have a basic vocabulary, as do painters, musicians, architects, sculptors. Why is it that actors don't, when there's one there, staring us in the face? Why is it that you can walk into a rehearsal room, with recent graduates or the great-and-good, and the director's approach with a new ensemble will still be basically hit-and-miss? Even if we've read about objectives and through-lines, why don't we *really* know what directors mean when they say 'Play your actions'? The truth of the matter is that we don't really understand Stanislavsky. We're afraid of his ideas from two points of view: an emotional one and an intellectual one. From one perspective, as Peter McAllister (of the Royal Scottish Academy of Music and Drama) pointed out, there's a general emotional conservatism in British actors in comparison to our American and European counterparts. This means that 'in plays that require a great deal of emotion, British actors are not nearly so successful as American or Polish or Russian actors'.[166] From the opposite perspective, another actor-trainer, Christopher Fettes (of the Drama Centre, London), stressed that 'the British have always distrusted the realm of ideas, the intellectual, the high-brow approach'.[167] So what on earth can we do? If we don't like being emotional and we don't like being cerebral, and we don't like being physical, and we can't trust intuition? How on earth can we get inside a part?

Answer: adopt Active Analysis!

Because the emphasis in Active Analysis is on acting, doing, experiencing, playing, it couldn't go to the heart of Acting-with-a-capital-A *via* a more direct route. It's simple, joyful, playful, contradictory, mischievous, experimental, applicable to all genres. It's emotional without bringing out 'dirty laundry'; it's intellectual without scaring off the anti-eggheads; it's physical without excluding the old, infirm or lazy. It seeks to incorporate personality with character, so that it appeals to each actor's 'spirit' or 'higher conscious' or 'subconscious' or 'intuition', without seeming cranky or weird. It accommodates those who advocate nothing but script and action, and it serves those who seek physicality and emotionality in rehearsal and performance.

It's a curious thing ... The Russians' own re-encountering of their theatrical pioneer, since the collapse of the Iron Curtain and beyond, has led to a re-evaluation of the understanding of Stanislavsky in the West. There's clearly some unconscious cross-global fertilisation going on, and now seems to be the time to invest in it. And in small, humble ways, it's happening. At the time of writing, Katya Kamotskaya works in the Acting Department at the Royal Scottish Academy of Music and Drama, and Vladimir Ananyev spends almost as much time in Britain and Europe as he does in his native Moscow.

To close this personal voyage into the heart of psycho-physical acting, I want to quote the words of Simon Callow in support of the Russian Summer Schools pioneered in the 1990s. He wrote to me of the 'extraordinarily rich tradition of teaching and working' in Russia today. He spurred me on with the belief that we should 'seize the moment to try and plug our own need for stimulation and growth into the Russians' need for moral and material growth. It could provide us with renewed life to carry British acting vitally forward into the twenty-first century.'

Endnotes

All direct quotations from Vladimir Ananyev, Katya Kamotskaya, Albert Filozov, Tatiana Storchak, Jenny Stephens and Mark Babych are either taken from workshops and rehearsals, or from interviews conducted by Bella Merlin, with thanks to David Kendall, John Albasiny and Asher Levin.

Prologue

1   Sharon Carnicke, *Stanislavsky in Focus* (Netherlands: Harwood Academic Publishers, Russian Theatre Archives No 17. 1998) p.154 It's also worth looking at Carnicke's chapter, 'Stanislavsky's System' in *Twentieth Century Actor Training* edited by Alison Hodge (London: Routledge 2000) pp.26-29

2   Ibid pp.26-29

Act 1   Myths, Methods, Systems and Superstitions

3   Stanislavsky cited in Nikolai Gorchakov's *Stanislavsky Directs* translated by Miriam Goldina (New York: Limelights 1991) p.157

4   Magda B. Arnold in her essay 'Perennial Problems in the Field of Emotion', ed. M. B. Arnold, *Feelings and Emotions: The Loyola Symposium* (New York: Academic Press 1970) p.177

5   Keith Strongman, *The Psychology of Emotions* (Chichester: Wiley & Sons 1978) p.37

6   Konstantin Stanislavsky, *My Life in Art* translated by J. J. Robbins (London: Methuen 1982) p.194

7   Cited by Eric Bentley in *The Theory of the Modern Stage* (London: Routledge 1976) p.277 from Ribot's *The Psychology of the Emotions* printed in English in 1897 in *The Contemporary Science Series* published by Havelock Ellis

8   Konstantin Stanislavsky, *Creating a Role* translated by Elizabeth Reynolds Hapgood (London: Methuen 1988) p.241

9   William James, 'What is an Emotion?' in *The Nature of Emotions* ed. Magda B. Arnold (London: Penguin 1968) p.21

10·   Konstantin Stanislavsky, *On the Art of the Stage* translated by David Magarshack (London: faber&faber 1973) p.253

11   These excellent books include Joseph LeDoux's *The Emotional Brain* (London: Weidenfeld & Nicholson 1998) and *The Subtlety of Emotion* by Aaron Ben-Ze'ev (USA: Massachusetts Institute of Technology 2000). Both are written in a very accessible and entertaining way for the non-scientific reader.

12   Daniel Goleman, *Emotional Intelligence: Why it can matter more than IQ* (London: Bloomsbury 1996) p.6

13   Stanislavsky cited in David Magarshack's *Stanislavsky: A Life* (London: faber&faber 1950) p.389 from his address to the students at the new Dramatic and Operatic Studio in 1935 (My emphasis)

14   Stanislavsky cited in Vasily Toporkov's *Stanislavsky in Rehearsal: the Final Years* translated by Christine Edwards (New York: Theatre Arts) p.58

15   Stanislavsky, *Creating a Role*, p.240

16   Stanislavsky cited in Toporkov's *Stanislavsky in Rehearsal* p.161

17   N. Chushkin in the Foreword to Toporkov's *Stanislavsky in Rehearsal* p.17

18   Stanislavsky, *Creating a Role* p.213

19   Letter from Nemirovich-Danchenko to Stanislavsky June 8-10th 1905, cited in Jean Benedetti's *The Moscow Art Theatre Letters*, edited and translated by Benedetti (London: Methuen 1991) pp.212, 219

20   Stanislavsky, *Creating a Role* p.239 (My emphasis)

21   Stanislavsky cited in Toporkov's *Stanislavsky in Rehearsal* p.131

22   Stanislavsky, *Creating a Role* pp.100–101

23   Toporkov's *Stanislavsky in Rehearsal* p.160

24   Stanislavsky, *Creating a Role* p.207

25   Ibid p.262

26   Ibid p.239 (My emphasis)

27   From 'What is an Emotion?' in *The Nature of Emotion* ed. M.B. Arnold p.25

28   From 'Perennial Problems in the Field of Emotions' in *Feeling and Emotions* ed. M.B. Arnold pp.176,177 (My emphasis)

29   From 'Feelings as Monitors' in *Feelings and Emotions* ed. M.B. Arnold p.43

30   Keith Strongman, *The Psychology of Emotions* p.36

Act 2   Working on Your Self

31   Michael Chekhov, *Lessons for the Professional Actor* (New York: Performing Arts Journal 1992) p.81

32   Stanislavsky, *On the Art of The Stage* p.151 (Original emphasis)

33   Cited by Jean Benedetti in *Stanislavsky – An Introduction* (London: Methuen 1989) p.36 from 'Sobranie Sochinenii Volume 1, p.310

34   Stanislavsky, *An Actor Prepares* p.101

35   Michael Chekhov, *To The Actor – On the Technique of Acting* (New York: Barnes & Noble 1953) p.144 (Original emphasis)

36   Chekhov, *Lessons for the Professional Actor* p.24

37   Michael Chekhov, *On the Technique of Acting* (New York: HarperCollins 1991) p.50

38   Stanislavsky, *An Actor Prepares* p.287

39   Chekhov, *To The Actor* p.7

40   Chekhov, *Lessons for the Professional Actor* p.147

41   Ibid p.67 (My emphasis)

42   Ibid p.68

43   Chekhov, *On the Technique of Acting* p.42

44   Konstantin Stanislavsky, *Building a Character* translated by Elizabeth Reynolds Hapgood (London: Methuen 1988) p.244 (My emphasis)

45   Chekhov, *On the Technique of Acting* p.56

46   Chekhov, *Lessons for the Professional Actor* p.63 (My emphasis)

47   Michael Chekhov's tape-recording *On Theatre and the Art of Acting: Tape 1 – Individuality through the Mask* recorded in 1955 at the Stage Society, New York (New York: Applause Books 1992)

48   Stanislavsky, *An Actor Prepares* pp.248, 249

49   Chekhov, *Lessons for the Professional Actor* pp.32-33 (My emphasis)

50   Mamet, David, *True and False: Heresy and Common Sense for the Actor* (London: faber&faber 1998) p.41

51   Chekhov, *On the Technique of Acting* p.58 Chapter 5: 'The Psychological Gesture'

52   Chekhov, *To the Actor* p.71

53   Chekhov, *On the Technique of Acting* pp. 81, 87, 88

54   Ibid p.88

55   Stanislavsky, *An Actor Prepares* p.217

56   Stanislavsky, *On the Art of the Stage* p.145

57   Chekhov, *Lessons for the Professional Actor* p.57

58   Eric Berne, *The Games People Play: The Psychology of Human Relationships* (London: Penguin 1964) p.26

59   Ibid

60   Arthur Wagner in his article, 'Permission and Protection' The Drama Review Volume 13, No 3 1969 p.108

61   Chekhov, *To the Actor* p.144 (Original Emphasis)

62   Konstantin Stanislavsky, *An Actor's Handbook* translated by Elizabeth Reynolds Hapgood (London: Methuen 1990) p.100

63   Chekhov, *To the Actor* pp.100-101

64 Konstantin Stanislavsky, *Building a Character* translated by Elizabeth Reynolds Hapgood (London: Methuen 1988) p.21

65 Constant Benoit Coquelin, *On the Art of the Actor* translated by Elsie Fogarty (London: Allen & Unwin 1932) pp. 32, 71

66 Konstantin Stanislavsky, *The Stanislavsky Legacy: Comments on Some Aspects of the Actor's Art and Life* translated by Elizabeth Reynolds Hapgood (London: Max Reinhardt 1958) p.152

67 Stanislavsky cited in Gorchakov's *Stanislavsky Directs* p.318

68 Oscar Wilde, *Salome: with an Introduction by Steven Berkoff* (London: faber&faber 1989) p.65

Act 3   Working in the Ensemble

69 Stanislavsky cited in Gorchakov's *Stanislavsky Directs* p.318

70 Stanislavsky, *On the Art of the Stage* p.151

71 Stanislavsky, *An Actor's Handbook* p.57

72 Stanislavsky cited in Gorchakov's *Stanislavsky Directs* p.368

73 Jennifer Kumiega, *The Theatre of Grotowski* (London: Methuen 1984) p.204

74 Jerzy Grotowski, *Towards a Poor Theatre* (London: Eyre Methuen 1976) p.207

75 For example Chris Johnston's *House of Games* (London: Nick Hern Books 1998), Clive Barker's *Theatre Games* (London: Methuen 1982), Augusto Boal's *Games for Actors and Non-Actors* translated by Adrian Jackson (London: Routledge 1992) and Viola Spolin's *Improvisation for the Theater* (USA: Northwestern University Press 1990)

76 Antoine de Saint-Exupéry, *The Little Prince* translated by T.V.F. Cuffe (London: Penguin 1995) pp.69-70

77 Grotowski, *Towards a Poor Theatre* p.101

78 Ibid p.35 (Original emphasis)

79 Ibid p.16

80 Ibid p.201

81 Stanislavsky, *An Actor Prepares* p.139, Chapter 10 'Communion' and Chekhov's *To the Actor* p.19

82 Mamet, *True or False: Common Sense and Heresy for the Actor* p.30

83 Gorchakov, *Stanislavsky Directs* pp. 314, 316

84 Chekhov, *Lessons for the Professional Actor* p.43

85 Stanislavsky cited in Gorchakov's *Stanislavsky Directs* p.187

86 Grotowski, *Towards a Poor Theatre* p.47

87 Ibid p.101

88 Ibid p.91

89 Ibid p.99

90 Ibid p.45

91   Ibid p.185
92   Chekhov, *To the Actor* p.38
93   Ibid p.41
94   Michael Chekhov, *To the Director and the Playwright* compiled and
      written by Charles Leonard (New York: Limelight 1984) p.52
95   Chekhov, *To the Actor* p.43
96   Grotowski, *Towards a Poor Theatre* pp.201-202 (My emphasis)
97   Ibid p.215

Act 4   Working on Your Role
98   Stanislavsky, *Creating a Role* p.239 (My emphasis)
99   Carnicke, 'Stanislavsky Uncensored and Unabridged' pp.34-39
100   Toporkov, *Stanislavsky in Rehearsal* p.152
101   Mikhail Kedrov cited in Toporkov's *Stanislavsky in Rehearsal* p.211
      (My emphasis)
102   Lee Strasberg cited in *Strasberg at the Actors Studio: Tape-Recorded
      Sessions* edited by Robert H. Hethmon (New York: Theatre
      Communications Group Inc. 1991) pp.111-112
103   V. Sologub's biographical leaflet entitled *Albert Filozov: A Biography*
      (publisher unstated) translated for this book by Jeremy Criddle pp.5-6
104   Ibid pp.23,27
105   Chekhov, *To the Actor* p.40 (Original emphasis)
106   Chekhov, *On the Technique of Acting* p.124
107   Stanislavsky cited in Toporkov's *Stanislavsky in Rehearsal* p.86
      (Original emphasis)
108   Chekhov, *To the Actor* p.45
109   William Shakespeare, *The Tempest* Act 1, Scene ii, line 319
110   *The Tempest* Act 3, Scene i, line 23
111   Stanislavsky cited in Toporkov's *Stanislavsky in Rehearsal* p.124
112   Ibid p.48
113   *The Tempest* Act 2, Scene i, line 207
114   Stanislavsky, *On the Art of the Stage* p.151
115   Grotowski, *Towards a Poor Theatre* p.215
116   Stanislavsky, *On the Art of the Stage* p.219
117   Michael Chekhov Recording: *On Theatre and the Art of Acting:
      Tape 4 – Overcoming Inhibitions*
118   Stanislavsky, *An Actor Prepares* pp.202-203
119   Chekhov, *To the Actor* p.45
120   Stanislavsky cited in Gorchakov's *Stanislavsky Directs* p.193
121   Grotowski, *Towards a Poor Theatre* pp.96-97
122   C.S. Lewis, *The Great Divorce: A Dream* (London: HarperCollins
      1977) p.83

123 Stanislavsky, *Building a Character* p.275

124 Stanislavsky, *Creating a Role* p.237

125 Charles Marowitz, *The Act of Being* (New York: Secker & Warburg 1978) p.69 (My emphasis)

126 Grotowski, *Towards a Poor Theatre* pp.200,199

127 Ibid p.99 (My emphasis)

128 Ibid p.91

129 Stanislavsky, *Creating a Role* p.213

130 Letter from Nemirovich-Danchenko to Stanislavsky June 8-10 1905, cited in *The Moscow Art Theatre Letters* translated and edited by Jean Benedetti p.222 (Original emphasis)

131 Mala Powers' essay 'With Michael Chekhov in Hollywood' from *On the Technique of Acting* p.160

132 Stanislavsky, *An Actor Prepares* p.49

133 Stanislavsky, *Creating a Role* pp.58-61 (Original emphasis)

134 Stanislavsky cited in Gorchakov's *Stanislavsky Directs* p.84

135 Chekhov, *On the Technique of Acting* p.154

136 Stanislavsky, *An Actor Prepares* p.238

137 Grotowski, *Towards a Poor Theatre* p.180

138 Stanislavsky, *On the Art of the Stage*, p.151

139 Bill Bruehl, *The Technique of Inner Action – The Soul of the Performer's Work* (USA: Heinemann 1996) p.52 (Original emphasis)

140 Michael Chekhov Recordings: *On Theatre and the Art of Acting: Tape 4 – Short Cuts to the Part*

141 Stanislavsky, *An Actor Prepares* p.234

142 Ibid pp.234-235

143 Chekhov, *To the Actor* p.97

144 Fyodor Dostoevsky, *Crime and Punishment* translated by Jessie Coulson (London: World Classics 1980) pp.304-305

145 Ibid p.309

146 Ibid p.309

147 Ibid p.304

148 Stanislavsky, *Building a Character* pp.75-76

149 Shomit Mitter, *Systems of Rehearsal: Stanislavsky, Brecht, Grotowski and Brook* (London: Routledge 1992) p.19

150 Evgeny Vakhtangov cited by Reuben Simonov in *Stanislavsky's Protégé, Eugene Vakhtangov* translated by Miriam Goldina (New York: Drama Book Specialists 1969) p.48 (Original emphasis)

151 Michael Chekhov Recordings: *On Theatre and The Art of Acting: Tape 4 – Short Cuts to the Part*

152 Alexei Popov from his essay, 'Reminiscences and Reflections about Theatre' in *Stanislavski Today: Commentaries on K. S. Stanislavski*

compiled and translated by Sonia Moore (New York: American Center for Stanislavski Theater Art 1973) p. 91

153   Ibid p.69 Georgi Tovstonogov in his essay, 'The Profession of a Director' (Original emphasis)

154   Dostoyevsky, *Crime and Punishment* p.314

Act 5   Working in the Theatre

155   Max Stafford-Clark, *Letters to George* (London: Nick Hern Books, 1990) p. 70

156   Ibid p.70

157   Ibid p.70

158   Interview with Max Stafford-Clark, Leicester Haymarket Theatre, November 1995

159   Mamet, *True and False* p. 30

160   Stanislavsky, *An Actor Prepares* p.14

161   Chekhov, *To the Actor* p. 28

162   Stanislavsky, *My Life in Art* p.165

163   Peter Brook, *The Shifting Point* (London: Methuen 1988) p.231 (My emphasis)

Epilogue

164   Doreen Cannon cited in Eva Meckler's *Masters of the Stage: British Acting Teachers Talk About Their Craft* (New York: Grove Wiedenfeld 1989) p.271

165   Michael Redgrave, *Mask or Face: Reflections in an Actor's Mirror* (London: Heinemann 1958) p.172

166   Peter McAllister cited in Eva Meckler's *Masters of the Stage* p.310

167   Christopher Fettes cited in Eva Meckler's *Masters of the Stage* p.72